WINGS FOR THE FLEET

A Narrative of Naval Aviation's Early Development, 1910-1916

United States Naval Institute: Annapolis

WINGS FOR THE FLEET

By Rear Admiral George van Deurs, U.S. Navy (Retired)

FOREWORD

More than half a century ago, as officer of the deck of the USS *Pennsylvania* in San Francisco Bay, I watched a daring young man make the world's first aeroplane landing aboard ship. Aviation was in its infancy then; less than ten years had passed since the Wright brothers had made the world's first powered flight. Few who watched Ely's sensational feat realized its historical significance, for that day marked the actual beginning of naval aviation.

The men who ventured into the air in the Navy's first frail aircraft, and the trial and error methods by which they developed naval aviation into the mighty weapon it was to become in World War II, are nearly forgotten now in a swift passing of history. They were not only daring—they had vision, persistence, and nearly unlimited determination, qualities which were required if they were to convince the skeptics that their playthings of the wind could ever possess military value.

Here, written by a naval aviator who knew many of those early birds—"Bald Eagles," we call them now—is the account of their trials, tragedies, and triumphs.

Admiral van Deurs relates events during the first seven years when naval aviation was, as it were, getting off the ground. He tells the story well. To him, and to all those who, like him, flew in the days when every flight was still an adventure into the unknown, the Navy and the nation owe a vast debt of gratitude. This book will enable many who were not so fortunate as I, who saw it all begin, to appreciate the heritage of modern seagoing air power.

FRANK LUCKEL
Captain, U.S. Navy (Retired)

PREFACE

The span of but half a century separates the first flight of an aeroplane off the deck of a naval vessel from the first ascent of a naval aviator into outer space. The early days of this extraordinary development seem now to have been of another age and era. Yet it is a fact that within the lifetime of many, man has moved from the achievement of successful heavier-than-air flights to the penetration of space beyond the limits of the atmosphere of the earth on which he lives. And today no man can foretell the limit of this progression.

In the United States Navy the first phase of this development came to an end with the entry of the United States into the first World War in 1917. It had commenced in 1910, a full seven years after the then hardly noticed and the now memorable flights of the Wright brothers at Kitty Hawk. During the ensuing seven years the airplane was either the hobby of some rich sportsman or the stock-in-trade of the daredevil flier, who eked out a hazardous living by exhibition flights at the primitive air meets of that day. The development of aircraft and of flying in the Navy was inevitably tinctured by the glamour of that early time.

The officers who pioneered in naval aviation were few in number. They were venturesome individuals, who became pilots by their own choice. They worked against great odds. It was their destiny to develop aviation into an effective arm of the Fleet. This development was more a matter of faith than anything else. Its contemporary performance was so strange and unique as to be hardly credible to conservative naval officers. The elder of these officers, exercising the great power of seniority, had trained in sail and had only recently accepted the steam engine. Those who sought to become naval fliers had much to overcome in the way of inertia, professional conservatism, and closed minds.

The miracle is that some of these pilots, having survived the hazards of early flying and of two world wars in which they were the pre-eminent leaders of naval aviation, have lived on into the day when their successors are seeking to blaze a trail into space.

Among those who have made generous contributions of their time and knowledge to the making of this book in the form of both letters and personal interviews are Vice Admiral P. N. L. Bellinger, U.S. Navy (Retired), deceased; Mrs. Eugene Ely, deceased; Colonel F. T. Evans, U.S. Marine Corps (Retired); Admiral A. W. Fitch, U.S. Navy (Retired); Mr. Paul Garber, National Air Museum, Washington, D.C.; Mr. George C. Gilmore, Pensacola, Florida; Captain F. A. LaRoche, U.S. Navy (Retired); Mr. M. W. McFarland, Library of Congress; Rear Admiral L. N. McNair, U.S. Navy (Retired), deceased; Captain Charles H. Maddox, U.S. Navy (Retired); Admiral George D. Murray, U.S. Navy (Retired), deceased; Fleet Admiral Chester Nimitz, U.S. Navy, deceased; Mrs. Edna Whiting Nisewaner; Mr. Lee M. Pearson, Historian, Naval Air Systems Command, Department of the Navy, Washington, D.C.; Admiral A. M. Pride, U.S. Navy (Retired); Captain Braxton Rhodes, U.S. Navy (Retired), deceased; Mr. M. C. Sloan, Air

Force Museum, Wright-Patterson Air Force Base, Ohio; Lieutenant Colonel Edna L. Smith, U.S. Marine Corps Women's Reserve (Retired); Mrs. J. H. Towers; Mr. A. O. Van Wyen, Head of Aviation History Unit, Office of Chief of Naval Operations, Department of the Navy, Washington, D.C.; Mr. Alfred V. Verville, pioneer aviation designer; Mr. Charles L. Wiggin, pioneer aviation mechanic; and last but not least, many patient librarians.

My special thanks are due Mr. Dudley C. Lunt, who himself served in the Navy in World War I, and who did most of the final editing.

To all those named, and to those helpers I have been unable to name, my thanks.

Rear Admiral
U.S. Navy (Retired)

Belvedere, California
1 February 1966

TABLE OF CONTENTS

WINGS FOR THE FLEET

CHAPTER ONE: FIRST AMERICAN FLIGHTS

The United States Navy, which pioneered in ironclad warships, submarines, and nuclear power, was pushed into aviation. Man had been flying heavier-than-air machines for nearly seven years when the Navy first officially noticed aeronautics. Its natural conservatism should be viewed against the backdrop of what had been happening in the field of aviation.

Even after the Wrights had successfully taken to the air in 1903, scientists and engineers, such as Professor Simon Newcomb and Admiral George W. Melville, continued to prove in print that flying machines were impracticable, if not impossible. The *Proceedings of the United States Naval Institute* reflected professional naval thinking; no mention of flying machines is to be found in its pages before 1907.

At that time George Dewey, Admiral of the Fleet and President of the new General Board, was one who wondered if flying machines could be used at sea. He had been in the Navy before it had armored ships; he knew changes were possible. In 1904, he had gone to St. Louis to see Santos-Dumont fly his dirigible. The gas bag split before it got off the ground. But this experience did not disillusion the Admiral. He kept an open and inquiring mind. "If you can fly higher than the crow's-nest, we will use you," he told inventors.

In those early days, most men were so sure that aeroplanes were fakes that no mere news report could convince them;

everyone had to see a flight for himself before he changed his opinion. Orville Wright's flights at Fort Myer in 1908 converted the first large group of Americans. But at the time, most ranking naval officers were at sea, taking Theodore Roosevelt's Great White Fleet around the world.

After the next Fort Myer show, the following year, the Fleet lay at anchor in the North River for the 1909 Hudson-Fulton Celebration. Navy men then had a chance to watch the Wrights and their aircraft fight bumpy winds above Riverside Drive. But most of them did not think the Navy had a place for such things. Seafaring men are usually a conservative lot and to them the machine looked altogether too puny for use at sea.

The *Proceedings of the United States Naval Institute* reflected this traditionally conservative attitude. A British source was quoted praising a professor who had "demonstrated the small efficiency of the aeroplane as a war engine," while it ridiculed a major who thought it might have military uses. A *Scientific American* author was also quoted as saying that no sane aviator would try to get off the ground if a breath of wind were stirring. He forecast a long wait before machines could land and take off with any degree of freedom. "The most absurd claim," he said, "is . . . their ability to sail over hostile territory and destroy cities, fortifications, and military depots by dropping high explosives." Other similar sources were presented arguing that artillery would force flying machines so high their bombs could not hit accurately, and anyway, the Russo-Japanese war had shown that good armor

3

1. Orville Wright flying an early Wright aeroplane, Fort Myer, Virginia, September 1909. (U.S. Army)

4   could not be punctured. In 1909, most military men agreed that flying machines had no present military value, could never be used as weapons, and offered only ultimate development as scouts.

But outside the Navy, the exhibition flights of the Wrights had triggered a considerable change of sentiment. From disbelief, the popular view changed to gullible credulity. Aviation magazines flourished. The science fiction of 1910 blossomed with aerial adventure stories. Men who had never flown, been to sea, or experienced a battle, wrote of bombed-out navies, blasted cities, and helpless armies. Not in the future, they asserted, but right then, flying machines had made armies and navies forever obsolete.

Inventors, sportsmen, millionaires, stuntmen, society leaders—everyone wanted to play a part in aviation. It was popular. It was stylish. But the Navy Department was unimpressed. Air shows were making big money for the Wrights, Curtiss, some far lesser-known aviators, and plain frauds. Reporters who knew nothing about flying wrote reams of improbable bunk about the fad. A few aviators soon achieved fame in the new business. Eugene Ely, a skinny, young mechanic in Portland, Oregon, was one. In April 1910, he pieced together a wrecked Curtiss plane and practiced taxiing it on a race track, until one afternoon it accidentally bounced into the air. That night he began contracting for exhibition flights. In July, he joined the Curtiss Exhibition Company, and by fall he was one of the nation's leading professional flyers, with Aero Club of America license number 17.

2. The first powered heavier-than-air flight in the first Wright aeroplane, Kitty Hawk, North Carolina, 17 December 1903. (U.S. Army Air Force Photo, National Archives)
3. The Wright brothers, 1910. (Library of Congress)
4. Secretary of the Navy George von L. Meyer. (National Archives)
5. The Wright 1901 glider, being flown as a kite, on the dunes at Kitty Hawk, North Carolina. (Smithsonian Institution)

The Navy still sat tight. In 1910, the *Proceedings* mentioned aeroplanes only once, using a quotation which proved that planes could never affect the outcome of a naval battle. The article ended, "The flying machine of fiction may be a very formidable monster, but the real thing is feeble enough, the sport of wind and a hundred mischances." However, in the Department, responsible men faced an increasing volume of mail from air-minded civilians.

The Secretary of the Navy was the Honorable George von L. Meyer, a Bostonian, who had inherited position and money, made more of the latter in business, and then served ably as an ambassador and as Theodore Roosevelt's postmaster general. He was a friend of European rulers, understood the political aspects of the Navy, and was proud of his reputation as an efficient administrator. He wanted to retain that reputation in spite of his ignorance of technical engineering and naval matters.

One July evening in 1909, Secretary Meyer took Senator Henry Cabot Lodge out to Fort Myer, in Arlington, Virginia, to watch Orville Wright make "a very successful and interesting flight." Meyer later wrote that he considered the plane to be the "beginning of

4

5

a new mode of transportation," and he speculated on how different planes would look in 25 years. At the end of the month he noted in his diary, that "the Wrights made their flight to Alexandria and back to Fort Myer, carrying a passenger and averaging 42 miles an hour."

For several reasons no naval use for aircraft occurred to him. He was not a technician. More important, both he and Rear Admiral Wainwright, his Aide for Operations, believed that Navy money should go into fighting machines, that planes would never fight. Even if bombing, which had been suggested, became practicable, it would never be used, he thought. He was certain, as was Wainwright, that the rules of chivalrous warfare would preclude such barbarity.

But what about all those letters to the Department from air-minded civilians? In September 1910, Secretary Meyer called in his Assistant Aide for Materiel and told him to answer the queries, to watch developments, and to bring up any that should concern the Navy. In this offhand fashion, 54-year-old Captain Washington Irving Chambers became the first naval officer to be permanently assigned to duties involving naval aviation.

One would like to think of man's first flight as a dramatic single achievement. But in so complex a field this view is oversimplified. Many dreams and long years of theoretical experimentation preceded the actual event. Four centuries ago, Leonardo da Vinci's drawings showed his grasp of

some of the fundamental principles of flight. 5 In the last half of the nineteenth century, inventors and experimenters were busy seeking their practical application. Such men as Otto and Gustave Lilienthal in Germany, Percy S. Pilcher in Great Britain, and John J. Montgomery and Octave Chanute in the United States, sought experience in building and flying gliders. Clement Ader built four unsuccessful planes, and the Frenchman, Alphonse Pénaud, designed a rubber-band-powered model that actually made a short flight.

These new developments were noted and studied by Samuel Pierpont Langley, the secretary of the Smithsonian Institution, who by 1894 had designed a model which flew for a few seconds. Two years later, his model was making flights of distances up to 4,000 feet.

Langley's "aerodrome" was a curious-looking contrivance. Four delicate wings, two on each side in tandem and braced with fine external wires, were attached to a central, keel-like frame. Weighing 26 pounds and 16 feet in length, this steam-powered model was capable of sustained flight for about a minute and a half, at the end of which time it would settle into the water with only minor damage.

Reports of these experiments reached Assistant Secretary of the Navy Theodore Roosevelt, and he initiated an investigation by a joint Army-Navy board. This resulted in negotiations with Langley by the Board of Ordnance and Fortifications and an undertaking by Langley to construct a large-scale version of his flying machine which would

6

be capable of carrying a man aloft. This was late in 1898.

Then followed four and a half years of delay and frustration in the course of which, failing to find an adequate ready-made motor, either in the United States or abroad, one was designed and built. It was a rotary engine, which weighed 120 pounds and developed over 50 horsepower. Much time also was spent in devising a complicated spring-powered catapult device to launch the craft.

In July of 1903, all was declared ready. The aerodrome sat on its catapult atop a houseboat on the Potomac River. There had been plenty of advance publicity, and the reporters were out in force. Then some hitch caused the attempted flight to be postponed. This happened again and again during the summer but, on 7 October, Charles M. Manly, Langley's assistant, got the machine up to 24 knots at the end of the launching platform. For a moment the aerodrome was airborne. According to a contemporary account, it "hovered a moment, then plunged into the Potomac." On 8 December, there was another try in which the rear wings collapsed. Nine days later, down on the Carolina dunes, without any fanfare at all, the Wright brothers made the first successful heavier-than-air flight.

The publicity subsequent to Langley's series of unsuccessful attempts and frustrating failures threw a vast cloud of doubt over the whole affair and indeed over the development of all aviation. The caustic ridicule broke Langley's heart, and he died in 1906. Sixteen years later, his prophetic

6. Langley's aerodrome, 7 October 1903. It ". . . hovered a moment, then plunged into the Potomac." (Wide World Photo)
7. The Wright 1902 glider in flight at Kitty Hawk. (Smithsonian Institution)
8. Wilbur Wright in prone position following landing of his 1901 glider at Kitty Hawk. (Smithsonian Institution)

genius was recognized by the Navy when the first aircraft carrier, the USS *Langley,* was placed in service.

Two years after Langley had started work on his man-carrying aerodrome, the Wright brothers, Orville and Wilbur, became interested in gliding. These young bachelors studied the records of Lilienthal and Chanute, and Langley's air pressure tables. In the bicycle shop where they earned their living, they built biplane gliders with bamboo outriggers holding an elevator forward and a rudder aft. Seeking to find a place with gentle slopes and steady summer winds, they wrote to the Weather Bureau, which recommended Kitty Hawk, a remote village on the Outer Banks of North Carolina. There they assembled and flew their gliders.

Two summers of trial and error made the Wrights the first experimenters to realize the need for lateral controls, and the sea birds soaring low over the surf suggested to their minds flexible wing-tip controls. Basically, Langley and the Wrights worked from the same data, but approached the problem of flight differently. Langley had measured inert bird wings, the Wrights watched birds soar. Langley had taught the

7

8

mathematics of ship stability. He applied these principles when he built a stable, self-propelled model of a flying machine, then scaled it up to man-carrying size. The Wrights first learned to fly rather unstable gliders, then scaled these up to carry a power plant. Later, a foot-square wind tunnel rigged up in Dayton gave them better data on the lift of cambered wings.

The next glider the Wrights took to Kitty Hawk had more efficient wings, with tips the operator could warp. That summer, more practice and tumbles taught them to glide straight, bank their turns, recognize stalls, and avoid them. When winter weather ended their 1902 gliding they knew less than Langley and Manly about ship stability, but far more about airmanship and wing design. They were certain they had the data to build, and the skill to fly, a powered machine.

During the spring and summer of 1903, they built a 4-cylinder, in-line, gasoline engine for a larger glider. Mounted, right of center, on the lower wing, it delivered its 16 horsepower through bicycle chains to two wooden propellers.

At Kitty Hawk two more months slipped by and winter arrived before the brothers had their machine ready. On 17 December 1903, just nine days after Langley's fiasco, they tossed a coin for the first ride. Orville won. He stretched himself prone on the lower wing, where he balanced the 152-pound engine, and braced his toes on a cleat tacked to the rear spar. When he shifted his hips, the U-shaped saddle under his belly simultaneously moved rudder and wing tips. His right hand opened the throttle; his left operated the elevator.

Then, in the teeth of a 27-knot wind, the plane lifted off and Orville Wright flew 120 feet in 12 seconds. Each of the brothers flew twice that day. On the last flight, Wilbur covered 852 feet in 59 seconds and smashed a wing in landing. That night, when the big day was over, the inventors wired the news to their sister.

Unlike Langley's experiment, theirs was a small, private venture. No advance notices, or big investments, drew reporters and official witnesses. Someone mentioned the flights on the Coast Guard party line along the Carolina-Virginia outer beaches. This word reached a couple of Norfolk newspaper men, who then offered garbled versions to distant papers. Conservative editors refused to buy; sensational papers printed implausible accounts of the machine's cabin and the big propeller underneath that held it up.

When the Wright brothers went home to Dayton they were just small business men with the problem of a successful but unmarketable invention. In February 1904, the New York *Independent* printed a brief factual account of the flights over Wilbur's signature. The *Scientific American* quoted it. Neither editor risked an opinion about the report.

That summer, from a leased field near Dayton, they flew and practiced turns in the air. Only a few farmer friends watched them. Big prizes were attracting many unsuccessful flying machine inventors to the St. Louis Exposition. But Orville and Wilbur stayed

10

9

8 away. They considered their machine too simple and too valuable to show publicly before they were protected by patents.

In January 1905, they made their first offer to demonstrate the machine to the Army at no cost to the government. The letter went to the Board of Ordnance and Fortifications. But its members, still touchy over the Langley debacle, wanted nothing to do with any flying machine. Even though no money was involved, they gave the Wrights a polite brush-off.

A year and a half later the brothers received a basic patent. It was so general that besides the warping of the wings, it covered every other system of lateral flight control that has ever succeeded. Nevertheless, the Board of Ordnance and Fortifications still refused a free look at their flying machine.

That summer, the Wrights planned to startle the government into action by suddenly appearing in their machine, as a float-plane, over the navies of the world assembled in Hampton Roads for the Jamestown Exposition. But they dropped the plan before the floats were ready because a British-French syndicate, which had quietly investigated their activities, invited them abroad to demonstrate their craft.

Their skill as fliers, acquired in seven years' practice, made the Wrights an immediate success. By the end of summer, European companies were being licensed to build Wright machines, and American papers were spreading their fame. President Roosevelt prodded William Howard Taft, his Secretary of War, and Taft pushed the Board of Ordnance and Fortifications, which at long last

9. *A 1907 Wright aeroplane in flight at Pilot Training School, Montgomery, Alabama, 1910. (Wide World Photo)*
10. *Glenn L. Martin taught himself to fly and built his own Wright-type planes. (National Archives)*
11. *Captain Thomas S. Baldwin flying his balloon over Fort Myer, Virginia, 12 August 1908. Glenn Curtiss is running the four-cylinder, 24-horsepower motor. This first water-cooled Curtiss engine had enough power to drive the gas bag at twenty miles per hour. (National Archives)*

got in touch with the Wrights. In December, the Board invited them to build and demonstrate, at no cost to the government, a machine that could take off in a short space, carry two persons for an hour at a speed of at least 40 miles per hour, hold enough fuel for a flight of 125 miles, and be easy to take apart and fold into an Army wagon.

In September 1908, by Army invitation, the Navy sent Lieutenant George Sweet and Naval Constructor William McEntee to be members of the Aero Board appointed to observe Orville Wright's demonstration at Fort Myer. His plane was larger; the engine produced 25 horsepower. The pilot sat on the leading edge of the lower wing, instead of lying on his stomach. A foot throttle freed his right hand to manage the lever that now controlled wing tips and rudder. The passenger seat beside him on the centerline was partly in front of the radiator and engine. The outriggers could fold to let the machine ride atop a wagon. For the short takeoff, the plane straddled a monorail with one of its landing skids resting lightly on the ground. A line led from the machine, over a head-sheave on the track, then back to a weight hanging from a timber tripod to the rear of the monorail.

11

On 3 September, at the Fort Myer, Virginia, parade ground, Sweet, McEntee, and a few hundred skeptics gathered around the Wright flying machine. Orville took his seat on the wing and raced the engine. Then he yanked a release rope, the weight fell, and the plane scooted along the rail and skimmed up into the air. Orville flew one and a half times around the parade ground in less than two minutes, then landed. He made it look easy and the crowd went wild.

Every day for the next two weeks, thousands of persons jammed the field to see a flight. Twice they saw Orville carry a passenger. When he stayed up for an hour and a quarter, it was a world's record. Sweet was enthusiastic. He talked to Orville about flying from a ship. The inventor thought it would be easy. He offered to help draw up practicable specifications for a suitable machine.

Then, on 17 September, Lieutenant Thomas Selfridge, United States Army, rode as Orville's passenger. They had planned a passenger-carrying test flight to Alexandria and back. Moments after they left the ground, a propeller tip cut a tail brace wire. The rudder flopped over, trailing at a crazy angle. Orville tried to avoid trees and rough ground ahead by turning back toward the field. On the turn, the machine stalled and dove into the ground. Selfridge, crushed by the engine and radiator, was the first man killed in an aeroplane.

George Sweet's original report of the trials proposed that the Navy take up Orville Wright's offer and get planes for shipboard tests. This suggestion stopped with his superior, Rear Admiral Cowles, Chief of the Bureau of Equipment. Two and a half months later, Cowles signed an emasculated revision which stated in part: "From recent tests at Fort Myer and reports of this machine from France . . . it has been demonstrated beyond a doubt that aeroitation [*sic*] is finally an accomplished fact . . . and man can fly when he wants to within the limits of the machine." The remainder of seven pages listed possible future aeroplane developments and obvious naval applications. There was no account of the Fort Myer flights, no mention of Orville Wright's offer of assistance, and no recommendation for Navy action. Consequently, nothing came of it.

However, George Sweet had a recompense of sorts. On 9 November 1909, Lieutenant Frank P. Lahm, one of the Army's first three pilots, who had been one of Sweet's fellow members on the observing team, carried him as a passenger in the Army's first Wright plane. Thus Sweet became the first naval officer to fly in a heavier-than-air machine.

Glenn Curtiss was a young man with an ingenious and inquiring mind who also got his start in a bicycle shop. His desire to get something to push his bicycle up the hills of Hammondsport, New York, led him to buy a mail-order engine, which he shortly improved upon. When other people saw his motorized bicycle, they wanted one like it, and soon Curtiss found his bicycle shop had turned into a motorcycle shop. He, like the Wrights, worked by trial and error, and his mechanical ability proved to be a great asset in designing his engines.

12

12. *Glenn Curtiss in his* June Bug, *4 July 1908.*
(Clara Studer)
13. *Curtiss took the wheels off the* June Bug, *added
two floats, or canoe-like pontoons, and renamed the
contraption the* Loon.

10   One of his 2-cycle gasoline motorcycle
engines was purchased by Captain Thomas
S. ("Cap") Baldwin, a builder of primitive
blimps of the day. Baldwin hung the engine
under a gas bag, called it an "airship," and
demonstrated it successfully at the St. Louis
Louisiana Purchase Exposition in 1904.
Would-be blimp builders, of whom there
were quite a few, were soon ordering Curtiss
engines. Later, Curtiss flew one of Baldwin's
blimps at Hammondsport; the event marked
the beginning of his lifelong interest in
aviation.

In January 1907, Curtiss assembled a
saddle, a pair of handlebars, a frame, two
wheels, and an 8-cylinder, 40-horsepower,
dirigible engine and took it all to Florida.
Dr. Alexander Graham Bell was one of the
group that watched Curtiss and his motorcycle roar down Ormond Beach at 137 miles
per hour. This record was destined to stand
as man's fastest speed on wheels for some
30 years. The Curtiss engine interested Bell.
He had been a friend of Langley's and had
lately been experimenting with man-carrying
kites. Could an engine be used on his kites?
He invited Curtiss to visit him and discuss
the possibility.

The following summer, at Bell's summer
home in Nova Scotia, the Aerial Experiment
Association was organized. Besides Bell and
Curtiss, its members were Lieutenant Selfridge (soon to die in a plane crash), and
two young Canadian engineers, John A. D.
McCurdy and F. W. Baldwin. It was agreed
that each in turn would take the lead in
designing a plane, and Mrs. Bell put up the
money to build the machines in Curtiss' shop

at Hammondsport, New York.

Selfridge designed the first plane, and late
in 1907, F. W. Baldwin flew it some 300 feet
over frozen Lake Keuka before he crashed.
In May 1908, Curtiss flew Baldwin's design
1,000 feet. Then on the Fourth of July he
flew a mile in a plane of his own design—
the *June Bug*. As the Wrights did not make
a first public flight at Fort Myer until September, this flight won the *Scientific American* prize offered for the first American
straightaway flight of more than a kilometer.
Despite the fact that the Wrights were still
the only Americans who knew how to control an aircraft so as to fly in circles, Curtiss
promptly advertised aeroplanes for sale with
flying instruction for each purchaser.

Meanwhile, "Cap" Baldwin, the blimp
builder, made the low bid for the Army's first
dirigible order. In order to qualify, the machine had to fly under power for two hours
and be able to maneuver in any direction.
In the spring of 1908, Curtiss built his first
water-cooled engine for this machine, and
helped Baldwin demonstrate his blimp at
Fort Myer. It consisted of a long, open frame
under a cigar-shaped balloon. Baldwin sat
aft and steered. Out in front, Curtiss manned
the engine and the elevator. While they flew,
and passed, the Army tests, Orville Wright
was assembling his plane on the same parade
ground.

Curtiss now went seriously into the aero-

13

plane business. He taught himself more airmanship, and he advertised. In 1909, he delivered a plane to the New York Aeronautical Association at Mineola and showed a couple of its members, who were wealthy sportsmen, how to fly it. Later, financed by them, he represented America in France at the world's first International Air Meet and brought home the Gordon-Bennett cup for speed. The Aero Club of America gave him the first Federation Aeronautique Internationale license issued in America.

Curtiss experimented with the hydroaeroplane, as he called it, hoping to recoup his fortunes with basic patents almost as valuable as the Wrights'. In 1908, he began by mounting his *June Bug* on a pair of canoe-shaped pontoons, but the plane could never get up sufficient speed to take off. Before the Belmont meet he tried hydroplane floats, got up to speed, but failed to break free of the water's suction; however, he was certain that he was close to success.

Curtiss won $10,000, on 29 May 1909, which had been offered by the New York *World,* for the first flight from Albany to New York City. He made the 137-mile trip in 152 minutes, with two stops for gas; his fame now began to approach that of the Wrights. He organized the Curtiss-Herring Company to build planes, and air show teams to advertise them. The Wrights met this competition with exhibition teams of their own, and patent infringement suits.

On 22 October 1910, the aviation world gathered at Belmont Park, New York, for the United States' first international air meet. The Wrights kept aloof from social functions, associating only with their own pilots. They looked on other fliers as chiselers, who by using bootleg craft sought to avoid the payment of license fees justly due the Wrights. The Curtiss clique and other pilots regarded the Wrights as dour, unfriendly, and unapproachable. This situation developed into a lengthy suit for patent infringement, initiated by the Wright brothers. The crux of the issue lay between the principle of wing warping, which they had developed, and the hinged aileron that Curtiss built between the wings of his biplanes.

This issue was most bitterly fought out. In the end the federal courts ruled that the principle of wing-warping, invented by the Wrights, had been infringed by Curtiss' hinged aileron. The legal quarrel quickly developed into a vicious personal feud which divided the aviation world during its early years and vastly complicated the whole aeronautical situation prior to 1917. The Wrights' cockpit control system was complicated and unnatural, and produced pilots who flew but could solo only if a weight was in the other seat. The Curtiss system used normal reactions somewhat like the Deperdussin, a system of stick control which had been developed in France, and which eventually became standard for all aircraft.

Nearly seven years had passed since the memorable flight of the Wright brothers on the dunes of Kitty Hawk. In the years to follow, the U. S. Navy would take the first moves in making this new plaything of the air a vital part of future fighting fleets.

11

Washington Irving Chambers, Captain, United States Navy, was of medium height with brown hair that was beginning to grow thin and a half-moon mustache above his soft mouth. He had stood twenty-seventh in his 1876 class of forty-one graduates from the Naval Academy. In those days, promotion was slow. Two decades after graduation, during the war with Spain, he was a lieutenant commander at the Naval Torpedo Station in Newport, Rhode Island. Then followed successive tours of duty at sea. His first command was the schooner *Frolic.* Next came the gunboat *Nashville,* followed by the monitor *Florida.*

During the following years, Chambers had finally achieved the line officer's goal—a battleship command—and wore his captain's stripes with self-confidence and pride. Chambers worked for Admiral Dewey in 1904, but he did not accompany him to St. Louis when the Admiral watched Santos-Dumont fly his dirigible. When the Wrights flew from Fort Myer in 1908 and 1909, he was Assistant Chief of the Bureau of Ordnance, but there is no evidence that he took a professional interest in them. When the Wright brothers flew up the Hudson River to Grant's Tomb, he witnessed the event from his command, the battleship *Louisiana,* but he was unimpressed.

1. Preparing for Eugene Ely's flight off the USS Birmingham, 14 November 1910. Sailors had constructed an 83-foot platform from the bridge rail to the main deck at the bow. Ely's Curtiss biplane was hoisted aboard, and, while the Birmingham got under way, the flier and his mechanics installed the engine and double-checked the plane.

Less than three months later, because of his familiarity with ordnance material, the Navy Department cut short his captain's cruise before it had well begun and ordered him back to Washington for duty. He asked to stay at sea, but was told his "special abilities" were needed in Washington, and in December 1909 he became assistant to Captain Frank Friday Fletcher, who was Aide for Materiel to Secretary of the Navy Meyer.

Nine months later Chambers was handed the aviation mail as an additional duty. There was nothing in his past experience to qualify him in the new field of aeronautics, so he proceeded to read everything he, or the naval librarian, could find on the subject. The mechanical details of the flying machines, both proposed and in use, fascinated him. But he had never been in the air, or closely observed any aircraft, and could only assess what he read against his own seagoing background. Thus he began his new career with some of Langley's fallacious reasoning and with no conception of a plane's weight-power-wing relationship. He pictured a naval plane as an unusually handy ship's boat. It cost about the same. The steering of it, up and down, or right and left, appeared to him as similar to the work of a boat's coxswain.

In October, his old boss, Admiral Dewey, nudged the Navy closer to aviation. He recommended that in the future the Bureau of Steam Engineering and the Bureau of Construction and Repair design scouting vessels with space for aeroplanes.

In those days Navy bureau chiefs had no military superior. Congress gave each bureau

2

14   an appropriation and held its chief personally responsible for the way the money was spent. By law each bureau head was the adviser on his specialty to the Secretary of the Navy, who alone could coordinate their activities. The chiefs were jealous of Dewey's General Board, and they frequently stood together to oppose its advice to the Secretary. At other times they were rivals. Always there was a scramble for control of any proposed new Navy equipment. Thus Rear Admiral Hutch I. Cone, the engineer in chief, used Dewey's recommendation to open a new round in this continuing competition. Within a week he was asking the Secretary to let him buy an aeroplane for the USS *Chester,* and hire an instructor to show an officer how to fly it. But the aides recommended waiting until planes were better developed. Chief Constructor R. M. Watt tried to belittle the General Board by proposing that an officer from his bureau and another from the Bureau of Engineering study aviation and advise the Department on its naval applications.

Secretary Meyer was busy inspecting Navy yards on the West Coast when these papers were put on his desk. Assistant Secretary Beekman Winthrop, who was "acting," pigeonholed the aides' recommendations and sent Cone's request to Dewey for comment. Then he told Watt and Cone that Chambers had already been detailed to advise the Department about aviation. He suggested they each appoint an officer to work with Chambers. The Bureau of Engineering appointed Lieutenant H. N. Wright, and the Bureau of Construction and Repair named Naval Con-

structor William McEntee, who had accompanied Sweet to see the 1908 flights at Fort Myer. Thus Chambers' letter-answering job expanded into one of liaison before it was a month old.

The next few years, Dewey and Winthrop were naval aviation's best friends. Their direct help, however, was limited. The General Board could only give advice, which the Secretary was not bound to accept. The Assistant Secretary dealt only with Navy yards, except when, in Mr. Meyer's absence, he was "acting" secretary. Chambers took full advantage of this exception. Most of the pioneering moves which required the Secretary's approval were signed, "Winthrop, acting."

Chambers sent a summary of his first studies to the General Board. He believed that the performance and reliability of aeroplanes would improve rapidly. They would soon be able to land on, or take off from, a ship. Someday, they might even fight, but for the immediate future he recommended they be developed for scouting only. This last opinion did not suit one new Board member, Captain Bradley A. Fiske.

Fiske was a veteran of the battle of Manila Bay. He had arrived in the Navy Department from command of the *Tennessee,* had been told to study war plans, and had quickly concluded that the plans to defend the Philippines were inadequate. Two years senior to Chambers, he was an inventor who experi-

3

mented with radio before Marconi and had developed a telescopic gun sight and an optical range finder.

Bradley Fiske had never seen a flying machine in the air. No aeroplane had yet flown either from a ship or from the water. The Navy had neither a plane nor a pilot. Despite all this, at a meeting of the General Board, this little man, who ignored bothersome details to tackle big problems, proposed to defend the Philippines with four naval air stations. Each was to be equipped with one hundred planes to sink transports and boats if the Japanese tried to land in the islands. If they made the planes big enough, Fiske said, they could launch torpedoes against the transports.

Rear Admiral Richard Wainwright protested, "Why waste the time of the General Board with wildcat schemes?" The proposal was dropped and everyone forgot about it, except, of course, Fiske. His idea was an arrow, shot into the future. Two years later he was granted a patent on a torpedo plane.

A few days after this General Board meeting, Winthrop, "acting," signed orders for Chambers and the two liaison officers to be present as official observers at the International Air Meet opening at Belmont Park on 22 October 1910. There, for the first time, Chambers closely inspected flying machines, met the men who had invented and were building them, and talked with the sportsmen fliers and professional pilots.

Most of the professional pilots knew little about the "why" of their machines. They had been parachute jumpers, balloonists, racing drivers, or circus stunt men. Few of them

ever formally learned how to fly. They took off by luck, superstition, and rule of thumb, and then landed by sheer audacity and agility. They would try anything for publicity and big money. These men were the mainstays of the exhibition teams, but they bored thoughtful men like the Wrights and Curtiss. Chambers found them uninteresting because they could only discuss flying in terms of muscular exercises and sensations.

Eugene Ely, the self-taught flier from the West Coast, was an exception. Chambers found him an amiable young man. Curtiss liked and trusted him more than his other pilots. Unlike the daredevils, Ely had a logical theory of flight and a keen interest in the machines. He spent a lot of his time on the ground working with Glenn Curtiss. Both men were interested in producing aeroplanes that would be more useful than merely providing sport.

When he first met Glenn Curtiss, Chambers was surprised to find that this 32-year-old inventor looked more like a quiet, shy farmer in an oversized coat than a spectacular speed king. At first Curtiss could only find disconnected monosyllables to explain his machines. He would lay hold of an elevator and say, "down," move it, and say "up." Chambers mentioned an intelligence report on the Frenchman, Henri Fabre, and his takeoff from the water at Rheims. Could Curtiss build a machine that would fly from the water? This question seemed to spark Curtiss' own enthusiasm and dispelled his self-consciousness. He talked more easily of his past failures and his present hopes. He and Chambers discussed hydroaeroplanes at

16 some length. When the meet was over, Chambers was convinced that Curtiss' hydro would soon succeed, and Curtiss believed that, when it did, the Navy would be his customer.

Among the aeroplane builders, Chambers thought the Wrights were using the best approximation of scientific methods. At the same time, he was appalled at how much they all relied on "cut-and-try" procedures.

They had to, the Wrights pointed out. No adequate aeronautical engineering knowledge existed. There was no aeronautical mathematics. Would planes improve faster if some sort of national laboratory developed basic information for all designers? Could planes fly from a ship? Chambers put these questions to almost everyone at Belmont Park, and the answer they gave him was yes to both questions.

The Wrights were cordial and obviously eager to interest the Navy in their work. However, Chambers felt some intangible, persistent reserve. Possibly, since they knew he was also talking with Curtiss, it was a shadow of the hatred engendered by the patent suit. After the Belmont Air Meet, Chambers and Curtiss exchanged ideas and frank opinions in personal letters. Chambers did the same with Loening, the Wrights' manager. But he had few such exchanges with the Wrights themselves. Whatever caused this personal stiffness in the Wrights, it never kept Chambers from doing business with them.

The mechanical details of the forty-odd machines at Belmont Park claimed most of Chambers' interest. Beginning with Santos-Dumont's tiny monoplanes, he studied them

4. Eugene Ely and J. A. D. McCurdy—both members of the Curtiss Exhibition Team. They and eleven other members of the team thrilled the countryside with their spectacular flying in 1910 and 1911.

carefully. He admired the way French fliers pulled parts from crates, quickly assembled them, and then took off. They never wasted time with preflight adjustments or warm-ups, like other pilots. Could similar machines be built with parts small enough to go through a cruiser's hatches? The obvious instability of all planes started the captain following Langley's thinking. He convinced himself that ship-design methods and automatic-steering engines, like those of a torpedo, could make an aeroplane as stable as a skiff on a pond.

He watched aviators who, in order to win big cash prizes, flew in bad weather, but he did not give their piloting the attention he gave their machines. Maybe he thought flying easy because the boasting of the daredevils sounded like old sailors' yarns, or because they broke a few machines but no bones. Without much investigation he concluded that any seagoing officer could quickly master an aeroplane. Once learned, he assumed, flying would be like riding a bicycle; the trick would never be lost.

Chambers left the eight-day Belmont Park meet convinced that the Navy could and should develop naval aircraft. He thought a naval aeronautical organization and a national aeronautical laboratory desirable to speed the project. Thereafter he became a missionary with a cause. Opponents' arguments always made him more certain that

4

he alone saw the light. No matter how many details of his conclusions would prove erroneous, he would remain dedicated to the improvement of naval aviation.

As naval aviation grew and spread into the Fleet, some unknown individual coined two terms which distinguished enthusiasts for naval aviation from their more conservative and skeptical brother officers. It derived quite naturally from an aspect of their dress. All naval officers wore black shoes; the aviators, brown shoes. Thus, flying officers were "brown shoes," while shipboard officers became the "black shoes." For some years before World War II, it was the "brown shoes" versus the "black shoes."

After the meet at Belmont Park, Chambers figuratively put on brown shoes for the rest of his life.

On 3 November 1910, another air show opened at Halethorpe Field near Baltimore. Again, Chambers left his desk in Washington to attend. Many of the Belmont pilots sent their planes to the Baltimore show, but an expressmen's strike held up delivery of most of the planes and, on opening afternoon, only two Curtiss planes flew. One of these was flown by Eugene Ely. Ely was feeling pretty confident. He liked to fly. He was making big money and a good name in an exciting business, which promised an unlimited future. His wife, Mabel, was also an aviation fan.

A rain storm stopped the show; by evening tent hangars were blown down and Ely's planes were smashed. Since nothing could be

done at the field in such weather, Gene and Mabel went shopping in Baltimore. When they returned to the hotel at the end of the wet afternoon, they met Captain Chambers.

During their conversation, Chambers mentioned he had just asked Wilbur Wright for a pilot and a plane to fly from a ship. Wright had flatly refused all help, saying it was too dangerous. He would not even meet Chambers to talk it over. Chambers was taken aback because it was Orville's suggestion in 1908 that had given him the idea. "I had hoped it would get the Navy interested in planes," he said.

Gene Ely quickly asked for the job. "I've wanted to do that for some time," he told the surprised captain. Ely would furnish his own plane and he asked for no fee. He had three reasons for his eagerness. He had argued shipboard takeoffs with other fliers and he wanted to show them it could be done, he wanted the publicity, and he wanted to do a patriotic service.

Chambers wanted to get Curtiss' consent. "Not necessary," Ely assured him. "I make my own dates under our contract." That was a happy chance. As a matter of fact, Curtiss did his best to talk Ely out of it. Maybe he agreed with Wilbur Wright and thought it too dangerous. He argued that a failure would hurt plane sales. Mabel Ely believed he feared success even more. It might detract from the naval value of his hydroaeroplane.

Back in Washington, Wainwright turned down Chambers' proposal to let Ely fly from a cruiser. Chambers' boss, Captain Fletcher, told reporters the Navy had no money for such things. Meyer returned to Washington;

18 in Baltimore that same day, Chambers asked Curtiss and Ely to back his appeal with technical arguments. Only Ely went to Washington with him to confer with Meyer.

Secretary Meyer was back at his desk after his long inspection trip. Undoubtedly Wainwright had coached him before the conference. Ely never forgot how the Secretary covered his technical ignorance of aircraft and ships with an imperious coldness, and he never forgave him for calling Ely's plane a mere carnival toy when he turned down the proposed shipboard takeoff.

Then John Barry Ryan, a millionaire publisher and politician, got into the act. Two months earlier he had organized financiers, investors, and scientists interested in aeronautics, with a few pilots, as the U. S. Aeronautical Reserve. He furnished this organization with a Fifth Avenue clubhouse, provided several cash prizes for aeronautical achievements by its members, and made himself commodore of the organization. One of these prizes was $1,000 for the first ship-to-shore flight of a mile or more. Ryan was in Washington to pledge the club's pilots and their planes to the Army and Navy in case of war, when he heard of the Chambers-Ely plan and reopened the subject with Secretary Meyer.

When Ryan urged Chambers' proposal, Secretary Meyer responded that the Navy had no funds for such experiments. Ryan then offered to withdraw the $1,000 prize, which the non-member Ely could not win anyway, and use it to pay the costs of the test. Meyer had little interest in planes, but he was an accomplished politician, and he

5. *Ely's plane on the USS* Birmingham, *just prior to his flight.*

knew Ryan could swing votes in both Baltimore and New York. After consulting the White House, he agreed that the Navy would furnish a ship, but no money. Thereupon he left town.

Winthrop, "acting," acted in a hurry. He rushed the *Birmingham*, commanded by Captain W. B. Fletcher, to the Norfolk Navy Yard and told the yard commandant to help equip her with the ramp which Constructor McEntee had designed. The ship was a scout cruiser, with four tall stacks. Her open bridge was but one level above the flush main deck. On her forecastle, sailors sawed and nailed until they finished an 83-foot ramp, which sloped at five degrees from the bridge rail to the main deck at the bow. The forward edge was 37 feet above water.

Meanwhile, Henning and Callen, Ely's mechanics, worked at Piny Beach, where later the Hampton Roads Naval Base would be built. Using bits shipped from Hammondsport and pieces salvaged in Baltimore, they built a plane. Ely got there on a Sunday in foul weather. He added cigar-shaped aluminum floats under the wings and a splashboard on the landing gear. Late in the day he saw the plane—without its engine—aboard the Navy tug *Alice,* headed for the Navy Yard. The engine had been shipped; no one know when it might arrive.

Gene Ely was not a worrying man. But the storm at Baltimore had cost him money. Shortly before Belmont, a speck of paint in a gas tank vent had robbed him of fame and

5

a $50,000 prize. In previous months other crack-ups had bruised his body and damaged his pocketbook. These mishaps taught him how tiny, unexpected flaws could foul up a flight. Each time he charged it off to experience and tried again. Since his interview with Mr. Meyer, the cruiser flight had become a must. To his original motives, Ely had added an intense desire to show Secretary Meyer the error of his ways. At the same time he knew that, if he failed in his first try, Meyer would never give him another chance. And so Ely was worried when he joined his wife and Chambers.

At the old Monticello Hotel in Norfolk, Ely told reporters, "Everything is ready. If the weather is favorable, I expect to make the flight tomorrow without difficulty." Mabel knew that her husband was whistling in the dark. He had not seen the platform. The plane was untested. He hoped his engine would come on the night boat. But she had complete confidence in Gene, so she enjoyed a seafood dinner and untroubled sleep. Ely ate little, turned in early, and slept poorly.

In the morning, as he worried into his clothes, the clouds looked level with the hotel roof. He skipped breakfast and took the Portsmouth ferry.

Callen and Henning had hoisted the plane aboard the *Birmingham,* pushed it to the after end of the platform, and secured it with its tail nearly over the ship's wheel. Only 57 feet of ramp remained in front of the plane. Henning was worried. But Callen reassured him. "Old Gene can fly anywhere," he said. Then Ely's chief mechanic, Harrington, arrived with the engine. The three were getting

it out of the crate when Ely and Chambers boarded the ship. 19

At 1130, sooty, black coal smoke rolled from the *Birmingham*'s stacks as she backed clear and headed down river. Two destroyers cleared the next dock. One followed the cruiser; the other headed for Norfolk to pick up Mabel Ely and the Norfolk reporters.

Going down river, Ely helped his men install the engine. He wanted to double check everything to avoid another failure; besides, the familiar work eased his tensions. He blew out the gas tank vent twice. In spite of squalls, they had the plane ready before the ship rounded the last buoy off 'Piny Beach. They had almost reached the destroyers *Bailey* and *Stringham,* waiting with Winthrop and other Washington officials, when another squall closed in. A quarter mile off Old Point Comfort, Captain Fletcher anchored the *Birmingham.* Hail blotted out the Chamberlain Hotel.

It was nearly two o'clock when that squall moved off to the north. Ely climbed to his plane's seat. Henning spun the propeller. Under the bridge the wireless operator tapped out a play-by-play account of the engine testing. When the warm-up came to an end, nobody liked the looks of the weather. Black clouds scudded just above the topmast. The cruiser *Washington* radioed that it was thick up the bay, and the Weather Bureau reported it would be worse the next day. Chambers nodded toward the torpedo boats. "If this weather holds till dark," he said, "a lot of those guys will go back to Washington shouting 'I told you so.' "

By 1430 the sky looked lighter to the south.

20 Captains Fletcher and Chambers decided to get under way. Iowa-born Ely could not swim, feared the water, got seasick on ferry-boats, and knew nothing about ships. He thought the cruiser would get under way as quickly as a San Francisco Bay ferry. He had no idea that the windlass he heard wheezing and clanking under the aeroplane platform might take half an hour to heave 90 fathoms of chain out of the mud. So he paced first the bridge, then the launching platform. Then he climbed into his seat and tried the controls. Sixty fathoms of chain were still out. Henning spun the propeller. Ely opened the throttle and listened approvingly to the steady beat. Under the plane's tail, the helmsman at the wheel took the full force of the blast.

Ely was ready. He idled the engine and waited. Then he gunned the engine to clear it, twisted the wheel for the feel of the rudder, rechecked the setting of the elevator, and looked back at the captains on the bridge wing. They looked completely unhurried.

Then Ely noticed the horizon darkening with another squall and he began to wonder why the *Birmingham* did not start. He looked at Chambers, pointed at the approaching blackness. The captain nodded. He knew it would be close, but he could do nothing. Thirty fathoms of chain were still in the water.

Gene Ely checked everything again, and stared at the squall ahead. He seemed about to lose his chance because the Navy was too slow. At 1516 he decided he would wait no longer for the ship to start steaming into the

6. The wireless operator tapped out, "Ely just gone," as the frail little biplane left the deck of the Birmingham, 14 November 1910, and the first flight from a surface vessel became an accomplished fact. (National Archives)

wind. If ever he was going to fly off that ship, it had to be now. He gave the release signal.

Harrington, who knew the plan, hesitated. Ely emphatically repeated his signal. The mechanic yanked the toggle, watched the plane roll down the ramp and drop out of sight. Water splashed high in front of the ship. Then the plane came into sight, climbing slowly toward the dark clouds. Men on the platform and bridge let out the breath they had held. One of them spoke into a voice tube, and the wireless operator tapped out, "Ely just gone."

In 1910, Curtiss pilots steered with their rudder, balanced with their ailerons and kept the elevator set, by marks on its bamboo pushrod, either at a climb, level, or a glide position. In order to dip and pick up a bit more speed, Ely took off with his elevator set for glide. Off the bow he waited the fraction of an instant too long to shift to climb. The machine pointed up, but squashed down through the air.

Gene felt a sudden drag. Salt water whipped his face. A rattle, like hail on a tin roof, was louder than his engine. He tried to wipe the spray from his goggles but his gloved hand only smeared them, so he was blinded. Then the splashboard pulled the wheels free of the water. The rattle stopped. He snatched off his goggles and saw dirty, brown water just beyond his shoes.

The seat shook. The engine seemed to be trying to jump out of the plane. Ely's sense of direction left him. There were no landmarks, only shadows in the mist, and that terrifying dirty water below. He swung left toward the darkest misty shadow. He had to land quickly. On the ground he might stop the vibration, take off again, and find the Navy Yard. He wondered if the bulky life jacket that fouled his arms would keep him afloat if the plane splashed.

A strip of land bordered by gray, weathered beach houses loomed ahead. Five minutes after the mechanic had pulled the toggle, Ely landed on the beach at Willoughby Spit. "Where am I?" he asked Julia Smith, who had dashed out of the nearest house.

"Right between my house and the yacht club," she said.

It sounded funny but it wasn't. He knew the splintered propeller would not take him to the Navy Yard. He had failed. He blamed himself bitterly for the split second delay in shifting the elevator. Now he knew how to do it without hitting the water, but would he ever get another chance?

Boats full of people converged on the yacht club dock. Their enthusiastic congratulations confused him. "I'm glad you did not head for the Navy Yard," Chambers told him. "Nobody could find it in this weather." Captain Fletcher agreed. John Barry Ryan offered him $500 for the broken propeller. "A souvenir of this historic flight," he explained.

Ely figured that in not making the Navy Yard, he had failed, and Chambers and Ryan spent the evening trying to convince him that he had succeeded. His particular landing place was unimportant. It would soon be forgotten. The world would remember that he had shown that a plane could fly from a ship, and that navies could no longer ignore aeroplanes. Ely did not cheer up until Chambers promised to try to arrange a chance for him to do it again. "I could land aboard, too," was Ely's comment.

The next morning Ryan's valet wrapped the splintered propeller in a bathrobe and carried it into his pullman drawing room. There Ryan gave a champagne party until train time, presented Ely with a check for the propeller, and made him a lieutenant in his U. S. Aeronautical Reserve. After the train pulled out, Gene spent the check on a diamond for Mabel.

The morning of 15 November 1910, the *Birmingham* flight filled front pages all over the United States and Europe. Foreign editors speculated that the United States would probably build special aviation ships immediately. American editors, more familiar with naval conservatism, said the flight should at least lead Secretary Meyer to ask for appropriations for aviation. But Wainwright's friends belittled the performance. A ship could not fight with its guns boxed by a platform. A masthead lookout, they said, could see farther than Ely had flown.

And so it went and so it would go for a long time, this argument between the Navy's black shoe conservatives and the brown shoe visionaries.

CHAPTER THREE: THE SHIP AND AIRCRAFT MEET

The first flight from ship to shore, from forecastle of the cruiser *Birmingham* to Willoughby Spit, resulted in a blaze of publicity. In Washington, Captain Chambers endeavored to take advantage of such favorable atmosphere. But the interests of the bureaucrats in that bureau-infested city soon proved to be different from the aims and desires of Chambers.

Nobody denied that aeronautical research was needed, and everybody wanted the appropriations and the prestige that went along with it. When Chambers suggested a national laboratory, he was quickly seconded by the National Aeronautical Society and the Smithsonian Institution. Charles Walcott, who had taken the Langley pictures to Theodore Roosevelt, headed the Smithsonian. He announced the reopening of Langley's old laboratory as a very inadequate nucleus for expansion.

But Chief Constructor R. M. Watt objected. A national laboratory would be needless—a costly duplication. Construction and Repair's ship model basin could do all the necessary research, if only a few extra pieces of equipment were added. H. I. Cone, engineer in chief of the Navy, claimed that his Bureau had the necessary equipment, and offered the use of the Engineering Experiment Station across the Severn River from the Naval Academy. President Taft opposed a separate laboratory and, in spite of continuous agitation by Chambers and his backers, no national aeronautical research organization was formed for over four years.

Another scheme that bristled with controversy was Chambers' plan for a small naval air organization. He wanted an Office of Aeronautics, headed by a director responsible to the Secretary of the Navy, to coordinate all aviation developments. Because Chambers thought naval planes would be like ships' picket boats, he assumed they would be similarly bought, maintained, and operated. The Bureau of Construction and Repair would take care of the airframes; the Bureau of Engineering would provide motors and wireless; the Bureau of Navigation would equip, man, and operate them. And someday the Bureau of Ordnance might arm them.

Chambers ignored the interbureau rivalry and blamed naval aviation's slow start on ignorance and lack of interest. Hence an informed coordinator to help everyone seemed a natural solution. He seems to have expected to have the office going within a week or so after he had suggested it. Although he knew Wainwright and the Secretary would oppose anything aerial, the stubborn opposition he encountered in other quarters took him by surprise. Watt, still trying for exclusive control of aircraft by the Bureau of Construction and Repair, said that no other bureau, except possibly Engineering, should be involved with planes. Since these two bureaus already cooperated on many things, they

---

1. *The first flight to a "carrier deck" was accomplished by Eugene Ely in San Francisco Bay on 18 January 1911, when he landed on the slightly inclined wooden platform, 30 feet wide and 120 feet long, which had been built on the stern of the USS* Pennsylvania *for the occasion. A ramp sloped downward at a 30-degree angle at the after end of the platform. Twenty-two years later, Ely received posthumously the Distinguished Flying Cross.*

24 needed no outside coordinator to get them together on this new item. Other bureau chiefs shoved in their oars.

In addition to this open maneuvering, there was a covert, foot-dragging resistance by many veteran bureaucrats. They were jealous. They suspected Chambers of empire-building in order to make aviation a sinecure for himself. Ships, planes, and fleets were nebulous things to these men for whom the only reality was their individual spot in the Washington sun.

When Chambers persisted in his campaign, the opposition got rough. Captain Fletcher complained that aviation took so much of his assistant's time that his regular work was being neglected. Then Chambers was refused clerical help for his aviation correspondence. So he answered letters in long-hand, using this circumstance as an additional argument for an Office of Aeronautics. Every letter, to anyone, on any subject, included a plug for his proposed organization. In addition, he set forth his aviation ideas in several magazines.

In March 1911, his article, "Aviation and Aeroplanes," was the first original work on aviation to be printed in the *United States Naval Institute Proceedings*. It comprised a lengthy report of the machines and the flying at Belmont Park and Halethorpe and told of Ely's work for the Navy. It stated the case for scouting planes, an Office of Naval Aeronautics, and a National Aeronautical Laboratory.

Soon after this article appeared, Secretary Meyer addressed a long, involved memorandum to Chambers, made him a handcuffed

2. Eugene Ely's "flying gear" consisted of an inflated bicycle tube tied over his stained leather jacket, a padded football helmet, and goggles. His "seat belt" was a length of rope looped over each shoulder which could easily be shrugged off in case of accident. His plane was a Curtiss landplane with pneumatic landing wheels. In case of a forced landing in the bay, metal air tanks were secured to each side of the plane to help keep it afloat, and a skid was placed forward to prevent "nosing up" in the water.

coordinator, and did nothing to check inter-bureau bickering. That day Chambers wrote to the Wrights' factory manager, saying he was "running into obstruction in establishing the Office of Aeronautics," but that he still hoped to have naval aviation started right.

In the spring, Admiral Dewey had Chambers ordered to the General Board. Ostensibly Chambers was to advise on aviation. Incidentally, the move made the Board's typists available to him, but this break lasted only a couple of weeks. Then President Taft approved an appropriation bill which included the first funds for naval aviation. Over Dewey's protest, Chambers was immediately assigned to the Bureau of Navigation to handle this.

Next to the chief of this Bureau, Admiral Reginald F. Nelson, Chambers was the senior officer attached. Nevertheless, the chief told him to work at home since there was no room for him, nor for aviation, at the Bureau. Instead, Chambers moved himself into Room 67, a hole under the basement stairs of the old State, War, and Navy Building. A caller described this as being about eight feet square, half filled with files, leaving barely room for a man and a desk. It

2

was a good place to take cold and was "so unsanitary," said Chambers, that no one wanted to take it away from him.

For over three years his proposal for an Office of Aeronautics was tossed out every time it was brought up. During those years, Chambers' unofficial cubbyhole under the stairs was headquarters for naval aviation.

After his successful flight from the *Birmingham*, Ely received a fulsome letter of congratulations from Secretary Meyer.

"That four-flusher has a crust to congratulate me," Ely commented. "He tried to stop me."

And with that, he threw the letter at the wastebasket. After he stamped out of the room, Mabel Ely salvaged it for a souvenir. Then it was discovered that it bore the initials "WIC." Chambers had drafted it.

Then came another letter, this time from Chambers himself. He asked if Ely still wanted to fly on and off a ship. If so, when and where would he be available? Ely wired his acceptance, suggesting San Francisco, where he expected to take part in an air meet during January 1911.

The commander of the Pacific Fleet was authorized to choose a convenient ship and arrange the details. Before Christmas, platform plans were sent to the Mare Island Navy Yard, with instructions not to spend over $500 on the project. The letter mentioned that the *Birmingham*'s platform had cost only $288, but it did not say the money had been put up by John Barry Ryan, and not the Navy!

In due course Rear Admiral Edward Barry, commanding the Pacific Fleet, named the armored cruiser *Pennsylvania* for Ely's second demonstration flight. This vessel had nearly four times the tonnage and was a hundred feet longer than the *Birmingham*. Late in December 1910, at the Los Angeles air show, the Admiral's liaison officer and Ely agreed to set the date sometime during the San Francisco air meet. Ely wanted to pick the weather and test his gear. He did not want to worry as he had in Norfolk.

Gene and Mabel Ely registered at the Palace Hotel in San Francisco on the evening of 4 January 1911. The *Pennsylvania* had moved up to Mare Island that morning. Her skipper, Captain Charles F. ("Frog") Pond, a classmate and friend of Chambers, was a square-faced little man with a shaggy gray mustache and laughing wrinkles at the corners of his eyes. Naval Constructor Gatewood, from the Navy Yard, supervised the building of a platform above the quarterdeck. It was 37 feet longer and 7 feet wider than the *Birmingham*'s platform, and it had a 14-foot apron drooping over the ship's stern. Forward of this overhang, the planking sloped gently up over the after gun turret to the bridge deck at the base of the mainmast. There were two low canvas barriers just aft of a two-inch timber backstop. Said Gatewood:

"We'll hang a canvas screen from that searchlight platform to catch you if the sudden stop throws you."

Ely announced stiffly that he intended not to crash, but to land. However, the thick steel mast, just forward of the platform,

3

4

26 flanked by two tall boat cranes, looked terribly solid. He did a lot of thinking on the ferry ride back to the city. He needed something on that platform to prevent a possible overshoot. The arrangement that he devised was essentially that used on the carriers of a much later day. Controversy still exists as to the source of the idea.

Curtiss, in his *Aviation Book,* noted that he went to Mare Island with Ely and told the Navy Yard people "just what would be required . . . across the runway we stretched ropes every few feet with a sandbag at each end."

Some years later, Hugh Robinson, a Curtiss man who had been present at the San Francisco meet, related how he had once worked in a circus where a pretty girl rode a car down a steep track, looped the loop, then stopped herself by plowing into sawdust heaped on the track. Robinson hated to see her covered with sawdust at every show. So he rigged hooks on the car to pick up weighted lines which would stop the car clean. Robinson claimed that at San Francisco he had suggested the same system to Eugene Ely.

In an interview more than 40 years later, Rear Admiral R. F. Zogbaum, Jr., who had been a young officer aboard the *Pennsylvania* in 1911, remembered that he had proposed the lines and 50-pound sandbags. Ely had told him that a blacksmith at the field could make him a hook.

But Mabel Ely claimed that they were all wrong. Gene had used this system to stop his racing cars long before he ever saw an aeroplane.

3, 4, 5, 6. White lines, with 50-pound sandbags secured at each end, were stretched at 3-foot intervals to prevent the plane from crashing into the mainmast at the end of the platform. Hooks were secured underneath the plane to catch on the lines, which were raised several inches above the platform by two longitudinal wooden rails. Tarpaulins placed on either side were to catch Ely if the craft skidded off the runway. His plane passed over ten of the arresting lines before it eased down and landed lightly on the platform, and the hooks began engaging the ropes. After a 30-foot run, the drag of the sandbags stopped the 1,000-pound aeroplane within 50 feet of the end of the platform.

These claims could all have substance. Quite probably a lot of people took part in discussions regarding arresting gear while Ely was trying out ideas on the aviation field at Tanforan. He tied a weight to each end of a rope, stretched it across two-by-fours and taxied over it. A blacksmith's hook usually skipped over the rope and, if it caught, the plane swerved alarmingly. By trial and error he found that, if he caught the rope dead center, carefully matched weights would slow him in a straight line.

After looking at the *Pennsylvania*'s mast, Ely knew he had to be right the first time. On the ship he could not go round again if the hook failed to catch. That worried him until he got three pairs of spring-loaded, racing-car hooks from a San Francisco friend and lined them up in tandem on a slat under his landing gear. With that arrangement he picked up the line on every run.

Glenn Curtiss did not like the plan. Ely was confident. For months he had been making short takeoffs and precision landings. He was certain of his skill. He had a new and heavier plane which let him land slower than with the old one. When he put aluminum

floats under the wings he felt ready for anything, even if the engine should quit over the water.

So Ely went back to Mare Island and told of his field tests. He wanted 50-pound bags at 3-foot intervals. Gatewood had spent the Navy's $500 on timber, so Captain Pond and Ely used their own money for sandbags, the necessary line, and guard rails. Gene told how the lines sometimes slewed the plane out of control and Pond promised to rig heavy awnings beside the platform where it was narrower than the ship. "If you skid too far," he said, "they'll keep you from being skewered on one of those stanchions."

Chambers had proposed that during the landing the ship should steam into the wind. Pond did not think the deep water area of the bay big enough. Ely thought the open sea, outside the Golden Gate, too far from Tanforan. He was more afraid of the ocean than of any landing. He was sure he could land aboard with the ship standing still. So it was agreed that the ship would be anchored. They all hoped it would swing into the wind at the right time.

The next morning the ship left the Navy Yard in a fog so thick she rammed a channel buoy before anchoring with the Fleet off the Ferry Building. That night the weather turned bad and for a week the ship logged rain in almost every watch. So they had to wait for better weather.

Curtiss, Ellyson, and Ely visited the ship one stormy day. As they left, reporters asked Glenn Curtiss for his opinion. "This is the first time an aviator has attempted to land on a battleship," he answered. "Ely will alight on the *Pennsylvania*. I'm willing to guarantee that much. The only question is, can he do it without damaging his machine?"

No one had yet been killed in a Curtiss machine. Glenn wanted to keep it that way. Until he left town, he kept on urging Ely to give up the stunt. Bad weather automatically extended San Francisco's air meet because its promoters had signed the pilots for ten flying days. Curtiss was bored. Even though exhibition flying was almost his only source of income, he did not like it. Since he did not drink and gamble like his daredevils, this waiting for exhibition weather was even duller. He wanted to work on his hydro down in San Diego. Furthermore, he knew he could not stop Ely, and he did not want to be there if he failed. So he left town.

On the seventeenth, the weather improved and Ely announced that he would land on the *Pennsylvania* at 1100 the following morning. Eleven o'clock had been picked so as to give any morning fog time to burn off and because the flood tide would then head the ship into the usual light west wind from the Golden Gate.

This forecast was only partially accurate. The next morning, the ships, anchored south of Goat Island (now known as Yerba Buena), rode to the flood tide but, by 1100, a light wind out of the east was coming from behind them. High clouds hid the sun. This 3-knot breeze filled the *Pennsylvania*'s canvas backstop like a mainsail running free. The sandbag lines were taut and evenly spaced along the platform's guide rails. Cap-

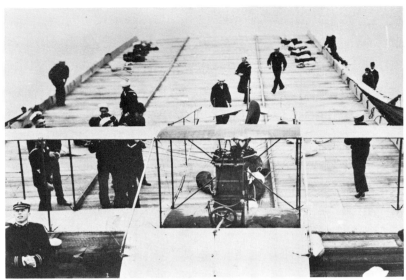

8

7

tain Pond put crews in lifeboats alongside
and stationed strong swimmers at the ship's
rail. Then he took Mrs. Ely to the after
bridge. Launches and chartered tugs carrying several hundred people surrounded the
ship. Thousands of spectators crowded the
San Francisco docks and peered at the ship
through the haze.

Twelve miles south at Tanforan, infantry-
men helped Ely's mechanics ready the plane.
Ely wore an inflated bicycle tube over his
stained leather jacket. The tube left his arms
freer than the life jacket he had worn on the
flight from the *Birmingham*. He tied on a
padded football helmet, hung his goggles
around his neck, and climbed to his seat.

Everything clicked. At 1048, right on
schedule, he was off, the engine purring
smoothly as the plane climbed to 1,200 feet
and swung across the green San Bruno hills.
Below, San Francisco's waterfront zigzagged from Hunter's Point to the Ferry
Building. Off shore, scattered craft smudged
the bay with smoke. Beyond them, haze hid
the anchored fleet.

A couple of minutes after Ely turned east
out over the dull, green water, he made out
the line of ships. He nosed over toward the
nearest one. When he rounded the *West Virginia*, and headed up the line toward Goat
Island, he was down to 400 feet. The steam
trailing from each ship's whistle as he
swooped by told him that he would be landing with the wind behind his shoulder. It was
fortunate that he had practiced cross-wind
landings along a chalk line.

The plane passed the *Pennsylvania*'s
stern at topmast height, and Ely checked the

7. *Sailors came running to give Ely a hand, while
the crowd cheered wildly, and the harbor whistles
announced the successful landing aboard the* Pennsylvania.
8. *Gene Ely was calmer than anyone else aboard the
ship. ". . . there was never any doubt in my mind
that I would effect a successful landing on the deck,"
he said. ". . . had the ship been in motion and sailing
directly into the wind, my landing . . . would have
been made considerably easier. . . ."*
9. *Mabel Ely, the flier's wife, kissed him and
shouted, "I knew you could do it!" Captain C. F.
Pond announced it was the most important landing
since the dove flew back to the Ark.*

platform as he flew along her starboard side.
Rounding the bow, he flew aft along her port
side. One hundred yards astern he banked
steeply, throttled his engine, and headed for
the platform. The nearest planks were 50
feet ahead when he cut his switch. In the
sudden quiet, he heard himself say:

"This is it."

It looked good. But suddenly, just as he
expected to land, an updraft boosted the
machine. He saw the weighted lines scooting
past, ten feet below. He pushed the wheel,
dove at the deck. Then the spring hooks
snagged the eleventh and succeeding lines.
They stopped him easily with room to spare.

Cheering people surrounded the plane. Ely
slid from his seat and his wife, bursting
through the crowd, flung herself into his
arms, kissed his cold face, and shouted:

"Oh, boy! I knew you could do it."

Captain Pond started pumping Gene's
hand and then, for the benefit of the pho-
tographers, he kissed Mabel. He declared it
the most important landing since the dove
flew back to the Ark. Then he maneuvered
his guests down to the quarter-deck; at the
cabin hatch, he turned to the officer of the

9

deck and gave an order that was destined to become historic.

"Mr. Luckel," he said. "Let me know when the plane is respotted and ready for takeoff."

Thus originated the order—"respot the deck"—that would later start many a carrier's crew into action.

In the captain's cabin, officers and guests lifted champagne glasses and toasted "Ely" and "the birth of naval aviation."

In a short while the gay party was interrupted by a report from the officer of the deck that the plane was gassed and ready. It was a few minutes before noon when Ely climbed into his seat. This time he was confident. At the same time, he remembered the cold spray that had hit his face on the first occasion. The engine roared and, for a second time, a plane rolled off a ship's ramp. He climbed away from the deck in a wide spiral, leveled off at 2,000 feet, and headed south. Thirteen minutes later he landed at Tanforan.

Later, aboard the *Pennsylvania*, the navigator, Lieutenant Commander W. H. Standley, approved the log with its matter-of-fact recital of this unique event sandwiched in with the routine without adding any comment of his own. Was he unimpressed? Thirty years later, would his thoughts return to Eugene Ely? In December 1941, Admiral W. H. Standley, U. S. Navy (Retired), was a member of the commission sent by President Franklin Roosevelt to evaluate and report on what Japanese naval aircraft had done at Pearl Harbor.

Captain Pond's report of the experiment was enthusiastic:

I desire to place myself on record as positively assured of the importance of the aeroplane in future naval warfare, certainly for scouting purposes. For offensive operations, such as bomb throwing, there has as yet, to my knowledge, been no demonstration of value, nor do I think there is likely to be. The extreme accuracy of control, as demonstrated by Ely, while perhaps not always to be expected to the same degree, was certainly not accidental and can be repeated and probably very generally approximated to. There only remains the development of the power and endurance of the machine itself, which, as with all mechanical things, is bound to come. There will be no necessity for a special platform. The flight away may be made either from a monorail or from a stay, and either from forward or aft, but preferably forward, while the return landing may be made on the water alongside, and the aviator and his machine afterwards brought on board.

No responsible naval officer of that day, not even Captain Chambers, envisioned an aircraft carrier. Chambers knew the 1911 "bamboo tails" needed a lot of improving before they could be used for operations at sea with the Fleet.

The *Pennsylvania* flights were the last Ely made for the Navy. He never wore a uniform, never drew a nickel of Navy pay, and he never liked the sea. But he tried to give aviation to the Navy because he believed it would strengthen his country. That fall he died in a crash while stunt flying at Macon, Georgia, after a career that had lasted less than two years. On the day he would have been 25 years old, he was buried near his Iowa birthplace.

The next steps toward aircraft carriers were made by the British. Early in 1917, the

30 Royal Navy tried flying Zeppelin chasers from a platform on the bow of a former ocean liner. Since more pilots survived than when the practice had been to fly from the turret tops, a "fly-off" deck was built in place of the forward 18-inch gun of the new battle cruiser *Furious*. Then a Royal Navy flight lieutenant, E. N. Dunning, talked her captain into letting him land aboard. With the ship steaming into the wind at 30 knots, Dunning brought his Sopwith Pup in from astern level with the deck, made an S-turn in front of the bridge, and slowed enough so that men were able to grab his wings and drag his plane to a stop. It was the first shipboard landing since Ely's. Five days later, Dunning tried it again. This time the plane got away from the deck crew and skidded over the side. Dunning was killed.

Shortly thereafter, the *Furious* had a "flying-on" deck added aft, where an American naval officer saw them experimenting with sandbags on lines like those Ely had used. Off-center landings caused planes to swerve. So they discarded the cross-deck lines, and the *Furious* went to sea in March 1918 with her flying-on deck covered with taut fore-and-aft wires high enough so that a plane's axle skidded along them with the wheels clear of the deck. Anchor-like hooks protruding from the axle snagged the wires and kept the plane from bouncing.

Fast landings and rough air from the stack ahead of the landing area caused discouragingly frequent fatalities. Nonetheless, in 1920, the United States paid the British $40,000 for the right to use this gear on the Navy's first carrier, the *Langley*. It was in-

10. While the Captain entertained at lunch and the guests toasted Ely and the birth of naval aviation, the sandbags were removed from the platform, and the plane turned around for the return flight.
11. At 11:58 A.M., 57 minutes after his landing, the plane rolled off the ramp, and under Ely's skillful handling the second flight from a ship's deck was accomplished.
12. The plane dropped almost to the water, then rose and leveled off at 2,000 feet. Thirteen minutes later Ely flew back over Tanforan.

stalled first on a big turntable set up at Chambers Field in Norfolk.

Commander Kenneth Whiting and Lieutenant Commander Godfrey deC. Chevalier, the captain and the officer of the *Langley*, respectively, turned the turntable over to a young aviator, Lieutenant Alfred Melville Pride, and told him to develop an arresting gear for the *Langley*. When Pride landed on the turntable, axle friction on the wires was seldom enough to stop him safely. Several times he ended up beyond the end of the wires with his plane on its nose or its back. Navy experts suggested that he wrap something around the wires in order to increase their drag, but Pride had other ideas. He knew all about Ely and, for sound engineering reasons, he liked his cross-deck lines. However, planes had changed so he could not use the little hooks on a slat.

His planes landed on two wheels and a tail skeg. His first problem was to find out how to attach a hook so the plane would not flip over on its back and also how to keep it on the deck until it caught up a cross-deck cable. He hung a weighted line across saw horses and practiced making passes at it with an Aeromarine, a plane so slow he could drift it backwards across the field

12

when flying into a moderate wind. After a practicable hook was perfected, he replaced Ely's dragging sandbags with weights that could be lifted in a tower. In this way the energy absorbed could be calculated. His first weights were 13-inch shells for obsolete guns, bridled so that several were picked up in succession as a cross-deck line ran out.

Thus the arresting gear developed by Pride and used in the early *Langley* operations consisted of lowered British fore-and-aft wires, superimposed on Ely's cross-deck cables connected to lifting weights. In landing, the hook caught a cross-deck wire; the plane came to a quick halt and was held down by the fore-and-aft wires.

A few years later, L. C. Stevens, a flying naval constructor, demonstrated that the fore-and-aft wires merely slowed up operations. Although they had been installed on the carriers *Lexington* and *Saratoga,* they were all eliminated in 1929. Since then the U. S. Navy's carrier arresting gear has been an improvement of Eugene Ely's system adapted to larger planes. Heavy steel cables have replaced his cross-deck lines, and they are attached to higher-capacity energy absorbers than his jury-rigged sandbags.

In 1933, the President of the United States posthumously presented the Distinguished Flying Cross to Eugene B. Ely for showing how to make carriers practicable. The existence of the U. S. Navy's carrier arresting gear was then a closely held military secret and it could not be mentioned. So the citation read in part:

> . . . for his extraordinary achievement as a pioneer civilian aviator and for his significant contribution to the development of aviation in the United States Navy. . . . His feat of flying aboard the USS *Pennsylvania* in 1911, assisted by retarding gear of primitive design, called attention for the first time to the possibilities of landing airplanes on shipboard. He had previously flown an airplane from a cruiser. These acts were the forerunners of our present aviation forces operating with the surface fleet.

By that time the U. S. Navy had named a ship honoring Langley, who could not, and the Wrights, who would not attempt to fly an airplane from a ship. Later it would name a ship for Curtiss, who did not want anyone to fly from a ship. But there has never been a ship named for Eugene Ely, who first did the trick. As the world's first naval aviator and the man who pointed the way for unnumbered carrier pilots, Eugene Ely deserves to be better remembered.

CHAPTER FOUR: THE CURTISS AVIATION SCHOOL

Exhibition work earned big fees for Glenn Curtiss, but the money went for team expenses, experimental work, and lawyers to fight the Wrights. As a result, he was usually broke. Shortly before the Los Angeles and San Francisco air meets, a disagreement with his partner, Herring, put the Hammondsport factory in the hands of a receiver. Undaunted, Curtiss got together what resources he could muster, and for $25 leased North Island in San Diego Bay. The barren island would later become one of the biggest naval air stations on the West Coast. There, with three planes and a couple of mechanics, he proposed to set up "a winter experimental station" and a flight school.

On 29 November 1910, before leaving for the West Coast, he wrote the Secretary of the Navy offering to train, without charge, "an officer of the Navy in the operation and construction of the Curtiss aeroplane." An accident of timing gave the job to young Lieutenant Theodore Gordon Ellyson, a husky redhead from Richmond, Virginia, who graduated from the Naval Academy in the Class of 1905. He had had two commands in submarines which, it was deemed, had given him the experience with gasoline engines that Captain Chambers had specified should, among other qualities, determine the choice.

Ellyson went with Curtiss to San Francisco and had accompanied him when he left for San Diego just prior to Eugene Ely's

remarkable exploit. On 19 January 1911, Ellyson became the first student at the flight school opened by Glenn Curtiss on North Island. Within a month the class grew to six —Ellyson, three Army lieutenants, and civilians Charles Witmer and Bob St. Henry. North Island was nothing but an uninhabited bulge at the northerly end of the sandspit separating San Diego Bay from Coronado Roads. Most of it was covered with sagebrush and undermined by rabbit burrows. It had no fresh water. In those days, Spanish Bight, a narrow arm of the bay, almost reached the ocean between North Island and Coronado. Curtiss thought its shallow, sheltered water ideal for testing his float plane. Before his arrival, his mechanics had set up shop in an old hay barn beside Spanish Bight and had cleared a runway through the sagebrush toward the center of the island.

On the island Curtiss used a 4-cylinder biplane for beginners' instruction. As in all of his early machines, the engine, centered between the wings, was directly connected to a pusher propeller. From the engine supports, two wooden braces angled down past the leading edge of the lower wing to the front wheel of the landing gear. The pilot sat on a seat affixed to these braces just forward of the wing. His feet rested on a little slat beside a foot throttle. In front of the pilot a steering wheel moved the rudder mounted aft of the propeller on four bamboo outriggers. By pushing or pulling the wheel on its hinged post, the elevators were operated. There was one such elevator on each side of the rudder and another on forward bamboo outriggers. The ailerons be-

33

---

1. With planes somewhat resembling grasshopping orange crates, Glenn Curtiss in 1911 set up an aviation school at North Island, near San Diego, California, where the Navy's first pilots were trained.

34 tween the wings were hinged to the outer rear struts. This was a fruitless attempt to evade the Wright patents. They were connected to a movable seat back, which fitted around the pilot's shoulders. Thus, in flight, when a flier leaned toward the high side, this device moved the ailerons so as to level the plane. The pilot leaned into a turn, so to speak, in order to bank it.

Students took their turns at sitting in a stationary machine and moving its controls. After several of these drills, when a man felt at home in the seat, Curtiss would have him taxi a plane on the field. Before turning him loose, a block was fitted under the throttle so that it would not open far enough to take off. The student was told to use the throttle and rudder to drive straight down the runway, as if he were in an automobile. All three wheels of the tricycle gear were free-swiveling. A hinged slat braked only the front one. This was no help in steering. At the end of the runway, the student pilot would lift the nose around and then drive back to the barn.

During Ellyson's second steering practice, the block under the accelerator dropped out. His foot went all the way down, and a burst of unexpected speed threw him back in the seat, still clutching the wheel. The machine leaped ten feet in the air, stalled, and landed on one wing. His face was red, but he was unhurt.

After the wing was patched, Curtiss replaced the block with a toggle pin inserted in a hole in a metal quadrant. The first hole permitted power enough for steering practice. When this had become routine, the pin would be dropped down a hole, and the stu-

2. *Lieutenant Theodore G. Ellyson was the Navy's first student at the Curtiss school on North Island. Later, he was designated Naval Aviator No. 1.*
3. *The "grasscutters" had two wheels near the trailing edges of the wings, while a third was mounted well forward, making it nearly impossible for a student to "nose over" the craft. A blocked throttle kept the student from flying higher than the sagebrush while training.*

dent would go up and down the runway with the front wheel off the ground. Another bit of power rendered the ailerons slightly effective, and then the student could practice coordinating all three controls on the runway. The next step was to use enough power to make several short hops into the air as the plane rolled down the runway. Then with full power the student would take off, climb a little, make a shallow "S" turn, and land again on the runway. After those turns were made smoothly, the student was turned loose beyond the runway to make a half circle and land headed back in the opposite direction.

The training machine was called "Lizzy," just as some years later a Curtiss training plane that was officially dubbed a JN-4 became universally known as "Jenny." Progress was slow because all of the students had to use Lizzy. The engine was cranky, hard to start, and ran like a rock-crusher. Any minor mishap delayed them all. After a few trips down the runway, it had to be stopped to cool a boiling radiator or replace some essential part that had shaken loose. Each morning about eleven, a breeze sprang up from the sea. This ended practice until it died near sunset. Only Ellyson and Witmer were impatient. Each morning at daylight, the two of them went over to the island and

3

divided Lizzy's time until their classmates arrived about nine and claimed their shares of the day. By dint of their extra effort, Witmer and Ellyson were soon well ahead of the others.

While Ellyson was still practicing straight-aways, Lizzy's crankshaft broke. No one could practice for over two weeks while a new one came from the East. A few days after Lizzy was back in commission, Curtiss promoted Ellyson and two other students to the 8-cylinder machine. Ellyson was delighted with this more powerful machine. It was similar to the trainer but it had enough power actually to fly instead of just staggering a few feet into the air, and it wasn't long before he was making turns in this plane.

From that point on, it was Curtiss' theory that everything was up to the student. He had been shown all the essentials. If he lived long enough, practice in the air would eventually smooth out his performance and make a flier out of him. Then, when his landings and turns were sufficiently perfected, he could pass the test for the Aero Club of America license.

At the end of March, Ellyson wrote Chambers that he felt qualified to fly the 8-cylinder landplane under good conditions, but that he needed more practice for short takeoffs and strong winds. He wanted to stay with Curtiss as long as he could because, he wrote, "he makes suggestions after every flight, which show me just what I did wrong or could have done better."

On 12 April 1911, Curtiss in turn wrote to the Secretary of the Navy:

Lieutenant Ellyson is now competent to care for and operate Curtiss aeroplanes and instruct others in the operation of these machines. Mr. Ellyson is a hard worker and has acquired considerable knowledge of the art of aviation. He has been especially successful in operating the machine and is easily capable of qualifying for a pilot's license. . . .

Curtiss wanted his students, when they were not flying, to overhaul and repair the planes. His experience with daredevil pilots had convinced him that a pilot's knowledge of his machine was an essential part of the business. The three Army students took no interest in this part of the course. They thought Curtiss just wanted some cheap labor because he was too broke to hire any. Anyway, they wanted to be pilots, not mechanics.

But Ellyson and Witmer agreed with Curtiss. The former's submarine service had convinced him that a man might live longer if he learned all about his craft. Also, he knew he would be expected to train the Navy's first aviation mechanics when the Navy got a plane. He liked to work with machines and had a genuine professional interest in Curtiss' hydroaeroplane.

Curtiss and Ellyson hit it off well. Both were adept with tools. Glenn Curtiss was always absorbed in a problem. Ideas came to him at strange moments. When he got one he sketched it on whatever was at hand—a scrap of board, an aeroplane wing, or the wall of the barn. Ellyson marveled at the man's ability to visualize and then, without slide rule or drawing board, to build a workable solution to a mechanical problem. In

4

5

Ellyson, Curtiss found a hard-working, serious friend, who believed in the hydro-aeroplane. Because his own schooling had ended with high school, he had an exaggerated respect for Ellyson's engineering education and experience, and welcomed his suggestions. Their hours of shop work led them into a lasting friendship, based on mutual respect.

Coincident with the operation of his school, Curtiss was testing, changing, and retesting the hydroaeroplane he had shipped out from Hammondsport. Ellyson, Witmer, and the two men from his factory were his principal helpers. They launched the machine from a beach near the barn. With a float made of tin and wood under the center section and a smaller one in the place of the front wheel, the plane floated with no more than an inch of freeboard. But, when Curtiss opened the throttle, it tried to dive like a loon. They dragged it out, used sticks and canvas to change the shape and size of the floats, and launched it again. This time spray soaked Curtiss and drowned the motor. So they towed it back and worked away with more sticks and canvas.

On 26 January 1911, Spanish Bight was choppy. Spray drenched Curtiss but he managed to keep his engine running. He was about to quit, when the little waves broke the bottom suction and the machine leaped into the air. After a few hundred yards, he landed easily. Everyone on North Island was elated. Ellyson wired a report to the Navy Department. The newspapers reported the beginning of a new kind of aviation, and

4, 5. Curtiss experimented with his hydroaeroplane at North Island. His students, as helpers, changed to bathing suits and dragged the machine through the slime down to the cold Pacific water each day. Finally, on 26 January 1911, the pontoon of Curtiss' hydroaeroplane broke its suction; the plane rose from the water and flew to a height of 50 feet for 31 seconds. Newspapers hailed the beginning of a new kind of aviation. When he added retractable wheels to the pontoon, he named the machine the "Triad." (Historical Collection, Title Insurance and Trust Company)
6. North Island, where Glenn Curtiss began training Navy pilots in 1911, was barren and flat, covered with sagebrush, and undermined with rabbit burrows. The San Diego Naval Air Station now occupies this site.

Curtiss filed for a patent while he went on planning improvements.

A few days later, Curtiss sketched a broad, box-like float with a shovel nose. Thereupon, one was built in a machine shop on San Diego's water front. It was stable enough to eliminate all of the auxiliary floats and surfaces that had originally been used. The plane flew well when mounted on it, but the spray was still a problem. Enough was thrown up to ruin a propeller after a few takeoffs.

One February day, Ellyson rode the pontoon in a bathing suit, hanging to the struts in order to see just where the trouble started. But when the plane took off, the spray blinded him. When he could see again, they were flying down the bay at the height of the ships' masts, and the world's first seaplane observer was startled at how far he could see below the surface of the water. That night he wrote Chambers he was sure a flier could see a submerged submarine. He thought it would be easy to toss bombs onto

ships. But he dropped the bomb idea upon realizing the kind of a target a slow-moving, low plane would offer to a shipboard sharpshooter. The spray remained a problem.

In January, before Curtiss got his hydro off the water, Captain Chambers informed the men at North Island that one of the first Navy planes had to be a hydroaeroplane, or possibly an amphibian. With an eye for this business, Curtiss hung wheels on the bow and sides of his big pontoon. They added so much drag in the water that he could not get up flying speed. Back in the shop, he built a rachet device that let him raise and lower the wheels while in the air. Then, calling his machine a "triad," because it moved on land, or water, and in the air, he flew it from Spanish Bight to the field and back again.

On 17 February, Curtiss taxied his hydro alongside the *Pennsylvania* in San Diego Bay. From a rowboat, Ellyson helped him hook onto the ship's boat crane, which swung the plane aboard. An hour later, the plane was out again, Ellyson spun the propeller, and Curtiss taxied back to North Island. It was a good publicity stunt. But everybody realized that shipboard aviation would need something better for the open sea.

Back in Washington, naval aviation was enmeshed in the gears of naval bureaucracy. By the fall of 1910, Chief Constructor Watt, Engineer-in-Chief Cone, and Captain Chambers were each on record as wanting aeroplanes for the Navy. Both bureau chiefs said they had funds that could be used. On the

surface the delay was due to professional conservatism, but a stronger, though less obvious, cause was the same interbureau rivalry that had bucked Chambers' proposal for an Office of Aeronautics. Before they put any cash on the line for naval aviation, powerful bureaucrats wanted to be certain of future control of it.

In October, the General Board recommended approval of Cone's request to buy a plane for the *Chester*, but Wainwright killed it in the Secretary's office. Right after the Belmont meet, Watt asked permission for his Bureau to buy one or more planes on the basis of McEntee's report. Chambers tried to help this request along, but again the aides stalled it.

Three days after Ely had flown from the *Birmingham*, it was proposed that Cone's Bureau should purchase two of each American type aeroplane for comparative tests and set up an aeronautical station with a ship attached for development work. A few days later, Chambers recommended the purchase of "several planes for further investigation of the principles governing their use." But none of these proposals resulted in the acquisition of any new planes.

Watt and Cone were bright young men, who were more than 15 years junior to Captain Chambers. They had been promoted from commander and lieutenant commander, to be temporary rear admirals while chiefs of bureau. Both of them avoided Chambers, curried favor with the Secretary, and ordered no planes. With the possible exception of Lieutenants Sweet, Wright, and McEntee,

7

8

only Chambers cared about the future of naval aviation.

After Ely's *Birmingham* flight, $25,000 of the Navy's annual budget request had been proposed in the Bureau of Navigation's list of operating expenses for "experimental work in the development of aviation for naval purposes." It was a trial balloon. If Congress voted the money, the Secretary's office could take it as tacit approval of naval aviation but, until Congress acted, that office would mark time. Only Congress could stop the interbureau rivalry and start plane orders. At this time Chambers and others assumed that eventually control of funds for naval aviation would be divided between the Bureau of Construction and Repair and the Bureau of Steam Engineering.

In January 1911, some off-the-cuff testimony by Secretary Meyer changed these expectations. When he appeared before the House Naval Affairs Committee, a congressman brought up the question of aviation. "In your report you touched on aviation and the fact that an airship had flown from the deck of a scout and reached the shore," he said. "Has the return trip been made? I understood that was to be part of the experiment."

This was two days before Ely's *Pennsylvania* flights. Secretary Meyer was indefinite. "No, I think that is going to be tried in the Pacific," he answered. "I would like very much to have that twenty-five thousand put in. It will be of incalculable value to experiment just on that line—the planes leaving the ship and coming back. . . ."

"That twenty-five thousand would enable you to purchase one or more planes and have

7. *In order to convince the Navy Department it needed planes, Curtiss accepted Secretary of the Navy Meyer's challenge to prove that a hydro could alight alongside a ship and be hoisted aboard. On 17 February 1911, he brought his hydroaeroplane alongside the USS* Pennsylvania *and taxied up under a boat crane.*
8. *Curtiss guiding the crane and hooking it onto the wire slings mounted on the upper wing.*
9. *There had been no opportunity to test the wire sling, so Curtiss slipped one leg over the crane hook and rode it up to the deck with his plane. Captain C. F. Pond is standing by to greet Curtiss. The single pontoon was one Curtiss had developed only a month before. It was about 12 feet long, two feet wide, and one foot deep. The bow sloped up sharply, in order to ride easily over waves.*
10. *Ellyson, attired in his bathing suit, checking the hydroaeroplane before it was lowered over the side for the return flight to North Island. Curtiss (with mustache) stands in the foreground.*

money left?" the same member asked.

"Yes," said Mr. Meyer. A few minutes later in answer to another question he was sure the same money would let them solve the antiaircraft problem, too.

Later, reporters asked him about the future of aeroplanes. The Secretary had not changed his opinion of aeroplanes. "That they will be used as fighting machines is very doubtful," he said. "It has been suggested that they could drop explosives on war vessels and forts. There are some barbarities, however, that are prohibited even in war. Besides, Germany has a gun that pumps lead into the air as thick as rain, and an aeroplane could be shot to pieces before it got near enough to work any damage."

Watt and Cone closed ranks. The Bureaus of Construction and Repair and Steam Engineering did not want the Bureau of Navigation buying planes and engines. Four days after the committee endorsed the avia-

10

9

tion item, Watt approved Chambers' report, which he had held up for a month:

> The Bureau believes that the maximum development of aeroplanes in the Naval Service will be obtained by their purchase, and is ready to submit joint requisition with the Bureau of Steam Engineering covering the purchase of such machines as the department may authorize.

Chambers then sent word out to Curtiss to get ready to bid because the Navy was definitely going to have aeroplanes. His first thought was that it would be wise to let Congress pass the appropriation before placing any orders. Then, within three weeks, he got impatient and asked Watt and Cone to buy a Curtiss plane as soon as possible for Ellyson's training. Nothing was done. After another three weeks, Chambers wrote Ellyson that he hoped to get the practice machine out of the $25,000 as soon as the budget was passed by Congress. He still wanted to establish the principle of joint bureau purchase by getting the standard hydroaeroplane in that manner. He asked Ellyson to rush the specifications for the training plane and then follow it up with his ideas for a service hydroaeroplane.

Thus the Navy's first plane specifications grew out of Ellyson's early experience with Curtiss. His shop work gave him a good idea of what could be produced and enabled him to add improvements as soon as Curtiss worked them out. Since he expected to use Curtiss' training system to teach other officers, he recommended a low-powered machine for the training procedure that had come to be known as grass cutting and also one of Curtiss' standard machines to finish

the training. In order to cut down on spare parts, he suggested interchangeable wings for the two machines. Since he agreed that the Navy should use hydroaeroplanes, or amphibians, aboard ship, he wanted the full-powered machine to be able to operate either from a field or on floats. Chambers' final specification also called for the triad gear.

In late February, while this correspondence was going on, the Wright Company offered the Navy their "B" model landplane for $4,900 and said they would build floats for it later. In early March, Congress passed the appropriation bill. The aviation money was not mentioned in debate. The next day, Wright's manager stepped up his sales talk. He recited all the records held by the Wright machines and offered to teach an officer to fly provided the Navy bought the "B" model for $5,000. After an exchange of several letters and wires, Chambers accepted this offer. Then he had to recant. He discovered that he could not use the $25,000 before the beginning of the next fiscal year. "Now I have to try getting the first planes under the appropriation 'Equipment of Vessels' and it will take longer," he wrote to Ellyson. In April 1911, the United States Navy still had no aeroplanes.

About that time, Curtiss unexpectedly recovered his factory at Hammondsport. Ellyson was pleased when invited to go east with him. After closing the North Island camp in April, they stopped in Salt Lake City with Eugene Ely for an air show. While this helped Curtiss' purse, it hurt his feelings.

12

11

When his hydro failed to take off from Great Salt Lake, the local papers called it a fake. No one had yet realized that a plane which could not reach an altitude of more than 200 feet at sea level could not possibly fly at an altitude of 4,000 feet, which was Salt Lake's height above sea level. After Chambers read Ellyson's report of this, he raised the power requirement in the specification he was writing.

Ellyson went to Hammondsport under orders to achieve three things. He was to get experience in the hydroaeroplane, teach another officer to fly, and act as inspector of the planes Chambers wanted built. The month of May was lost to all three of these purposes. Curtiss wrecked his hydroplane before Ellyson had a try at it. Chambers could not get the second officer released from his sea billet, and neither bureau would order any planes. Curtiss had crashed due to taking off without realizing that water had leaked into the pontoon. When he nosed the plane down for a landing, the water ran forward and he never was able to get the nose up again. The forward outriggers and controls chewed him up when he went through them in the crash landing. When he rebuilt the plane, he subdivided the float with watertight bulkheads and dropped the forward controls below the pilot's feet. He wanted a man to clear them if he should be catapulted out of his seat, or if he was just trying to get out from under the engine in a crash.

Chambers finally gave up as far as Cone and Watt were concerned. But, in personal letters to the Wrights, Curtiss, and Ellyson,

11. The Curtiss A-1 was the U. S. Navy's first plane. Lieutenant T. G. Ellyson was sent to Hammondsport in 1911 to act as inspector of the A-1 and instruct another officer. Captain Washington Irving Chambers, holding his life preserver, is perched alongside Ellyson, ready for a demonstration flight. Note the pivoted steering column. The plane had a 50-horsepower engine.
12. J. H. Towers reported to Hammondsport for training on 27 June 1911. He later became Naval Aviator No. 3.
13. During the summer of 1911, Ellyson instructed Towers in flying. When he qualified for his Aero Club license, Towers considered it the perfect ending to a wonderful summer.

he kept up a steady exchange about plane designs, specifications, and progress, while he inched the official papers through departmental red tape. Finally, on the first of June, the plane builders received official invitations to bid.

A few days later Ellyson flew the rebuilt hydroaeroplane. A week later its propeller broke in the air. The pieces missed the outriggers and wires, and Ellyson became the first man to glide a floatplane without power. He was pleased—and a bit surprised—when he landed without cracking up.

After Curtiss got the formal order, there occurred another serious delay that was characteristic of the early days of naval aviation. A new janitor was tidying up the shop by himself. Coming upon a pencil-marked wall, he whitewashed it, thus obliterating the only working drawings Curtiss had for his planes. Curtiss could not remember all of the dimensions he had used in his sketches or the changes to them. Production stopped. It took him nearly two weeks to reconstruct the sketches and get the shop going again.

13

On 1 July 1911, Captain Chambers arrived in Hammondsport to inspect the U. S. Navy's first plane. The A-1 sat on its boxlike, 16-foot pontoon by the shore of the lake, awaiting its first flight. It looked like the rebuilt Triad with a single float and a low forward elevator. A pivoted steering column could put the wheel in front of either of its two seats. It was powered with one of the Curtiss 50-horsepower engines, loaned for the occasion. The bigger one, built for the Navy, was still in the shop after several failures on the test stand.

In the early evening, when the air was almost still, Curtiss flew the plane off the lake for a short demonstration flight. Then Ellyson went with him for another short hop to prove its balance. After that, the latter took it up for two flights, totaling half an hour, before the light failed.

On the following evening, Chambers watched Ellyson qualify in this new plane for his Aero Club of America license. Then Curtiss took Chambers up. It was the first time the officer in charge of naval aviation had been in the air. He flew again in mid-July at Dayton, where Orville Wright demonstrated the Navy's first Wright machine and then took the captain up for half an hour. Chambers never tried to handle a plane himself. In the next two years, he rode briefly as a passenger on one other occasion. In that time his self-confidence grew. He became known through his writing and speeches as the Navy's aviation expert. He was always enthusiastic, but his aerial experience was too limited to correct errors generated by the Langley-type thinking.

In these early days, naval aviators kept rough notes of their aeroplane records. These logs on loose-leaf sheets were written up in duplicate in order to provide Chambers with file copies. The first entry in the A-1 log ended thus:

"Lieut. (j.g.) Towers, J. H., U.S.N., reported for duty."

John Henry Towers was a slim, blonde, and unusually shy young man from Rome, Georgia. He had graduated near the top of the Naval Academy Class of 1906, a year later than Ellyson, and in 1910 he was the foretop spotter on the *Michigan*. She was the Navy's first dreadnaught and her big guns could shoot farther than he could see from her tops. Towers had never seen a plane, but he thought a flying machine might be the answer to the need for better spotting. Early in November of 1910, before Ely's flight from the *Birmingham*, Towers asked "for instruction in aeroplaning in case the Navy adopted them." His skipper begged him not to spot his record with so unorthodox a request. The Department filed it, and Towers sailed for Europe in the *Michigan*.

In the spring of 1911, Chambers was successful in his argument that, since he was ordering two Curtiss planes, the Navy needed two pilots who could fly them. Thereupon Towers' request was exhumed, but it took several months to get him transferred. In France he had seen French planes and had watched their spectacularly uniformed pilots strutting about, and he expected something equally grand when he arrived in Hammondsport.

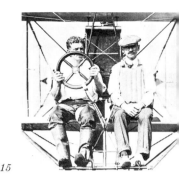

15

14

42 That quiet little country town in central New York state was a shock. Curtiss, quiet and unassuming, in an ill-fitting business suit, completed the surprise. Small talk was outside the scope of these shy men and, when silence got embarrassing, Jack Towers asked to see the plans for the Navy planes. Curtiss showed him the whitewashed wall covered with pencil lines, whereupon conversation stalled. Then Curtiss led Towers across the road to the porch of his cottage and disappeared. Re-appearing, he handed him a big glass of buttermilk. Jack loathed the stuff, but he could think of no graceful way to refuse it. So he braced himself, gulped a big mouthful, and promptly lost his breakfast over the porch rail. This broke the ice; the two were friends for life.

At Hammondsport, Towers shared quarters with "Spuds" Ellyson, who had been impatiently awaiting his arrival. The first morning Spuds had him down at the field before sunrise. He showed Jack a barnful of old planes, most of which never flew. Then he wheeled out old Lizzy, the grass cutter.

As he explained the Curtiss method of flight instruction, Ellyson whittled a stick with his jackknife. Fitting the stick under the throttle, he drove Lizzy down the field. At the edge of the lake he lifted her nose around and drove back. Only then did Jack realize that Spuds, not Curtiss, was to be his flight instructor.

"O.K.," said Ellyson. "You drive it up and down like that for a while. Push the throttle all the way down. You can't take off."

14. *The Navy's first plane, the Curtiss A-1, at Hammondsport, June 1911. Left to right: Charles Witmer, civilian pilot; John Cooper, mechanic; Dr. A. F. Zahm, engineer; 1st Lt. J. W. McClaskey, USMC (Ret.); Jim Lamont, mechanic; Glenn Curtiss; Lt. T. G. Ellyson; Captain W. I. Chambers; Lt. J. H. Towers; Mr. Pickens, Curtiss Exhibition Company; an unidentified mechanic.*

15, 16. *Ellyson, left; Curtiss, right. The two photos demonstrate the dual control Curtiss developed at the insistence of the Navy. The yoke permitted the wheel to be passed from one pilot to the other. Later, two wheels were mounted on the Y-shaped control.*

17. *Curtiss is at the controls, with Ellyson riding as his passenger, in the first Curtiss Triad. Curtiss devised a way of raising the wheels for a water landing, or of lowering them for a ground landing—the first retractable landing gear. He named the plane the Triad because it would operate on land, sea, or in the air.*

Jack Towers took his seat in a flying machine for the first time. Scared of the machine, more scared of doing nothing, and much too shy to question a senior whom he did not know well, he jammed his foot down and headed for the lake. Halfway down the field, the plane met a catspaw of wind. Towers was twenty-odd pounds lighter than Ellyson and the old grass cutter jumped into the air, stalled, fell on a wing, and rolled up into a bundle of broken sticks and tangled wire. Jack crawled out of the wreckage. He had assorted cuts and bruises, a broken ankle and, strangely enough, a strong craving to fly.

"Good God!" cried Spuds. "I did the same thing, but not on my first run. I worked up to it."

A couple of weeks later, Towers laid aside his crutches. His ankle was still stiff, but he began grass cutting in another Lizzy. The Navy trainer, the A-2, was delivered in mid-

16

17

July. He soloed it up and down the field on two successive days. After 25 normal landings, the front wheel collapsed. The plane skidded to a stop with broken main braces and outriggers. It went into the shop, and Towers shifted to another machine.

While Towers was accumulating solo time, he also learned from the experiences he shared with Ellyson. They began on the evening Spuds had attempted to fly Chambers to the foot of the lake to catch the train to Washington and had had to taxi all the way because the engine would not lift two big men. For the solo hop back to Hammondsport, he took off easily. Twilight was fading when he landed, only part way back, and ran up onto the beach. The long taxi had used up all his oil. It took an hour in those early days of the automobile to locate some more. By then it was dark, but the town's lights let him see well enough to take off. Eleven minutes later, as he neared the Curtiss factory, the lake was a black shadow. The only light came from the stars. He thought he still had at least 20 feet of altitude when the nose of the float hit. The plane bounced. Spuds jammed his foot down on the throttle, squared away, and then eased the machine down again. This time it settled slowly, power partly on, nose a little high. Again, it hit before he expected it to, but it stayed down. This was naval aviation's first night landing, and the first "power stall," a technique that became standard for seaplanes at night.

Although the A-1 had flown, it was still not finished. None of the bamboo tails had any stability. In the air, they were as touchy as tightrope walkers. The practice in those days, when a plane was assembled, was to approximately balance it statically. Then it was test-flown for balance. After this flight, the pilot shifted weights, seat, pontoon, or engine, to relieve the pressures he had felt on the controls. This trial and error work continued until the plane was rigged to please him. Each time he changed the landing gear or the engine, Ellyson had to go through this procedure all over again.

Towers got in his solo work between hops in the A-1 with Ellyson. This could be flown from either seat, but not both, and hence was unfit for dual instruction. The throw-over wheel had been intended only to allow pilots to relieve each other on long flights. There were no long flights that summer. Almost every landing was a forced landing.

The 80-horsepower engine was an expansion of an earlier freehand design and was the biggest motor Curtiss had thus far built. There had been repeated test stand failures and, after it was installed in the plane, all the main bearings burned out. On the next flight test, there were eight forced landings in a row before it was sent back to the shop for another overhaul. When Ellyson filled out the log forms later, he wrote: "No record was kept between the above dates (23 July and 30 August) because the engine failed in so many respects that it had to be rebuilt." Then he filled three pages with descriptions of the failures. Almost everything had broken several times—cylinders, pistons, valves, the radiator, pipes, and mani-

43

18

44 folds. The Curtiss Company footed the bill, Jack and Spuds flew when they could, and the rest of the time skinned their knuckles on wrenches.

Oil, water, and gas leaks plagued them. They tried gaskets of lead, blotting paper, wrapping paper, flax, and rubber. They smeared joints with shellac, white lead, soap, chewing gum, and paint. Lines clogged. Vibration loosened everything from propeller nuts to timing gears. They drilled and inserted cotter pins and installed safety wires. Many of their expedients later became industry standards. They improved the A-1, but they never cured her of all her ills.

The airfield was so small that, when the A-1 was used as a landplane, it could only take off while the wind came off the lake. Then the plane had to swing wide across the water to get back over the land. Before operating the A-1 as a landplane, Ellyson put flotation tanks under the wings of the practice plane, the A-2, and intentionally landed it in the lake. It stood on its nose. He shifted the tanks and tried it again next day. It floated, undamaged, on an even keel.

He then fitted similar tanks under the A-1's wings. But when a faulty magneto dropped that machine into the lake, it dove. Ellyson and Towers clawed their way up through the wings, then spent two and one-half hours in the icy water riding the plane's tail to balance it while a boat worked it inshore for salvage. Years later, Towers said they built a fire to thaw out, and Spuds was so done in that he fell on his face into it. At the time, Ellyson wrote to Chambers,

18. *T. G. Ellyson and J. H. Towers in the A-2, August 1911, Hammondsport, New York.*
19, 20, 21. *In his search for a means of launching aircraft from ships, Curtiss devised a launching wire, which was tried at Hammondsport on 7 September 1911. One of the Curtiss hydros was hauled up the steel cable from Lake Keuka to a platform on the hillside. Two lighter wires balanced the wings. Ellyson took his place at the controls, ran up the engine, and released. The plane soared out over the water after a run of 150 feet. The wire launching device was tried only once and abandoned when catapults promised a better technique.*

"Some kind friend brought us a pint of whiskey, so no ill effects."

In early September, Ellyson flew the A-1 half a dozen times as a hydroaeroplane in order to compare different propellers. Before he took off the last time, a 25-knot wind had built up three-foot waves. When he tried to taxi, after his landing, a wave licked the end of the propeller, and the blade snapped off near the hub, breaking a rudder wire and tail outrigger. He cut the switch but the unbalanced stub spun long enough to wreck the engine bed, radiator, and most of the plumbing, while waves bashed in the bow of the float. While he salvaged and repaired, Ellyson blamed himself for poor judgment.

Captain Pond's report on Ely's flights had suggested takeoffs from a monorail, or a stay, as simpler than from a platform. After the *Pennsylvania* had taken the Curtiss hydro aboard, Ellyson had got down to details in a letter to Chambers. He suggested three parallel wires held apart by spreaders. One spreader would be secured on the forecastle at the bow. The other could be hoisted up the foremast by winch until it was about

19

20

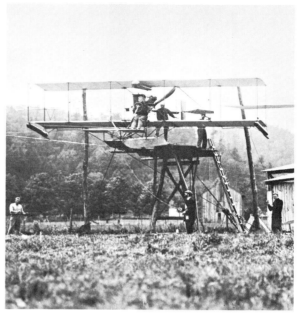

20 feet above the forecastle with the wires taut. The hydroaeroplane, with its keel on the center wire, would be secured to and hoisted with this after spreader. It was Ellyson's idea that the pilot could then release his machine with the engine wide open, slide down the wire, and take off. The side wires would steady the wings until he had aileron action. He estimated it would take 15 minutes to rig the gear, take off, and re-stow the wires. Chambers gave his approval and Curtiss volunteered to try out the scheme.

There was considerable delay in assembling the gear and solving the rigging problems. The wires were stretched from a piling in the lake up to sheer legs on the beach. Finally, on 7 September, with a metal channel on its keel, one of the Curtiss hydros was hauled up the wire from the lake. In case the side wires were not enough, Curtiss stationed men alongside with wing-tip steadying lines. Ellyson ran up his engine, set his controls with down flipper to insure plenty of speed before he left the wire, and released. The wing-line men were not needed. The hydro took off from the wire after 150 feet and, thought Ellyson, astonishingly quickly and easily.

In the *Scientific American,* Chambers praised Ellyson for "successfully performing the daring experiment of showing the

possibility and facility with which a hydroaeroplane can be sent in flight from a ship in smooth water over an improvised single wire cable." But, as he wrote the article, Chambers knew that something better was needed. Above a rolling ship, a plane would never balance on a wire.

Ellyson had accepted the A-2 in mid-July, but it proved too underpowered to be even a good Lizzy. After Towers' first two days of practice in it, nobody wanted to use it. In September, after the wire experiment, both pilots flew the A-2 and Towers kept it up for five minutes, which was two minutes longer than anyone else had ever done with that engine. The next day Curtiss loaned them an 8-cylinder, 60-horsepower engine, and Towers used it to qualify for his Aero Club of America license.

For three more days, they flew the A-2 with this borrowed engine. Towers nearly doubled his solo time. Qualifying for his A.C.A. license he considered a perfect ending to the best summer he could remember. He and Ellyson had been bumped, banged, skinned, and dunked, but pioneering in the air was the most wonderful and exciting sport in the world. John Towers was in naval aviation for the rest of his professional career, which ended upon his retirement with the rank of admiral after World War II.

45

CHAPTER FIVE: AVIATION COMES TO ANNAPOLIS

The second man in the U. S. Navy to qualify as a naval aviator was John Rodgers, the last of four men of that family to serve their country as naval officers. The original John Rodgers had commanded the USS *John Adams* at Tripoli in 1802, and as a commodore led the Navy against the British in the War of 1812. His son John became a rear admiral and had a distinguished career during the Civil War. Third in line was John Augustus, who also became a rear admiral and was the father of the naval aviator, who was plain John Rodgers once again.

Rodgers, who graduated from the Naval Academy in 1903, was attached to the *Pennsylvania* at the time of Eugene Ely's famous flight, was detached shortly thereafter, and ordered home to await orders. At this time, Chambers was in correspondence with the Wright brothers, who had offered to train a pilot. Young John Rodgers was named for this honor.

Over the next few years, the Wrights and a good many others came to believe that John Rodgers had some powerful friends in Washington. That they may have been right, later events might seem to confirm. Be this as it may, when Chambers was forced by lack of funds to cancel these arrangements with the Wrights, things began to happen with a speed unusual in bureaucratic Washington.

The Wrights' manager wired back an offer to train Rodgers unconditionally, urging speed since the head of the school was to leave Dayton on the first of April. That same afternoon Winthrop, "acting," wired the Navy's acceptance of the unconditional offer and signed Rodgers' orders "for instruction in the art of aviation."

And so John Rodgers went to Dayton, Ohio. The instruction routine there was quite different from the course that Ellyson was then following at North Island. The Wright controls were completely non-instinctive. There were two levers, one at each side of the pilot's seat. The left lever moved forward and aft and made the machine's nose go down or up. The right lever was pushed forward to bank the plane to the left and pulled back to bank the other way. Also, the top of this right lever was hinged. Laying it over to the left applied the left rudder, and vice versa. In order to accustom a student to this system, an old plane was mounted on sawhorses. When this original flight simulator's controls were moved, clutches grabbed a moving belt and tilted the machine. The motions were too jerky, however, to simulate the feeling of flight.

Dual instruction in the Wright B model was the mainstay of the course. In this machine, as in the single seaters, the left seat and engine were offset so as to balance each other. In a centerline seat, the second man could use the regular turn and bank lever with his left hand. A duplicate elevator lever was at his right.

This system resulted in two kinds of Wright pilots. Those who were trained in

---

1. *At the Greenbury Point aviation camp the pilots did most of the work on the planes themselves. The only way to develop Navy planes seemed to be to fly them until they quit, fix what broke, and then start all over again. (Courtesy U. S. Naval Academy Museum)*

the left seat steered with their right hand, and could solo with the center seat empty. Right side fliers steered with their left hands, and they always needed a man for ballast in the left seat. For them flights were logged "in control," rather than "solo." John Rodgers was a left side pilot.

Even when both men were light, dual instruction flights could never last more than seven or eight minutes, and they never could go very high. On the first few flights, the student just rode. Then he was allowed to follow through with a light touch on the levers while the instructor flew. The next step was to handle one lever in the air for a part of each flight. Later he handled them simultaneously. When he had acquired sufficient coordination, he was instructed in take-offs and landings.

After he had soloed in April, Rodgers stayed on at Dayton until he could act as inspector of the Navy machine when it was ordered. During this period, he flew occasionally as an advanced student. Years later, an Army officer, who had trained at Dayton with him, said, "The two Rodgers boys never showed good flying sense. I always knew they would kill themselves." Others were agreed that their records showed more guts, perseverance, and ingenuity than judgment and flying skill.

The reference to "two Rodgers boys" includes a cousin of John Rodgers, Calbraith P. Rodgers, a civilian, whom John quite early in the game talked into joining him as a student flier at Dayton. Cousin Cal, as the other fliers came to call him, was a big man, a 200-pound, six-footer, and an in-

2. Sports-loving Cal Rodgers in the open cockpit of the biplane in which he made the first coast-to-coast flight from Sheepshead Bay, Long Island, to California, in 1911. (Wide World Photo)
3. Cheered on his way, Cal Rodgers takes off on 17 September 1911. Forty-nine days and 69 stops later he landed in Pasadena, California, and became the first man to fly coast to coast. Almost every piece of the plane had been replaced at least once by the end of the flight. (Wide World Photo)

veterate cigar chewer. He had an impediment in his speech and was very deaf, both of which infirmities had been caused by scarlet fever.

After Chambers had visited Dayton and had flown with Orville Wright in the B-1, he asked the latter to store it until he should send shipping orders, through Rodgers, when the Navy had a field. This was so different from his instructions at Hammondsport that one wonders if Chambers, also, did not question Rodgers' skill.

Long before the Navy plane was ordered, John wanted a flying machine, and he wanted to play a part in the current aviation show business. For some time he did nothing about it because he knew the Department would object, and in addition he did not have the money. Then the National Cash Register Company offered him $3,500 to fly around their new smokestack in Dayton for the purpose of taking publicity pictures. John said a naval officer could not do such a job, but there was Cousin Cal. He could and he would.

This set in motion a comic opera sequence that was entirely characteristic of this barnstorming era of early aviation. In view of the defect in Cousin Cal's speech, it was quite

3

natural that Cousin John should do the talking and negotiating for him. Throughout, the two Rodgers boys worked so closely that many people thought they were brothers. Indeed, later research fails to reveal clearly on some occasions just who did what.

When John volunteered him for the smokestack job, Cousin Cal, who was a right-seat man, had never soloed. So on that job, left-seat John rode as his "mechanic." The money went as a down payment for a Wright plane. John negotiated the sale. Later, when Cal needed a new engine, it was John who wrote for prices and specifications. Still later, it was John who asked the Wrights to license Cal to build Wright planes on the West Coast.

The Navy's B-1 was in storage at Dayton in early August when John qualified, perhaps in Cousin Cal's plane, for his Aero Club of America license. Four days later, Cousin Cal chalked up the next license. And right after that, they took Cal's plane to the Chicago air meet.

In Chicago, John informed Towers and Ellyson he was not flying the Navy plane because Chambers had told him not to. He said he was the half owner of Cal's machine, but that he was not flying it because he thought the Department would object. Instead he was riding as "mechanic" for right-seat Cal. He must have been a good one. Cousin Cal was credited with more time in the air than any other pilot at the meet. He pocketed $11,285 cash as a prize, and this more than finished paying for the plane. The news stories mentioned John only as a relative, not as mechanic, manager, or part-

ner. They never reported that he arranged Cal's barnstorming dates after the Chicago meet. Nevertheless, the next issue of *Aero* carried this notice:

The Rodgers Aviators. (Wright biplane) Now Booking. Permanent address: R. S. Richardson, Manager, Dayton, Ohio.

During the next month, Cousin John visited Cousin Cal wherever he put on a show. After a few days, he would leave, either on Navy business or to find new bookings for Cal. The last of August, John had the Wrights move the Navy's B-1 to Annapolis, where the Greenbury Point field was reported ready. But he did not use the field. Instead he took his plane to College Park, where the Army fliers were operating.

Half a year later, when he started the B-1 smooth log from his notes, Rodgers entered all the September flights in an unlikely sequence, dated 3 September. This included several flights at College Park, a hop from Annapolis to College Park via Washington, and a return via Baltimore and Havre de Grace, where his parents lived. He entered only total flying time without any stops, elapsed time or mishaps. Still later Captain Chambers cited, in the Secretary's annual report, the flight from College Park to Annapolis (an airline distance of 25 miles) as the Navy's "first notable cross-country flight." If it occurred as logged, on the same day as the other flights, or on any other date, without mishaps, it was a record that neither plane nor pilot ever achieved again.

Cousin John had arranged for Cousin Cal to try for a $50,000 prize offered by William Randolph Hearst for the first man to fly

4

from coast to coast within a period of thirty days. The Armour Company also contracted to pay Rodgers by the mile for advertising their new soft drink, Vin-Fizz, along the route. A special train was chartered to follow the flight. It carried mechanics, a carload of spares for the new Wright single-seater the Rodgers boys had bought for this venture, and also Cal's wife.

On a mid-September afternoon, a big crowd assembled at the Sheepshead Bay (Long Island) race track to watch Cal's flying start. He reached Middletown, New Jersey, on that hop. But the next morning he took off into wires and trees and made junk of the plane. He blamed himself for not seeing the obstructions and for using too small a field. But others conjectured that his deafness may have been the cause of this and many another of his crashes. Planes had no instruments and, unlike other pilots, Cal could not hear his engine begin to misbehave.

When this news reached Annapolis, John left the B-1 in a Greenbury Point hangar in care of Dale B. Sigler, electrician's mate first class, who may well have been the first Navy enlisted man detailed to aviation. Then, with Chambers' blessing, he went to help Cal. When the mechanics had rebuilt the plane, John went on ahead to find landing fields and to arrange for servicing. Frequently he backtracked in order to help patch up the results of another crash. At the end of the specified thirty days, Cousin Cal was repairing the plane in east Texas. His crashes and poor navigation had saved Hearst $50,000, but Vin-Fizz was still paying by the mile. So the

4. *Autumn of 1911 saw the establishment of the Navy's first aviation camp on Greenbury Point, across the Severn River from the Naval Academy. The camp was moved to a privately owned beach beside the Naval Academy's Experimental Station in 1912. This rare aerial photograph shows the Navy's aviation camp at its second site, with Greenbury Point in the background.*
5. *Left to right: H. H. Wiegand, T. G. Ellyson, J. H. Towers, and D. Sigler, with the A-1. Wiegand and Sigler were two of the first enlisted men assigned to naval aviation.*
6. *The Curtiss A-2 in front of the hangars at Greenbury Point, 1911. Left to right: Chief Carpenter's Mate Erickson, Chief Gunner's Mate H. H. Wiegand, and Chief Electrician D. L. Bronson.*

Rodgers boys went on to finish what they had started. John zigzagged them westward with stops wherever a carnival, fair, or advertiser could put cash on the barrel head for Cal's appearance.

Both Cousin Cal and the machine took a beating. Before they reached Pasadena in November, almost every piece of the plane had been replaced at least once. Cal had made some hops with his leg in a cast and crutches lashed to a wing, so he could move about after his next landing or crash. Early in November, he left Pasadena for Long Beach, which had bid highest along the coast for the honor of being his terminal. Before he neared Long Beach, the engine quit and he crashed again. This time the machine was finished. Cal, unconscious, was dug out of the mud and transported to a hospital where he remained for over a month.

Cousin John could not wait. He returned to Annapolis to fly the B-1.

Calbraith Rodgers did not win Hearst's $50,000 prize; nonetheless, he became the first man to fly coast to coast, even though

5

6

he had to make 69 stops en route in order to do so.

Even before Chambers had ordered the first Navy planes, he was looking for adequate motors. He found none. At Annapolis, the Navy Engineering Experiment Station was in operation on Greenbury Point beside the Naval Academy rifle range. Rear Admiral Cone offered its help for engine development. Chambers accepted and, during the summer of 1911, he arranged for a small hangar and a small field between the target butts and the beach of Greenbury Point. The only practical access to this aviation camp, which had no living quarters, was by boat from the Naval Academy across the Severn River.

In September 1911, Ellyson, Rodgers, and Towers were ordered to report to the Superintendent of the Academy and to Captain Thomas W. Kinkaid, the officer in charge of the Experiment Station, "for duty . . . in connection with the test of gasoline engines and other experimental work in the development of aviation. . . ."

Towers was the first to check in. Kinkaid offered him desk space, asked for a weekly report to forward to Washington, and showed no further interest. Captain John H. Gibbons, the superintendent, ignored the existence of aviation and aviators except when he signed "forwarded" on their scanty official mail. Nobody in the Navy, save Captain Chambers, spent any time worrying about the Navy's first three fliers.

Army pilots, who were flying at nearby College Park, were held in similar low esteem by the rest of the Army. Some of them had trained with the Navy pilots. The two groups swapped parts, parties, information, and other help in greater quantities than the surviving records show. But, when the Army group suggested that the Navy pilots join them at College Park and work together to advance service flying, Ellyson declined. He never wanted a separate air force and shied away from the reporters who frequented the Army camp. He foresaw that a lot of unspectacular development would be necessary to make planes useful to the Fleet and, he thought, this could best be done at Greenbury Point.

The aviators lived in Carvel Hall, an inn just outside the Academy gates. To cross the Severn to their hangar, they used an open motor launch. The same boat was their only means of reaching a plane in trouble on the water. It was equipped with a Norfolk engine, a 2-cycle monstrosity that for many years caused more profanity than anything else the Navy ever had. The starter was a fathom of rope, which the boat engineer would wind around the flywheel. Then he pulled and prayed. If he had lived right, if he had squirted just the right prime into the pet cocks atop the cylinders, if the magneto was dry—plus a lot of other "ifs"—the engine might start. But usually it just coughed and lay still. On cold mornings the most stubborn mule was a comparative paragon of willing cooperation. On some of these mornings, all of naval aviation worked on this marvelous marine engine before it would carry them across the Severn.

The Navy plane at Dayton had not flown.

7

At Hammondsport, Glenn Curtiss had supplied parts, gasoline, oil, and some labor for repairing the Navy planes, all at no cost to the government. At Annapolis, Ellyson and Towers asked for mechanics, but even after Chambers sent them two electricians, they did most of the work themselves. Then they got a few men nobody else needed at the moment. A cook, a coxswain, and a gunner's mate arrived—but the fliers had no galley, boat, or guns. Using their Hammondsport experience, Towers and Ellyson turned these unsuspecting sailors into the Navy's first aviation mechanics.

The three pilots were financial, as well as professional, outcasts. No supply officer was authorized to issue them tools or materials. They got some by begging, more by midnight requisitions. They spent their own pay for gasoline, travel, flight clothing, and other essentials they could get in no other way. Air-meet prizes helped meet these extra expenses. Before checking in at Annapolis, Rodgers had barnstormed with Cousin Cal. Ellyson took leave, rented a plane, and won $700 racing it at a Brooklyn air meet.

When the A-1's engine reached Annapolis after another rebuilding, Towers assembled the hydro, flight-tested it, and worked on it for a week. Then he discovered a new hazard —on each Wednesday and Friday midshipmen on the firing range spattered the aviation camp with high shots which punctured the machines and drove everyone out. After the first week, the fliers abandoned the place on those afternoons and patched holes before flying the next day.

7. Towers and Ellyson at the dual control devised by Curtiss which permitted control of the aircraft to be passed from one to the other in flight by means of a pivot at the lower end of the wheel column. Originally intended to improve student training by eliminating the "self-teaching" phase, the changeover proved too slow in emergencies and the device was later modified by adding a second wheel. 8. Some of the difficulties which beset Ellyson and Towers on their flight to Fortress Monroe are recounted by Ellyson in this entry from the A-1 log.

When Ellyson arrived, they worked four more days on the A-1's erratic engine. The only way to develop Navy planes that could function like ships seemed to be to fly them until they quit, improve what broke, and then do it all over again. For such a purpose, Ellyson and Towers took off for Fortress Monroe, Virginia, one October day.

After half an hour Ellyson landed, to secure the gas tank which had shaken loose. Towers then flew 20 minutes before having to land again to repair other vibration damage. A half hour after Ellyson made the third takeoff, the engine clattered, clanked, spat black smoke, and put them down at Smith's Point, 75 miles south of Annapolis. The main bearings had burned out. A torpedo boat running wireless tests in the bay took the plane back to Annapolis. The fliers shipped the engine back to its maker. This time Curtiss gave up. He sent a new 75-horsepower model to replace it.

Cold north winds were hitting Annapolis when the plane was ready again. On 23 October, Towers took it out to test the new engine. He lasted three minutes, then a wave grabbed a wing-tip float and broke a wing. They put on a spare and tried it the next

NO. OF FLIGHT.	REMARKS.

77 — Lt. Ellyson driving. Landed at 2:05 p.m. at Smith's Point, Va., owing to #3, #4, #7 and #8 crank bearings burnt out. Total distance 79 miles in 85 minutes. Disassembled the machine and placed it on the U.S.S. Bailey which had been summoned by wireless, and returned to Annapolis, Md.

Oct 12 — Unloaded machine from U.S.S. Bailey and commenced setting up same. Shipped engine to Curtiss Aeroplane Co., Hammondsport N.Y.

Oct 13 — Finished assembling machine.

Oct 19 — Installed non-skid planes. Painted machine where necessary.

Oct 21 — Received new 75 H.P. engine from Curtiss Aeroplane Co., and installed same. Fitted auxiliary oil tank to right side of engine bed.

Oct 22 — Installed new magneto and made new carburetter adjuster.

78 — When landing buried right wing owing to wind. Lower panel broken where wing tip pontoon made fast to rear plane beam.

79 — Renewed right lower end panel. Day very rough. In turning on water broke end of propeller.

80 — The objective point of this flight was Fort Monroe, Va., and the purpose of the flight was to determine and eradicate the weak points of the machine, to determine the physical strain caused by a long trip, and to thoroughly test the shift control.

80 — Lt. Towers occupied the right seat which can be disconnected from the controls, and several times during the trip he was able to tighten water connections and make minor repairs, doing away with the necessity of landing. Once he stopped a bad water leak by climbing partly out of his seat to the engine section, and tightening the water manifold. Lts. Ellyson and Towers drove alternately for fixed periods, thus preventing fatigue

Landed at 2:17 p.m., at Milford Haven, Va., having covered 112 miles in 122 minutes. The landing was made through a 6 foot surf with a 20 mile wind astern, and was made because the engine ran hot due to loss of water from the radiator. The radiator was leaking in the honeycombing at the lower right hand corner, the water connection at the upper right hand corner had broken due to vibration, and there were leaks around the packing nuts on the water manifold. It was impossible to rise from the rough water in the Bay, so the machine was taxied into Milford Haven where the water was smooth. The leaks were temporarily repaired, radiator filled, and five gallons of gasoline added. The metal pipe connecting the auxiliary oil tank to the oil case was found to be

80 — broken in two places, so the auxiliary tank was unrigged and shipped to Fort Monroe, Va.

One copy to be retained for aviator's log. Duplicate to be sent to Navy Department. Bureau of Navigation, for filing in Department Aviation Records.

Signature: T. G. Ellyson, Lieutenant, U.S. Navy

54 day. Everything went well until they tried to run toward the beach after their hop. The propeller hit the water and shattered.

On the day of the third flight, there was a 25-knot wind from the northwest. At noon they took off and headed for Fortress Monroe without waiting to test the new propeller in the air. Twenty minutes later, with the bay beneath them a rolling surface of white caps, the engine manifold began to spew water. Towers motioned Ellyson to keep on going, unlatched the back of his seat from the aileron control and, facing aft, knelt on the seat. Hanging to a wire brace with his left hand, he fished a pair of pliers from his pocket, tightened the leaking packing nuts, and then squirmed back into his seat.

For two hours they periodically swapped the controls while the north wind booted them down the western shore of Chesapeake Bay. Several times Towers had to disconnect his seat and stretch back to tighten something that worked loose. However, he was helpless when both the core and top connection of the radiator broke. They landed in rough water off Milford Haven and had good luck in beaching through a six-foot surf without damaging the machine. With the strong wind, they had covered 112 miles in 122 minutes.

A curious waterfront crowd watched them patch the cooling system with chewing gum, whittled sticks, wire, and friction tape. They tightened things up generally and took on gas and water. In the late afternoon a boatman towed them into quiet water where a takeoff was possible. Twenty-five minutes

9. The Navy's Wright plane, the B-1, in its original configuration, before the Burgess floats were fitted to it. Ensign Victor Herbster and Lieutenant John Rodgers are in the foreground.

later, with Fortress Monroe in sight, five miles ahead, the radiator let go again. Its rusty water drowned the magneto and they landed with a dead engine. They dried the magneto, started the engine, and drove downwind through the heavy surf beating on Buckroe Beach. Before they worked into a quiet little cove, the pontoon split.

The next morning, having telegraphed for a new pontoon and radiator, with the gale still blowing, they put soft patches on the float and radiator, took out everything they could to lighten the plane, and put in only five gallons of gas. Then Towers, the lightest of the two, took off alone in the 200 feet of smooth water inside the surf line and five minutes later landed at their destination.

Their trip was hailed in the press as a record for hydroaeroplanes in distance and passenger carrying. The New York *Sun* said "the flight will justify Secretary Meyer in asking Congress in December for a liberal appropriation to equip the Navy with airships of the amphibious class." This lengthy article reviewed the development of the hydroaeroplane and concluded that, while limited to inland waters, "its value as a naval auxiliary for reconnaissance and dispatches cannot be seriously disputed . . . although its employment for damaging an enemy's ship with explosives may still be debatable."

Foul weather held them after the plane was set up with the new float and radiator.

9

After the storm passed, the return trip took another week. Without their Hammondsport shop experience, it would have taken much longer. Bad gasoline stopped their first take-off. A broken water pump shaft put them down at the York River. Before they reached Annapolis again, they had used borrowed tools and whatever metal they could find to make four pumpshafts, assorted pins, bushings, and braces. They soldered the radiator, patched the boat, tuned the engine, and waited out foul weather. When night caught up with them, they slept in whatever was at hand. Once fishermen ran away when they saw the strange machine taxi toward the beach. The nearly frozen fliers felt like heroes when they taxied up to their ramp on Greenbury Point. They had finished the trip in spite of the innate orneriness of weather, man, and machine.

Nobody greeted them. Nobody came to put a bowline on the plane. Deflated, they stepped stiffly off the nose of the pontoon, whereupon a couple of spent bullets kicked up sand at their feet. The day was Friday and the camp was deserted because the midshipmen were on the range. Said Jack and Spuds, "To hell with it." They threw a line on the plane and headed for hot toddies at the Carvel Hall bar.

The next event at the Navy's aviation camp was the arrival of prospective pilot Ensign Victor Daniel Herbster, graduate of the Naval Academy's Class of 1908. Short, swarthy, and husky, Herbster was a stub-

born, determined little man with a Napoleonic manner and a belligerent strut. The year before he had been at Brest in the USS *Minnesota* and from there he had gone to visit the Antoinette Aircraft Factory at Mour-Melon le Grande. He sent home a full report of their construction methods and of the seaplane they were designing. But he was unable to verify rumors that the French Navy was working out a system for ship-based aviation. Then about a year later, he was detached from the *Minnesota* to become a flier.

Captain Chambers wanted him trained entirely in a floatplane. While Ellyson and Towers agreed with Chambers that the Fleet had no need for landplanes, their view of training was different. They knew that a hydro was too tricky on the water for anything like the basic grass-cutting routine. Also the throw-over control wheel in the A-1 was unfit for dual instruction. Hence they thought a landplane trainer was essential as the first step. Chambers argued that pilots could be trained entirely in floatplanes using the Wrights' dual instruction system and thereby eliminate the need for Navy airfields. If he could find a float that the B-1 could carry, he was going to try it; but nobody, not even the Wrights, had built one. Up in Marblehead, Massachusetts, a yacht builder named Burgess was producing planes under license from the Wrights. He had flown one on twin floats, which he had built with vented steps, and he offered them to the Navy. On theoretical grounds, Chambers was suspicious of twin floats and dead against a

10. *The Wright B-1, the third plane purchased by the U.S. Navy, in Baltimore Harbor, after being fitted with the Burgess floats.*

56   step. He went shopping elsewhere; but sent word that Rodgers was to train Herbster in the Wright B-1.

When Rodgers reached Greenbury Point from California, Ellyson was on emergency leave. Towers and the Curtiss A-1 were weather-bound. Rodgers pulled the Wright B-1 from its hangar and flew a quick test from the little field. Then he gave Herbster a short ride. The next day he flew again and for a brief moment he let Vic handle the warping lever. That night he wrote to Chambers that the field was so small the plane had to keep turning all of the time to stay near it. Hence a student had practically no chance to learn anything. Moreover, he thought "teaching was a more or less dangerous occupation that should be done only when all conditions were favorable."

The next day Chambers asked Burgess to rush a set of floats to Annapolis and told Rodgers and Herbster to go to Marblehead to learn about them while they were being put together.

On 15 November, Towers flew from the water in the A-1. The first short flight went well in spite of the rough air churned up by a 20-knot wind above Greenbury Point. Three minutes after his second takeoff, with a hundred feet of altitude, a gust flipped the plane on edge and stalled it. There was not enough room for Towers to regain control and the plane hit the water nose down. He was thrown out and then smacked by the plane as it went over on its back. Struggling to it, he hauled himself up onto the bottom of the pontoon floating in the icy water.

Towers lashed himself to the float with his belt. For nearly an hour, over by the hangar, the boat crew frantically yanked the starting rope of the stubborn Norfolk engine. By the time they reached Towers, his face was blue and twice its normal size. His left leg was a sprained mess. This was the Navy's most serious aircraft casualty up to that time. Everyone thought Towers fortunate in not having been fastened to his seat and in being thrown clear without being knocked out.

When Rodgers reported the accident, he asked for a skiff, so they could row out if the boat engine balked again in such an emergency.

Jack wired Ellyson that he "had been shaken up a bit." It took Herbster and Rodgers two days to get the wreck onto the Experiment Station dock. There they left it and went on up to Marblehead to see the Burgess floats. A week later Ellyson came back from Richmond. He was shocked to find Towers still in bed and the A-1 a tangle of splinters and wires. Salvage work and salt water had ruined everything the crash had left unbroken. He overhauled the engine, salvaged the plane's nameplate, and swept the rest into the trash bins.

Using spares, he built a new A-1 around the engine and the nameplate. He was still working at this, when Rodgers and Herbster returned from Marblehead. On four out of the next five days, they flew a total of five and one-quarter hours in 22 flights. These included Ellyson's first ride in a Wright plane and 14 instruction flights for Herbster. This was the only concentrated instruction he ever received. The little man learned quickly and Rodgers reported to Chambers that he was "ready to go it alone now."

Then the Burgess floats arrived. It took three days to fit them and fix the wing that had been broken by cornstalks on the last field landing. When the B-1 was ready for a test, Rodgers, remembering Towers' crash, sent the boat out into the Severn near the place of his intended takeoff and told the coxswain to keep the engine running. The Burgess floats weighed only a hundred pounds more than the original landing gear, but this was almost too much. With the throttle wide open, the plane took off at 32 knots and, with throttle still wide open, flew level at 33 knots. The added weight was hung so low that the plane swung like a pendulum and level flight was trickier than ever. For half an hour Rodgers did well enough. Then, just after another takeoff, he turned to stay near the boat, and the plane stalled and crashed. When the boat fished him out, he was cold but unhurt. The B-1 was finished for the season. She needed nearly as many new parts as had been used to rebuild the A-1. Rodgers asked for two motor boats so they could be spotted in the seaplane flying area; but it was a long time before naval aviation got them.

When the problem of winter operations came up for discussion, Chambers favored Guantanamo, where the Atlantic Fleet might be impressed. Ellyson thought they would make more progress working with Curtiss at North Island and the Pacific Fleet ships. Then Chambers suggested that it might be undiplomatic to send the Wright machine to Curtiss' camp. Could Ellyson go out there and the other two to Cuba? Ellyson had objections to this. There were not enough spares for a winter in Cuba. Also he maintained that the planes should not be separated. Aviation was short of men and there was only one set of tools for the three planes. Furthermore, experimental flying was a two-man business. It would be unwise to separate Towers and himself when they had developed mutual confidence in the air. He was sure Rodgers and Curtiss could get along all right.

A week after Rodgers crashed the B-1, Towers and the A-1 were back in commission. It had been too cold to work in the hangar so the plane had been rebuilt as a landplane in the Experiment Station. They tested the engine, then took the wings off to get it out the door. Ellyson set it up, flew it from the narrow beach, and landed it in front of the hangar. The next day, Towers made four flights. Then the winter closed in. Finally, Washington decided to send them all out to San Diego.

The pilots closed up the Greenbury Point camp, sealed the planes in box cars and, after Christmas, took trains for San Diego. John Rodgers stopped in Dayton to see about a new engine for Cousin Cal, who had recovered and was in the flying game again.

CHAPTER SIX: CRASH, REPAIR, AND FLY AGAIN

When the planes were sent to North Island early in 1912, the Navy Department directed separate camps be established at "places designated by Curtiss, who has offered the use of the land." Ellyson, the number one aviator, was "entrusted with the care and control of the Navy Curtiss machines," while the Navy Wright machine was "independently under the control of Lieutenant John Rodgers," who was senior to Ellyson on the Navy list. This arrangement resulted in frequent references thereafter to the "Curtiss camp" or the "Wright camp" which designations meant, not that Glenn Curtiss or the Wright brothers were present, but merely that their planes were.

Near the northeast corner of North Island, Ellyson built a ramp to the water and set up his camp beside the Curtiss camp. New tents from the Mare Island Navy Yard and other gear from the USS *Iris* augmented the equipment shipped from Annapolis. A few days later, Rodgers established a similar camp near the inner end of Spanish Bight.

Towers and Ellyson had the A-1 flying as a hydroaeroplane on 30 January; but repairs on the Wright B-1 kept it grounded until the middle of February.

Generally, these two did more shop work than flying, with minor improvements accumulating as a result of their forced landings. They also tried out the Curtiss double control. It replaced the throw-over wheel with a "Y" that held a wheel in front of

each seat and made dual instruction practical. It also established a precedent. In reporting on this innovation, Ellyson wrote that the pilot sat on the left—"as he is in charge of the machine." He would take off and land, although, Ellyson continued, "this can and has been done equally well from the right seat."

Just why the left seat was so chosen is a mystery. This Curtiss plane did not have the balance problem that existed in the Wright B-1. Nonetheless, from that day to this, the first pilot has occupied the left-hand seat.

On the day this innovation was tested, as Ellyson taxied out for the seventh flight, the engine conked out. An internal bolt had sheered off, and it bounced around until it nearly wrecked the engine. The A-1 was grounded for a month and a half while parts were ordered and the engine rebuilt.

Five days later Rodgers had his plane in operation. After seven short dual flights, Herbster went up for his solo. The little man never liked to be behind in anything. After his solo flight, he practiced in the machine at every opportunity and he began to chafe because he had to divide its flying time with Rodgers. The latter gave rides to fleet officers, instruction to Towers and Ellyson, and even gave a couple of solo rides to Cousin Cal, who came down from Long Beach, where he was operating. In spite of this competition, Herbster was able to qualify for his Aero Club of America license nine days after his first solo. Thereupon, as the Navy's fourth pilot, he strutted around with a swagger.

As a hydroaeroplane, the B-1's performance was mediocre. With two men aboard,

---

1. *Narrow escapes and crashes were frequent with the fragile aircraft of 1911–1912. C. C. Witmer, a member of the Curtiss Exhibition Team, crashed in this Curtiss plane near Pittsfield, Massachusetts.*

2

60 she never got off in a calm, and she never carried them above two hundred feet. After he won his license, Herbster took a passenger up in this overloaded craft. A hundred feet above Spanish Bight, he thought a gust of wind knocked his right wing up. He knew the plane headed down to the left and refused to respond to the controls. The crash wrecked the B-1 but tough little Vic was not hurt. In a letter to the Wrights, he described the experience and asked them what had happened. Could it have been water in the floats?

Orville did not think so. He admitted that the plane was loaded "about at its limit." The mushy controls sounded "like it was due to what we call 'stalling.'" The Wrights cautioned their students about stalls, but for a long time most fliers failed to grasp the idea. Stalls got many a good man into trouble, and they explain many of the "air-hole" yarns of that day. When a plane had but a single-knot margin between flying speed and the lack of it, even a small air bump could cause it to stall.

While all the Navy planes were under repair, Towers began test flying for Curtiss. Mrs. Curtiss had long been apprehensive about her husband's flying. The year before, he had come into the polo field at nearby Coronado fast and low. In a hair-raising display of precision flying, he zipped around the oval several times, three feet above the ground, barely missing obstacles. The normally silent Lena Curtiss grabbed him when he stepped from the plane, and the reporters were delighted at her outburst. Glenn promised to do only experimental flying, but re-

cently she had been after him to stop that as well. So, when Towers began doing the testing, home life became calmer for Curtiss.

For Jack Towers, the arrangement was perfection. He loved to fly, and flying something new was the most interesting flying of all. He received no flight pay. He flew for fun, excitement, and experience. Forty years later, he would wonder if highly paid test pilots got as much satisfaction from their work and pay as he had found in doing this favor for a friend. That spring of 1912 he did far more flying than any other Navy pilot. He got himself into and managed to get out of several strange aerial predicaments. But he was the only Navy pilot who never wrecked a plane that season.

The wrecked Navy planes were still being repaired when Naval Constructor Holden Chester Richardson arrived at North Island. In the preceding September at Philadelphia, he had sketched floats for aeroplanes and had asked for duty with aviation. Thereupon Chief Constructor Watt had ordered him to the model basin on temporary duty. Captain Chambers welcomed him to Washington as a potential link between his office and the Bureau of Construction and Repair. Richardson wondered if the formula developed for ships' hulls could be used without change

3   4

for aeroplane floats. Maybe he should fly himself to check this? Moreover, that would let him try out his own designs. A few days before Christmas, he went to Annapolis to see the Navy planes and to talk about floats. Towers carried him on the last flight before the planes were packed for shipment. But the pilots all argued against his ideas.

At North Island, lacking a Navy hydroplane, Ellyson started Richardson up and down the field in a Lizzy. It was the middle of March before a Navy plane, the A-2, was back in commission. After a night of rain, that morning was clear and windless, and the runway steamed in the bright sun. Richardson wanted to start early, but Curtiss and Ellyson decided that it would be wise to make an air test first. Five minutes in the A-2 convinced Ellyson the air was too rough for anyone. He found it the same on later tests and, when Towers went up at a quarter past eleven, little dust devils were swirling up out of the field.

The next day Towers described what ensued in a letter to Captain Chambers:

> . . . I had one of the bumpiest rides of my life. I was alternately lifted and dropped at least 30 feet, probably more, and was thrown from one side to the other. At one time I was turned through nearly 90 degrees. Fortunately I was over 200 feet high, so had plenty of room to regain control. After having a great time jockeying for a landing I got down all right and advised the others not to go up or even grass cut. They had already decided on this after seeing my antics, so we went to luncheon.
>
> After luncheon Richardson was very anxious to get a chance to grass cut, so Ellyson, thinking that things must surely be settled by this time, said he would run down the two-mile straight way, staying close to the ground, land, turn around, and come back the same way. He went down all right but was badly tossed about. He had gotten about a third of the way back when he took a sudden drop, recovered, then a second one caused him to shoot straight into the ground, at an angle of about 45 degrees, and from a height of about 25 feet. It was so sudden that he had no time to do anything, and there was not room enough to recover anyway.
>
> The machine plowed an awful hole in the field and then turned over. As near as I could tell from the conditions, Ellyson was thrown from the seat through the front controls to the ground, striking on his helmet, then going on over and striking on his back and hips; the machine sort of scooped him up as it turned over.

The crash put a kink in Ellyson's neck that grounded him for over two months and troubled him the rest of his life.

Five days after Ellyson's crash, at the "Wright camp," Richardson saw the B-1 ready on a pair of his experimental pontoons. Rodgers took him out for the second flight, but the plane would not lift off the water with two hundred pounds of Richardson aboard. When the wind picked up a bit, John managed to get off with Herbster who weighed 127 pounds; when it died, he could not even solo.

Rodgers spent the next day taxiing. The V-bottom floats were hard to maneuver. At rest, their rear halves were submerged. The third day John soloed twice, and then staggered into the air with Richardson aboard. But, as soon as he began to instruct him in the Wright controls, the engine missed and down they went. With 25 knots of wind on their tail, they hit hard. From the "Curtiss camp" it looked like a crash,

61

5

but Richardson's pontoons took it without apparent damage.

On the third hop the next day, the right pontoon tore loose while Herbster was landing. The plane turned over, and the pilot flipped out unhurt, but the B-1 was a mess again.

In mid-April, Herbster almost got her in the air once more. The Navy floats had proved difficult to break out of the water, so, during the rebuilding, Richardson put hydrovanes under their sterns. Then, when Herbster started to take off, the vanes jumped one float out of the water while the other one dragged. The plane pivoted, but he cut the power before it capsized. So they removed the vanes and John Rodgers took her up.

There are at least three accounts of the wreck that followed. According to Richardson, the plane leveled off five feet above the water for a downwind landing "but between there and the water something, perhaps a puff of wind, changed the attitude so the pontoons entered the water about five degrees down by the head. . . ." The water being shallow, they stuck in the mud, and the machine turned slowly over, dropping John clear and unhurt.

John logged the accident as "failed to level off enough, catching the bow under water. . . ." Charles Wiggins, who had been Cousin Cal's mechanic, saw the crash and was one of those who waded out to help John ashore. To him, John confided the real cause. He had just bought one of those new-fangled wristwatches and, after leveling off, he took a peek at it to time his landing. In

5. *Naval Constructor Holden C. Richardson asked for aviation duty because he was interested in designing pontoons for aeroplanes. To try out his ideas, he learned to fly. Later, he became Naval Aviator No. 13.*
6. *A Curtiss hydroaeroplane with a single pontoon, on the beach at the Navy's training camp, Annapolis, spring of 1912.*

that instant of inattention, he let the nose drop.

Meanwhile, in the "Curtiss camp," the A-1 was in commission again, and Towers began teaching Richardson to fly. A month later, after 21 dual instruction flights, totaling four hours, Towers turned him loose to solo. The first time he did all right, and he thus became the first student taught to fly in a floatplane by dual instruction.

Richardson was keen about flying, and he was out the next morning for another try at it. In attempting to turn on the water in a cross wind, he got up too much speed. The plane suddenly took off, skidded in on its right wing, and went over on its back. Richardson emerged spluttering.

This was the end. When they got the A-1 ashore, it looked like junk again. Ten days later both camps closed up shop and the wrecks of the planes were shipped to Annapolis.

Richardson's schemes for pontoons had come to naught. While Towers had been instructing him, two pontoons had arrived from Washington. The formula which produced fast ships had been considered more scientific than the adverse opinions of Curtiss, Ellyson, and Towers, the world's most experienced hydroaeroplane pilots. The long, slim, sharp pontoon that Richardson had

6

patterned after a torpedo boat dove when Towers opened the A-1's throttle. Even when he pulled the elevator up as far as he could, he was unable to turn out of the wind and head back to the beach. And whenever he stopped, the pontoon began to sink by the stern. A boat finally caught up with him and took the plane in tow, with Towers straddling the bow of the pontoon to keep its tail surface out of the water.

From a statistical angle, the 110 days at North Island had been dismally unimpressive. In the "Curtiss camp," the A-2 had flown on only one day. The A-1 had logged a total of 13 hours and 15 minutes on 22 days. Over in the "Wright camp," the B-1 flew one day less but it did slightly better on hours. There were only three days when two planes were in the air. On 66 days none could fly. At the end of the season, Ellyson was on the sick list, the planes were wrecks, the Navy's floats had failed, and the B-1 had been proved useless as a hydroaeroplane.

Nevertheless there were items of progress. Herbster had qualified. The dual instruction system in a hydro had been initiated with the training of Richardson, who had learned about pontoons at first hand. Towers had become a successful test pilot and a competent instructor, and John Rodgers got married.

There was also a note of tragedy. On 3 April 1912, Cousin Cal lost his life in a crash at Long Beach.

At Annapolis in the spring of 1912, the two camps, on a privately owned beach beside the Experiment Station, were separated from each other only by a little dock. While this new site had no field, it was no longer in the line of fire from the midshipmen's practice range.

There then ensued the usual sequence of crashes, repairs, rebuilding, engine troubles, and intermittent flying, in the course of which John Rodgers gave his bride a hop in the B-1. In the middle of June, after surviving several forced landings, Towers and Ellyson managed to fly around the Fleet at anchor off Annapolis. Then there was the big day when they flew across Chesapeake Bay to Centreville, Maryland, and back, a round trip of 30 miles.

Near the end of the month, Towers tested the A-2, rebuilt as a hydroplane with a new 75-horsepower engine. Then all three planes started for the battleship *South Carolina*, which was lying at anchor off Baltimore. Ellyson, carrying his classmate "Fuzzy" McNair, failed to take off when the wake of a launch drowned his engine. After he had dried it, he did manage to get off and flew 16 miles before the engine quit. He was ignominiously towed home by boat.

Jack Towers, flying the A-2, carried Ike Dortch to the *South Carolina*. But halfway back they had to land to refill the overheated radiator. Then starting trouble delayed them until dark. They finished their flight by moonlight.

Rodgers could not get the B-1 in the air until he put Herbster ashore; then he soloed to the ship. Towers had left. The B-1 would not start, for the return trip, until a mechanic arrived by boat and tightened the parts that had shaken loose.

63

On the few other June days when the B-1 was flyable, Rodgers experimented. One day he carried Richardson to see how the pontoons would throw spray. On another he brought back the Navy's first aerial photograph. The rest of the time he was occupied trying to keep the engine running. After a year's experience, the Navy's planes were still far too unreliable for Fleet use. At Chambers' request, the four pilots recorded their ideas of practicable requirements for a Navy plane. It should fly from the water only and be so fitted as to be hoisted aboard ship and be disassembled there quickly for stowage. They wanted a top speed of at least 55 miles per hour, four hours endurance with two men and 100 pounds of wireless equipment at 50 miles per hour. Ellyson and Towers thought 100 feet per minute an adequate climbing speed, but Rodgers held out for 150.

The great trouble was—there was no engine that would log regular performances of sustained flight for four hours.

Richardson added his ideas. Instead of rigid requirements, he suggested rewards and penalties as incentives for high performance, prompt delivery, and the development of automatic devices. The hull should be divided into compartments and be constructed as a part of the plane and not just hung under it as an extra load. Plane makers should furnish a complete stress analysis and show that their machine could ride out 20 knots of wind on the surface. He also proposed demountable engine mounts to speed engine changes, which came into service 20 years later.

7. *John Rodgers, Naval Aviator No. 2.*

During this summer of 1912, a wireless message was first received from a Navy plane. When Towers had been attached to the USS *Michigan,* he had known Midshipman Charles Maddox, who was a competent wireless operator with a good working knowledge of the equipment. At the same time Towers went to Hammondsport, Maddox, then an ensign in the torpedo boat *Bailey,* began making reception tests for the Navy's new transmitter in Arlington, Virginia. In the fall, when Towers reported to the Experiment Station at Annapolis, the *Bailey* was based there. Maddox talked aircraft wireless with his old shipmate. Towers appreciated its potential value, but his immediate problem just then was staying in the air. Maddox soon understood why he did not relish either the weight or a trailing wire antenna near the pusher propeller. Nonetheless, he reappeared in December with orders to work "in connection with wireless telegraph for aeroplanes."

After a cold half-hour flight in the B-1, Maddox worked for the rest of the month with a transmitter he installed in the A-1, which was then being rebuilt. Towers took him up twice with it, but was never able to get the belt-driven generator working before the planes left for San Diego. In January, Maddox designed an aeroplane transmitter, and went to Harvard to take a course "in wireless."

In 1912, Maddox spent his summer vacation at Annapolis with his new wireless set, which weighed 40 pounds, including its belt-

7

driven generator. The spark-gap, helix, and other parts were in a skeleton crate on the lower wing. Under the upper wing, there stretched from tip to tip a four-wire antenna. On 27 July, he flew three times with Rodgers and worked the transmitter. The signal was merely a simple "dash dot dot"—International Morse code for the letter D—the *Bailey* picked them up a mile away. Maddox hung a receiving set around his neck and wore headphones under his helmet, but the magneto interference, noise, vibration, and wind prevented useful reception. Ensign Maddox made the first wireless transmissions received from a Navy plane; serviceable aircraft communications, however, remained far in the future.

After his wireless flights, Rodgers tested a Gyro engine in the B-1. While it took off consistently, after four or five minutes it would just as consistently overheat, lose power, and let the plane down. On the second day, as he was landing, it quit cold. He stalled and fell in on one wing. In Washington, the Gyro Company reworked the engine and sent it back. He got it into the air for a single, four-minute hop. Then it had to be torn down for more repairs. The experience was typical with the engines of those early days.

This was the last flight that John Rodgers logged for many years. He was absorbed in unfinished flight experiments when he suddenly received orders to sea duty. Ten years later, Rodgers came back to aviation in assignments that required him to do little or

no solo flying. In 1925, he commanded the flying boat PN9-1 on its hop from San Francisco to Hawaii. After better than 25 hours in the air the plane ran out of fuel and was forced down at sea, with no power for its radio. Rodgers and his crew made sails out of wing fabric and laid a course for Hawaii; they had sailed better than 400 miles when the submarine R-4 found them, only ten miles from Kaui.

In the summer of 1926, Rodgers, who was then Assistant Chief of the Bureau of Aeronautics, took off from Anacostia in a VE-9, a sweet-flying little Vought biplane. His first pass at Philadelphia's Mustin Field was high. He pulled away in a tight turn. One hundred and fifty feet above the Delaware River, the plane stalled, whipped into a spin, and crashed nose down in four feet of water. Rescuers splashed 100 yards out from the beach and pulled Commander Rodgers and Aviation Machinist's Mate Schultz out of the wreckage. Rodgers died that day at the League Island Hospital. Schultz eventually recovered and became a pilot.

Rodgers' detachment in 1912 was never noted in the weekly camp reports. In 1957, the Bureau of Naval Personnel could only say that his record "seemed to indicate" that his transfer from flying was a routine policy at that time. The Bureau could not state what the policy was or say why it had not affected Towers and Ellyson. Did they escape by remaining bachelors? A year later Towers assumed that another officer's married status would keep him out of aviation. If this was

65

NO. OF FLIGHT	REMARKS.
1	Trial flight alone with B-2. Forced to land & return on account of vertical rudder, turning
2	Trial flight with B-2 with passenger. Machine functioned excellently in the air. Boat proved an excellent for planing. Engine O.K. Boat has insufficient buoyancy aft & suction drags down tail on the water. Eight landings.
3 4	Conducting joint exercises with the submarine flotilla. Report will be sent in later. Submarines were discussed with principles planning. Chesapeake Bay.
5	Flight. slightly puffy
6	"
7 8	Conducting joint exercises with submarines. Chesapeake Bay
Oct 30 31	Overhauled B-2. All hands erecting new hangar
Nov 1 2 3	General cleaning up & overhauling.
5	Repaired pontoon & propeller
Nov 7	Magnets stripped motor on trial run. Removed & 8 gear wheel found stripped cause by screw in armature blocking out aileron jammed. Made all tail
9	pontoon. Tore all over thoroughly cleaning. Painted all tail wires with P&B Compound. Overhauled B-2.

Signature V. D. Herbster

(One copy to be retained for aviator's log. Duplicate to be sent to Navy Department, Bureau of Navigation, for filing in Department Aviation Records.)

8

66 established policy, why did it take over four months for the Navy Department to react to Rodgers' spring wedding? Was this bachelor policy originated by his influential family?

Herbster did not care. Indeed, he was glad to see Rodgers go. It left him free to have his own way in the Wright camp. He carried on the unfinished engine and wireless tests.

Early in September 1912, while Towers and Ellyson were away on duty, Herbster acted as officer in charge of the Navy's aviation camp for nearly two weeks. He sought and received permission from Chambers to build the B-2, a Wright type, which he proposed to assemble from spare parts. Herbster was loyal to the Wright design, but he resented an underpowered, waterlogged ma-

8. V. D. Herbster obtained permission from Chambers to build the B-2, a Wright-type plane, from spare parts. It took him a month. The B-2 was tricky, but he loved it because it would fly oftener than the old B-1 ever had. Above, entries from Herbster's B-2 log.
9. Powerplant of the B-2, fitted with a Curtiss six-cylinder motor.

chine that seldom was able to take off with a passenger, and always climbed like an overloaded oxcart.

His B-2 was a Wright plane with a 6-cylinder engine and a single Curtiss float. It took him a month to tailor the parts for this hybrid. The finished plane turned out to be a tricky and unstable craft, but Herbster loved it both because it was his baby and because it would fly more regularly than the old B-1 ever had.

RECORD _Annapolis, Md._ U. S. NAVY AEROPLANE No. _B-2_, DATE _Nov. 11_, 191 2, to _Nov. 21, 1912_, 191 .

DATE. 1912.	WEATHER	WIND.		BAR.	THER. DRY.	NO. OF FLIGHT.	OPERATOR.		PASSENGER.			TIME AT BEGIN- NING OF FLIGHT	DURA- TION OF FLIGHT	APPROX IMATE ALTITUDE ABOVE SURFACE.	EXTRA LOAD CARRIED.
		Direction.	Force.				NAME.	WEIGHT	NAME.	WEIGHT					
Nov. 11	Cldy	SE.	1	29.70		9	Ens. Herbster.	127	Lt. Childs.		150	4.55	20	500	
12	Clr.	SW.	1	2986		10	"	127	Lt. Gilbron.		170	9.02	28	500	
13	"	NW.	2	"		11	"	127	Lt. Edwards.		150	10.23	40	600	
14	C&C.	NW.	2	29.90		12	"	127	Lt. Smith.		170	2.40	20	500	
"	"	NW.	2	"		13	"	127	A.E.Tangren, SF1C.		170	3.30	14	400	
"	"	NW.	2	"		14	"	127	B.Rhodes, B'sth.		170	4.12	14	450	
15	"	"	2	29.95		-									
16	"	"	2	29.97		-									
17	Sunday.														
18	C&C.	NW.	3	29.80		-									

NOTE.—On the reverse side, opposite the corresponding "No. of Flight," desirable remarks, such as object of flight, character of flight, places of starting and landing, result of any experiment made, description of any accident however slight, damage sustained, repairs made, any unusual consumption or economy of oil or fuel, meteorological notes, time required to assemble and to disassemble, when occurring.
Enter full data in the first six columns each day, whether flights are made or not.

_9_

CHAPTER SEVEN: CATAPULTS AND FLIGHT PAY

The problems involved in learning to fly and in the training of pilots were by no means the only ones that existed in these early days of naval aviation. Chambers and his pilots hoped to develop a plane better suited to Navy purposes than either the Wright or Curtiss machines. To be acceptable to the Navy, an all-purpose scouting plane would have to be developed, and one capable of being launched from ships.

While Ely's flights to and from a shipboard ramp may be said to have anticipated flights from the deck of a carrier, it was clear that with the then existing planes and ships it was an economically impracticable method. Those two memorable flights had shown one way. Later, at Hammondsport, the successful launching of a plane from a wire showed another possible method. However, seagoing officers felt the wire-launching would prove too hazardous to achieve from a vessel in a seaway. But what about a track? There had been experiments with them. The Wrights had used a monorail at Fort Myer, but its falling weight seemed impracticable on shipboard. Langley had used a spring-driven device, and cross winds had caused him to clamp his model to the track for its take-off run. This experience seemed to have been forgotten. If anyone had read of his difficulties, Ellyson might have been saved a dunking in the Severn.

Chambers, drawing on his experience with the Bureau of Ordnance, devised a catapult, using compressed air as the propulsive force. The Wrights, hearing of this contrivance, offered him their release hook, which had served without failure for over a thousand launchings.

Before Richardson went to San Diego to take flying lessons, he helped with the planning of the catapult and, on his return, he took charge of improvising the machine at the Washington Navy Yard. The catapult, built out of old ordnance parts, was simple enough. Driven by compressed air, a piston and an arrangement of cables hauled a car along a pair of rails. The plane with its engine turning up full speed was perched on the car. The plane was expected to attain flying speed and fly off as the car reached the end of the track and dove into the water. In June 1912, Ellyson and Richardson set up the machine on the Naval Academy's Santee dock. Getting high pressure air to the dock took a bit of doing. Then Richardson started firing dead loads—timbers that had been bolted together and which weighed the same as the plane. Late in July, he found that 290 pounds of air pressure made a sudden start, but gave adequate speed at the end of the run.

On 31 July, everyone then in naval aviation watched Ellyson warm up the A-1 on the catapult car. Carefully setting his elevators for level flight and bracing his head against a board behind his seat, Ellyson shoved the throttle wide open and gave the ready signal.

---

1. *Lieutenant T. G. Ellyson (on wing) supervises preparations for first attempt to launch a hydroaeroplane by catapult, Naval Academy dock, Annapolis, 31 July 1912. (Photos 1 through 6, courtesy Mrs. C. G. Halpine.)*

1

70   The sudden acceleration gave him a terrific kick in the back, jamming him against his seat, yanking his hands and the wheel aft, and locking his head to the board. He sensed the plane gathering speed, saw the nose of the float rise, and looked straight up at the sky. Halfway down the track the machine stalled, rolled off the car, and corkscrewed into the Severn River.

"We all knew what was wrong as soon as it started," said one of the mechanics afterwards. "It was like a man being tackled low, from behind, when he was standing still."

When the plane sank, Ellyson let go and swam to the surface. "A little bump like that should never bother a good aviator," he said, as they fished him out. The A-1 was a pile of wet junk again. Ellyson shipped the catapult to Washington and turned his attention to testing flight instruments. In his opinion, a flier who needed air speed meters was incompetent, but Chambers had specified them, and so he tried to develop them. Then he and Towers devised a fitting to hold the plane on the car to the end of the catapult track and, when Richardson rebuilt the machine with a new valve, designed to cut down the starting jerk, he included such a device.

In November, Richardson set up his improved catapult on a barge at the Washington Navy Yard. On the twelfth, the barge was moved and anchored in the Anacostia River. On the catapult car, the new Curtiss hydro, the A-3, faced squarely into the wind. Ellyson warmed up the motor. Bracing his elbows against his ribs so the starting jerk could not shift his hands and the wheel, he leaned hard against the seat back and gave

2. The A-1 is mounted on a car which slid on rails secured to the dock. The compressed air actuating-cylinder, piston rod, and nest of sheaves and cable are shown behind the plane. The wing-tip pontoons were removed before the launch in order to clear a bollard on the dock.
3. Ellyson is seated in the plane, before starting the engine. Just prior to this, he had removed his cap and shoulder marks, anticipating a possible ducking.
4. As the plane shot forward, the heavy impelling force acting at the heel of the pontoon threw the plane into a stall. The left wing is starting to settle.
5. There was no time for Ellyson to "cut the gun"; the plane's nose dropped sharply and it dove into the water with the motor running wide open. This picture was taken at the instant the plane struck the water. Part of the pontoon may be seen through the spray, which rose about 50 feet into the air as the plane disappeared below the surface.
6. The plane came to the surface almost immediately—Ellyson, unhurt, surfaced a minute later, and calmly set about directing the salvage of the plane. The launching car is floating in the foreground.

the signal. This time Richardson's new valve made him wait a little longer, but it eased the blow on his back. The catapult car shot forward. At the end of the track, a cam tripped the hold-down device, and the car splashed into the river. Ellyson in the A-3 went climbing smoothly away.

Glenn Curtiss turned to Chambers:

"This is the most important advance since wheels were put on land machines," he said.

Both men were confident that hydroaeroplanes would soon be riding catapults on all the Navy's major ships. Their expectation would not be true for a dozen years.

The next month the Navy's first flying boat, the C-1, which Ellyson had meanwhile gone to Hammondsport to inspect and accept, was available. He flew it from the catapult on the barge and reported his experience no different than that with the hydroaeroplane.

The catapult would thrust either type of plane into the air with equal ease.

Meanwhile, Richardson had picked up some new ideas. He went to work to design a catapult to be built from new material, instead of being accumulated out of old parts. A year later he had it ready, but a year and a half passed before it could be tested.

This early development of a successful catapult was one of the outstanding achievements of the first decade of naval aviation.

Still another facet of this early period of naval aviation was the uneven and chaotic development of the theory and practice of flight training. In 1911, Captain Chambers believed that the Fleet could be supplied with officers who could pilot a plane whenever the occasion demanded. He did not envision anything like an aviation arm or branch of the naval service. His idea was that a man could learn and retain the knack of flying just as he learned to sail a boat or ride a bicycle.

In the *U. S. Naval Institute Proceedings*, he spelled out the details of the requirements for licenses of the Aero Club of America and the Federation Aeronautique Internationale. He supposed any pilot so licensed could act as a naval aviator when required. This belief was generally accepted, for fatalities had not yet demonstrated the need for regular practice. In line with these prejudiced notions was his suggestion that naval officers might qualify as pilots on their own time.

These ideas were reinforced by his belief that a scientific approach would soon evolve an all-purpose Navy-Marine aeroplane. Like a torpedo, it would be equipped with automatic stability and guidance mechanisms and hence would be both stable and foolproof. Thus any officer could check out in one, just as he might in a new automobile. Flying would be like boating. Anyone in the Fleet could be detailed to fly on a scouting mission.

At first, because he lacked the experience of a pilot, Chambers relied heavily on Ellyson's opinions. But as time passed he tended to discount some of them, because he found the pilots themselves were seldom in agreement, and some of their recommendations were in conflict with the theoretical ideas he was forming from his reading and from corresponding with hopeful inventors. For example, Ellyson did not agree with him that a pusher amphibian was the only suitable war plane or that all services would eventually shift to amphibians because no war had ever been fought entirely away from water. Ellyson felt that the electric automatic-stabilizer Chambers offered to the Aeronautical Society was completely unsuited for aircraft.

The two of them did agree, however, that Navy pilots needed a naval diploma. The orders which had sent the first officers to flight instruction had said, in effect: when you can fly, tell the Department. On their own initiative, Ellyson, Towers, Rodgers, and Herbster had all qualified for Aero Club of America licenses. These were not legal permits to fly. Neither law nor organization regulated aviation. All over the country unlicensed men were flying. Actually, the li-

cense was a certificate of competency and professional status. It showed that the holder had passed the flying tests prescribed by the Aero Club of America and the Federation Aeronautique Internationale. As the only widely recognized aviators' diplomas, they were highly prized by all early aviators.

To get such a license, a man practiced flying until he thought he could pass the tests. Then he asked the Aero Club to appoint official observers to certify his performance. In 1911, when Chambers had suggested that officers should qualify on their own, a candidate had to rise 50 meters above his starting point and make two "distance flights." Each of these was a series of figure eights around two posts set not more than five hundred meters apart. Each flight was to total five kilometers and it was to terminate with a precision landing—that is, the pilot cut his switch before touching the ground and stopped within 50 meters of a mark.

In July 1912, Richardson was practicing flying at Annapolis. In August, he passed the Aero Club of America test in a hydroplane at Hammondsport. A little later Ellyson asked for observers to check the performances of volunteer students Isaac F. Dortch and Laurance N. McNair. The Aero Club refused, and it also held up Richardson's license. The difficulty was that they had decided not to recognize tests unless at least one landing was made on a field. Richardson argued with the club's officials. He had qualified under the existing rules, and they should issue the license regardless of any subsequent changes of policy. Eventually they gave in. Richardson and Herbster were the only fliers

7. *Lieutenant Ellyson in the A-3, preparing for launch from H. C. Richardson's improved catapult, Washington Navy Yard, 12 November 1912. (National Archives)*
8. *The catapult car shot forward, then splashed into the river. Ellyson in the A-3 climbed smoothly away.*
9. *Later, Ellyson successfully flew the C-1 flying boat from the catapult on the barge at the Washington Navy Yard.*

ever issued these licenses on the basis of seaplane work alone.

That year the Navy had no landplane operations; so Dortch and McNair could not qualify for Aero Club licenses. They continued to fly without licenses. Since dual instruction was working so well in the hydro-aeroplanes, Towers and Ellyson no longer saw any naval need for landplanes. They suggested that the Aero Club requirement be ignored and that Naval Air Pilot Certificates be issued, based upon a similar but more comprehensive test, including an examination on the engines and plane construction. Chambers liked this idea.

Later Ellyson and Chambers wrote the first set of requirements for a Navy certificate. After the Secretary approved them, the Bureau of Navigation published them in a pamphlet dated 19 April 1913. They required that a student flier should submit a written request for flying duty and pass a physical examination. After instruction and practice, the student was to ask for a test that was to be observed, as in the Aero Club procedure; also, he was required to write an essay covering the theory of flight and the construction of the machines. After the essay had been approved by the senior qualified aviator present, "a board of at least two

9

qualified officers" was to conduct the tests.

These tests included several requirements. There was an altitude flight to 2,500 feet; a flight flying crosswind on a straight compass course between two markers five miles apart; and a 20-mile reconnaissance flight, at the conclusion of which the student was to make a sketch of what he had seen. Finally, there was a full spiral from 1,000 feet to a landing with the engine fully throttled, and Ellyson's pet—shooting the buoy. For this the candidate climbed to 500 feet, stopped his motor and landed, coming to a stop within 150 feet of a buoy "without upsetting." Then he had to restart his engine, take off, and land again, cutting when he touched the water, and stopping within 50 feet of the buoy. After some pilots had crashed the marker to keep from overshooting, the requirement "without touching the buoy" was added. In this form, shooting the buoy re-

mained a part of a naval aviator's tests until the Navy abandoned primary training in seaplanes in the 1930's.

While Chambers and Ellyson were working on these pilot requirements, extra pay for flying personnel was being discussed. Ellyson opposed it. It would be unfair on an hourly basis, he said. For example, flying as an instructor had given Towers much more time than the experimental flying which had been Ellyson's lot. Furthermore, it was his belief that extra pay would retard aviation development by attracting disinterested officers with influence.

Other views prevailed. In March 1913, the Navy Appropriation Bill granted an increase of 35 per cent of pay and allowances to not over 30 officers below the rank of commander, who were active heavier-than-air fliers, and who had been so designated by the Secretary of the Navy. This was the origin of flight pay.

73

CHAPTER EIGHT: FLIGHTS WITH THE FLEET

Along with other achievements, the year 1912 marked development of naval aviation from the standpoint of a growing number of pilots. The year before, when the Navy received its first planes, Chambers had encouraged his pilots to take up any interested line officers and to give flight instruction to those who desired it. His motive was two-fold: He sought to make a dent in the shell of conservatism that held so many officers in its grip; also, some unofficial pilots might be trained. But the results were nil.

When the winter season at San Diego ended and the aviation camp at Annapolis was re-established in the spring of 1912, things began to happen. The pilots began to interest friends and classmates they met at the Officers' Club, and in the bar at Carvel Hall, in learning to fly. Several lieutenants started to take flight instruction in their off-duty hours, but only two of them stayed through the course.

These were Laurance North McNair from Warsaw, New York, and Isaac Foote Dortch from Alabama, who had been Ellyson's classmates and were now assigned to duty at the Academy. In June, they began to fly with Towers and Ellyson, whenever their duty and the planes' perverse engines permitted.

That summer Towers gradually took over the camp administration and almost all of the instruction work. His enthusiasm for flying was contagious and he made it seem easy. His students soon discovered that he knew what he wanted, and that he could make them understand his wants. All of his students learned quickly.

Inspection, procurement, and experimental flying began to take more and more of Ellyson's time. During the summer, he was repeatedly called to Hammondsport to test the hydroplane and the flying boat that had been ordered from Curtiss. The Bureau of Engineering and of Construction and Repair spent money on planes for the first time. They bought on Chambers' recommendation, and as he momentarily expected some radical improvement to render all existing planes obsolete, he ordered them as cannily as if each one cost millions. Hence the A-3 and the C-1, which Ellyson inspected, tested, and flew from the catapult, were the only planes delivered to the Navy in the year 1912.

In the previous summer, when Curtiss had suggested a flying boat to Chambers and Ellyson, they had dismissed it as a wild dream. But out at San Diego in January, Curtiss had shown Ellyson a tractor-type flying boat. However, this failed to satisfy either Curtiss or the Navy fliers. That spring, back at Hammondsport, Curtiss reworked his design and Chambers ordered one. Richardson was probably responsible for the rough water tests that Ellyson had Curtiss put it through on Lake Ontario.

In the spring of this same year the Marine Corps first took up aviation, through the

1. *They flew, but what else could they do? Sailors aboard USS* North Carolina, *anchored off Seattle, Washington, in 1911, appeared more interested in looking over the side than they were in watching these early aircraft. Such aircraft were still not ready for fleet use, nor were they in 1913 when Secretary of the Navy Daniels said ". . . it is confidentially expected that within the next year their development will have reached such a stage. . ."*

76 activities of First Lieutenant Alfred Austell Cunningham, who was about the only officer who had tried to follow Chambers' suggestion that officers learn to fly outside the service. On duty at the Philadelphia Marine barracks in 1911, he had rented an aeroplane from its civilian builder, who had never been able to make it work. He persuaded the commandant to let him test the machine on the Navy Yard parade ground. He could not make it fly even when he bounced it into the air from a ramp, and his shipmates kidded him unmercifully. Undaunted, he joined the Aero Club of Philadelphia, and then convinced Marine Corps Headquarters that the Marines should have aviators and that he should be the first one of them.

Cunningham reported to the Naval Academy for aviation duty in May 1912, on the same day the carload of broken planes arrived from San Diego, and he figured that it would be some time before they could fly. In less than three days, he asked to be trained in the Wright type, talked himself into orders, and was on his way to the Burgess school at Marblehead.

In July, Cunningham visited Greenbury Point for a couple of weeks. He flew once with Towers, who was balancing the A-2 after it had been rebuilt. Twice he went out with John Rodgers, who was testing the Meade engine, but it never got them into the air. Then he went back to Marblehead, where he soloed on 1 August.

In September another Marine, Second Lieutenant Bernard L. Smith, reported for flight training. Two days later Towers began instructing him in the A-2. He proved

2. First Marine to train in aviation was First Lieutenant Alfred A. Cunningham, here propping the "Noisy Nan," which made plenty of noise but never flew. The hopeful pilot is unidentified.
3. Cunningham, at the controls of the Curtiss seaplane, later became Naval Aviator No. 5.
4. Second Lieutenant Bernard L. Smith, the second Marine to enter aviation, became Naval Aviator No. 6.

an apt and enthusiastic pupil, and he flew with Towers and Ellyson at every opportunity. Younger than Cunningham by four years, he had entered the Corps just a few days later, but these days were enough to put him six months behind Cunningham, when they were promoted to first lieutenants.

At this time, Ellyson, who had been the senior aviator since Rodgers' departure, reorganized the aviation camp. He named Herbster officer in charge of the B-2 and turned the B-1 over to Cunningham. Towers took charge of the A-2 and B. L. Smith, of the A-1. On paper the camp was unified, but of course it did not work out that way. Herbster kept to himself as the "Wright camp." Cunningham brought in a Marine mechanic named McGuire and became the "Marine camp." And the others, including Smith working with two planes, were for all practical purposes the "Curtiss camp."

When the aviators were given their first appropriated money and supplies, Ellyson sent Chief Wiegand ashore to spend 50 dollars, the open purchase legal limit, for the tools that had so long been needed. The chief lost the list. In the hardware store he could remember none of the needed items, so he went back to camp with 50 dollars worth of cotter pins and safety wire. The tool shortage continued.

4

Towers now rigged the A-2 with an extra 10-gallon gas tank and a reserve rubber water tank over the radiator; in order to carry this added weight, he added an extra bay of wing panels on each side. Then he gave it a flight test. Up to this time, the longest flight logged by any Navy plane was two hours and two minutes. Ellyson always opposed headlines, but Towers and Chambers believed that what naval aviation needed was some favorable publicity, and it was for this purpose Towers refitted the A-2.

While McNair and Dortch acted as official Aero Club observers, Towers took off a few minutes before seven in the morning on 6 October. When he landed, after 6 hours, 10 minutes, and 35 seconds in the air, he had hung up the world's hydroaeroplane endurance record and the American record for any type of plane. Aviation magazines dramatized the flight and made it sound quite risky and daring, but Towers logged it as "uneventful." Then he removed the extra gear and returned to more routine work.

Cunningham's experience with the B-1 was typical of these early days of flight training. Two days before Towers made his record-making flight, Herbster had flown the B-1 to show Cunningham that it would really fly with the Gyro engine. Then he turned the machine over to Cunningham who, for the next nine months, was the only pilot to fly it.

On eight different days in October, he flew it for self-training and experienced an assortment of failures and forced landings. Then he began to rebuild the plane with Burgess parts. As these were only approximately the same as the originals, he had to

tailor so many to fit that it was December before he got it together to test a Sturtevant engine. That morning the Severn River was rough. Before he reached a take-off position, a wave hooked his right wing and capsized him. Then repairs took until 18 December, the day the camp closed. In three months, the B-1 had given him five hours in the air.

Late in October of 1912, Ensign Godfrey de Courcelles Chevalier, U. S. Navy, reported for flight training. Small, unusually handsome, he moved with quick, restless energy. If his reckless resentment of authority had let him live at peace with discipline, his native intelligence might have caused him to stand much higher in the Academy Class of 1910 than he did. As it was, he might never have graduated at all but for his extraordinary charm, which made everyone who knew him want to excuse his offenses.

Chevalier had his first instruction flight the day after he checked in. That day a group of submarines anchored off the Academy. Ellyson's friend and classmate, Lieutenant Chester Nimitz, was commander of the Atlantic Fleet submarines, and he had arranged for the first aero-submarine experiments. He wanted to see if aviators could spot submerged boats in the murky water of Chesapeake Bay as easily as reports said this had been done off the French coast. Lieutenant Patrick N. L. Bellinger, the skipper of the submarine C-4, visited the air camp and arranged to fly the next day as Herbster's observer. Slim, dark, handsome Pat Bellinger had already requested aviation duty and was wondering why he had not heard

5

from his request. Afterwards he found that there had been a mix-up of names in the detail office and, as a result, Ensign William Devotie Billingsley had been ordered to aviation. When Billingsley was sounded out, it developed that although he had not asked for aviation duty, he was delighted with the prospect. He wanted no swap.

Mix-up or no, Bellinger persuaded the detail officer to let them both fly.

As Bellinger left the camp, McNair, who was practicing in the A-2, swooped down beside his motorboat. Bellinger watched him try to land downwind, a routine maneuver in those days of low flying when engines quit often. But McNair "stubbed his toe" and splashed over on his back. Bellinger began to wonder if he really was going to like flying. The next day Herbster made him wonder again.

Herbster had entered the Academy with Bellinger in the Class of 1907, but his troubles had kept him there for five years. So in the B-2 he proceeded to haze his more fortunate friend. For a final stunt after landing, he made Bellinger ride the nose of the float "to keep from sinking by the stern," he said. When they beached, Bellinger was cold and wet, and even more dubious about aviation. But he never considered trying to get his orders changed. He always hated to make decisions, but was noted for sticking stubbornly to every one he ever did make. He had decided on aviation and he stayed with it for 35 years.

After McNair's crash, the Curtiss pilots were grounded until the A-2 could be repaired. Then Towers continued Chevalier's

5. *The Navy's first aero-submarine experiments, conducted in Chesapeake Bay in 1912, were initiated by Lieutenant Chester Nimitz who then commanded the Atlantic Fleet submarines. In this 1909 view of USS* Plunger, *the officer on the bridge is believed to be Nimitz.*
6. *Another early submariner was Patrick N. L. Bellinger, who began flight training in 1912. The plane is a Curtiss, the AH-3.*

and Smith's instruction. All through November Herbster worked periodically with the submarines. Before reporting for flight duty, Bellinger flew with him again and once with Towers. Then he asked for training in the Curtiss machine.

Bellinger never realized that it was Herbster who had pushed him into that choice. Little Herbster did not want any senior, even an old friend, to displace him as the head of the "Wright camp," and the day Bellinger came aboard Herbster wrote a rambling letter to Ellyson, in Hammondsport. He wanted engine data, a trip to Dayton, spares for the winter and, since Bellinger desired Curtiss training, could he "have Billingsley," who was a year his junior.

Herbster got what he wanted; he was delighted to have an ensign to order about his "Wright camp." Although they came from different backgrounds in widely separated parts of the country, these two officers were alike in many ways. They were husky, stocky, short men with steady nerves and stubborn determination. Of the two, Billingsley was the more sympathetic, friendly, and good-natured man. Herbster started Billingsley's flight instruction promptly, but winter weather and engine troubles kept him from

6

learning much before the camp moved out of Annapolis in late December.

Away back in June of 1912, the General Board had come up with the suggestion that whenever the pilots were ready, they should operate with the Fleet. The general idea was that Fleet operations would answer the General Board's questions on ship-based aviation, scouting, and wireless. The acting Aide for Operations told the Bureau of Navigation to comply and, when Chambers was informed he said, ready or not, the pilots would be glad to go south with the Fleet in January 1913. He knew they would hardly be equipped to answer the Board's questions, but his hope was that they would interest Fleet officers, especially the seniors, in naval aviation.

And so on the eighteenth of December, packing up began, with pilots of both Curtiss and Wright machines in last-minute scrambles for parts, although this move had been in the offing for six months. Towers spent Christmas week loading the collier *Sterling*. He worked slowly so as to let as many spares as possible arrive before he finished, but there were many still missing when the ship sailed near the end of the year.

Ellyson had shipped the first flying boat from Hammondsport and was visiting his new mother-in-law in New York City when Chambers sent him word that he was to remain in the States until the Burgess boat, the D-1, was delivered. So it fell to his lot to work out of Chambers' office after the rest of naval aviation sailed for Guantanamo Bay. He rounded up the spares that missed the *Sterling*, got extra engines, crated up the C-1, and shipped them all down to Cuba. But

he would have preferred the fresh air of a ship's deck or an aeroplane cockpit to all the frustrations of Chambers' dank office.

The *Sterling* finally sailed from Annapolis carrying B. L. Smith, Chevalier, the aviation enlisted men, and the A-2, A-3, B-1, and B-2. For the first time, Navy planes went to sea in a Navy ship. The crated planes had been lowered into a hold on top of the *Sterling*'s cargo of coal; a collier's hatches were about the only ones in the Navy big enough to take a crated wing.

When the *Sterling* arrived at the Fleet's winter base in Guantanamo, Smith checked in aboard the station's ship, the *Cumberland*, landed the gear, and set up camp at nearby Fisherman's Point. Three days later, Towers, Herbster, Cunningham, Billingsley, and Bellinger arrived in the battleship *Utah*.

Before Towers left the States, Chambers had told him to do what he could about the General Board's questions and to qualify the new students. Then he had added:

"Your main object, though, is to interest as many senior officers as possible in aviation. Show what the planes can do for them. Get them to ride with you."

Naval aviation had nothing to lose. If the admirals enjoyed their flights, their opposition might ease up. Certainly it could not get worse.

The A-2 took to the air on 15 January 1913, and all four planes were set up a week later. Each morning, flying started at daylight and it ended about nine when the trade winds began to blow too hard for safe sur-

7

face operations. At the end of January, Towers decided that Chevalier was ready for his first solo.

"Take off," Jack told him. "Make two wide circles. Then land."

As he taxied out, young Chevy gripped the wheel tight. He was careful to do everything just right. Determination tightened him up. He came down to land with nerves and muscles that were as taut as piano wire. To avoid a stall, he kept too much speed until his pontoon smacked the water. The plane bounced mast-high. He closed the throttle, tightened his lips, and came down again. At the last moment, the machine, over-controlled by his taut muscles, hit the water so hard that again it leaped aloft. He circled back, glided into the wind and bounced again. By now everyone in the camp was at the water's edge with fingers crossed. Again and again they watched him bounce, circle and bounce again. Eventually he stayed on the water. Chief Gunner's Mate Wiegand put their feelings into words. Said he: "I thought we were going to have to shoot him down!"

Chevy beached the plane, climbed ashore, and went in search of a couple of quick drinks. It was a long time before he had any trouble with a plane again. Before they left Cuba, he was known as an excellent pilot and instructor, who always did his best flying after he had taken a couple of shots of rum to relax.

Bellinger was a most interested observer of this first solo by Chevalier. Two weeks later, it was his turn. That morning he chewed his gum a little faster than usual.

7. *Handsome Ensign Godfrey deC. Chevalier, Naval Aviator No. 7, had ten years of great accomplishment before he lost his life.*
8. *The C-1 arrived at naval aviation's winter camp in Guantanamo Bay, January 1913.*

Pressure only stepped his tension up to a good, fast-action level. When he had to do something, he just up and did it. When his solo was over, he felt that it was an anticlimax. He had not looked for trouble, but he did like to be noticed.

Proof of this attitude has survived. Soon after these two soloed, all the aviators were guests at a shipboard smoker, after which they liberally sampled their host's wine mess. When they were kept waiting on the quarterdeck a bit too long for their boat, Bellinger suddenly said, "Hell, I can swim home faster than this," whereupon he dove overboard. In a complete white service uniform, he was swimming strongly in the wrong direction when Towers overtook him in the motorboat and made him climb aboard.

Billingsley's progress was slower than the other two. He enjoyed flying and Herbster worked hard on his instruction, but Vic never was as adept a teacher as Smith or Towers. Early in February the B-2's Wright engine wore out, and there was no spare in Cuba. The two of them worked long hours to achieve occasional short flights. Billingsley complained mildly about the delay, but otherwise he enjoyed working with Herbster. He never asked to shift to the Curtiss type and no one suggested it. Certainly not Herbster, who enjoyed having a junior officer on hand to boss around. Hence it was not until March that Billingsley made his solo flight.

8

High flying was regarded throughout the Fleet as just a foolhardy exhibition. The line officers saw no need for more than a reasonable clearance of surface objects. Neither did some aviation editors when they commented on the altitudes of the cross-country flights they reported. Had not Glenn Curtiss said that a flying boat need never go higher than 95 feet?

Towers always suspected that this assertion by his friend Curtiss was a justification for some of his overweight and under-powered crates which could do little better. On the contrary, he could think of several good uses and reasons for altitude. Thus, when the question was discussed at lunch one day, he remarked:

"Anyone who gets above 3,000 feet will get his name in the papers."

To avoid Fleet criticism, Navy pilots always got Towers' O.K. each time they intended to go above 2,000 feet. The very next morning Bellinger decided he would have a go at it. In a quarter of an hour, he dragged the A-3 up to 2,650 feet. This made him the camp altitude champion, and Towers put this exploit in his weekly report to Captain Chambers. Then three mornings later, he stayed up until the trade winds were blowing before he landed. He did not know how to sail a seaplane either crosswind or downwind on the surface. Maybe nobody did then. When he tried stubbornly to force it around with power, the machine capsized and dunked this new altitude champion.

Late in January of 1913, the C-1 reached Guantanamo in the collier *Vulcan*. Towers immediately installed a wireless transmitter in the plane. Later, when a Fleet exercise was scheduled to divide the ships into opposing groups for maneuvers, he arranged a scouting demonstration. Having worked on his plane and wireless until they were in prime condition, he told the flagship operator to pick up his signals. On the big day, he flew over the horizon, sighted his quarry, and then poked his transmitter key. Nothing happened and nothing he did would make the wireless work. The Fleet commander did not care. He had always known that aeroplane scouts were no good.

Forced landings were frequent but Cunningham and Herbster had the most trouble with their Wright planes. Only once was Towers able to report a week in which all the planes had operated without accident or failure. By that time, every pilot had tried spotting submarines and mines. After they learned to search at the proper down-sun angle, this was easy to do in the clear Caribbean water, but a little scum of oil on the surface of the harbor made it a bit uncertain inside.

During the entire season, most of the flights for any purpose carried Fleet officers who came over to the camp on Fisherman's Point in response to Towers' invitations. A day or so after they had soloed, Chevalier and Bellinger began carrying passengers on their practice flights. At the end of the season, Towers listed over two hundred officers who had been carried aloft. Some of these, like John Hoover, Ralph Wood, and R. E. Byrd, got their wings, years later, when they were ordered to aviation duty. But in 1913 less than a dozen men had accepted the

81

9

offered flight instruction. The first and the most persistent volunteer student was a 39-year-old lieutenant commander—Henry C. Mustin of Philadelphia. Although quite an athlete in his Academy days, he was a slightly built little man, quiet and soft-spoken. Before joining the cruiser *Minnesota* as executive officer, aviation had fascinated him at the War College. There he had planned catapult installations for cruisers and had suggested fighter escorts for bombing planes. At Guantanamo he received instruction from Smith and Towers, and he soloed on the last day that the planes flew in Cuba.

On 10 March, Towers and Chevalier flew the C-1 along Cuba's south shore to Santiago as their last demonstration of the season. This flight was unusual enough to be guarded by three destroyers, and it was reported in detail in the aviation magazines. They waited until the next morning in order to start at dawn, when the wind was lowest, and then flew back in a little over an hour.

In their two months with the Fleet at Guantanamo, the fliers had given many officers their first knowledge of aircraft; no one had been hurt; and they had made favorable headlines for naval aviation. But their equipment had not been adequate to furnish any answers to the General Board's questions, and they failed to make an aviation enthusiast of the Commander in Chief.

At noon on the thirteenth, just after Mustin had soloed, flight operations ceased, and they began packing for the return to the States. On one of the last flights that morning, Bellinger took up a battleship captain who had once given him a bad fitness report.

9. Lieutenant Commander H. C. Mustin asked for duty with aviation in 1913. He was first Commandant of the Pensacola Naval Air Station. He is pictured here as a captain.

Now he thought he would have his revenge, and he gave his former skipper a dizzy ride filled with near misses. But instead of being scared, the old man was so pleased he invited Bellinger to use his guest cabin for the trip north. This comparative luxury was accepted with alacrity.

By 29 March, the aviators were again camped beside the Experiment Station on Greenbury Point. Two days later a storm blew down all the tent hangars. Most of the planes were still crated and thus escaped damage, but there were those at the camp who wondered if tent hangars were any real protection.

Two weeks later the new Secretary of the Navy, Josephus Daniels, and his young assistant, Franklin D. Roosevelt, came to Annapolis to inspect what there was of naval aviation. Lieutenant Towers, from a small Georgia town, got on well with this editor-politician from a small Carolina town, and also with the man from Hyde Park. Each of them flew with him in the C-1. To strengthen the favorable impression the Secretary had formed at Annapolis, Captain Chambers ordered Towers to ship the C-1 to Washington for a demonstration. After the machine had been assembled at the Washington Navy Yard, Chevalier and Towers flew it from the Potomac for a couple of days. Towers carried a Mr. Semple, an inventor of bombs, on one flight to test Semple's invention. Semple had little faith in either his bombs or the plane. The instant they were airborne, he began pitching bombs over the side as fast as he could. He got rid of all of them long before the plane was high enough to allow their fuses to arm. Fortunately there were no explosions.

Towers and Chevalier flew the C-1 down the Potomac, then up the Chesapeake to Annapolis, making the 171 miles nonstop at an average speed of 55 miles per hour. The plane proved more reliable than the A-1 had been on the Fortress Monroe flight, but luck was still an essential ingredient in a flight of that length.

The performance of the Wright planes was miserable. They failed more than they flew. Almost every time Herbster, Cunningham, or Billingsley coaxed one into the air he would have to make a forced landing a few minutes later. Cunningham tried new carburetors, magnetos, fuel lines, propellers, in fact everything anyone suggested. It took most of the month of May to get the plane into the air long enough to pass the test for the Seaplane Certificate, which the Aero Club of America had at length established for pilots who made their tests exclusively from water. On 4 June, Cunningham logged the first flight in three months when "the engine ran properly." Then the next morning a rudder wire snapped as he taxied out for a takeoff. The B-1 was an old lady.

The B-2 was little better until the 30-horsepower Wright engine was pulled out of it and a 75-horsepower Curtiss engine replaced it. On a test hop it seemed a bit over-sensitive to the controls, but Herbster was delighted when it climbed to 4,450 feet in 45 minutes. He displaced Bellinger as the altitude champion of the camp. Bellinger grinned at Herbster's cracks, tuned up the A-3, and began trying for the top again. By mid-June he had set the American seaplane altitude record at 7,200 feet and found the absolute ceiling of the A-3. There was no attack angle that would let it climb higher. The slightest pull on the wheel made all controls feel soft and mushy. Bellinger did not like the feel of it. He quit trying and nosed over. Soon after this record flight, he went to Hammondsport to test and inspect new planes and to work on the automatic stabilizer with Sperry and Curtiss and did not rejoin his fellow pilots until late fall.

The spring of 1913 brought two events which affected naval aviation. First, Lieutenant Commander Mustin asked for duty with aviation; secondly, the Navy Department decided to expand naval aviation moderately. In order to end interbureau competition in aircraft, General Order Number 41 was prepared. It made the Bureau of Construction and Repair responsible for planes, hangars, and launching gear. The Bureau of Engineering was to provide aircraft engines, radios, generators, and lighting equipment. Finally, the Bureau of Navigation was charged with instrumentation, personnel, training, and operations. A dozen officers were scheduled for flight training. The material bureaus ordered a flying boat and a hydro from Burgess and two hydroplanes

11

10

84 and five flying boats from Glenn Curtiss. Bellinger was ordered to inspection duty at Hammondsport. Murray, the Navy's newest pilot, was told to stay in Marblehead as inspector at the Burgess factory.

James McClees Murray, born in Murray, Nebraska, was an amiable, attractive, pipe-smoking classmate of Bellinger's. He had been in submarines until he returned from the Far East to the States in time to report for aviation duty at the Burgess factory in January 1913. There, while he inspected the work on the D-1, the Navy's first Burgess flying boat, he learned flying with Wright controls.

In the spring of 1913, Towers made cross-country flights part of the weekly routine. His purpose was to improve piloting and to promote mechanical reliability. On the chosen days, all the operable planes would fly at approximately the same time to some nearby town. Occasionally a landing was made at the destination, but more often the flights were nonstop round trips. Baltimore, Cambridge, Chestertown, and Galesville, Maryland, were among the places visited.

Friday, the twentieth of June, was a cross-country day and, at the scheduled time, Chevalier and Dortch, in the C-1, took off for St. Michaels, Maryland. Billingsley and Braxton Rhodes, a mechanic, were about to follow them in the B-2 when Towers waved them down from an approaching boat. He wanted to make the trip. No other plane was ready, so he took Rhodes's seat.

As the B-2 climbed above the bay, the air was bumpy. To stay in his seat, Billingsley gripped the control levers hard, and Towers

10. *The wreck of the B-2 on the dock at the Naval Experiment Station, Annapolis. This was the plane from which Ensign W. D. Billingsley plunged to his death while on a cross-country flight with Towers. Billingsley was the first Navy man to be killed in an aeroplane accident.*
11. *Ensign W. D. Billingsley, Naval Aviator No. 9.*
12. *V. D. Herbster's report of the accident to the Navy hydroaeroplane B-2.*

hooked an arm around a strut to steady himself clear of the controls. The outbound trip was routine, and they swung over St. Michaels and headed for home. The wind shifted and nearby rain squalls made the air rougher. At 1,600 feet, they were flying fast, still trying to overtake Chevalier and Dortch in the C-1. Suddenly the B-2 lurched violently forward and down. Both men were thrown from their seats. Billingsley clung to the control levers, yanking them forward. The plane did part of an outside loop and a quarter roll. Billingsley lost his toehold on the foot rest, then his grip on the controls, and, when the plane was some 1,200 feet in the air, he fell clear.

Towers' casual hold on the strut kept him from plunging with Billingsley. After Billingsley fell, Towers tried to hook the elevator lever with his foot, but it was out of reach. The plane flopped and shook, but Jack clung to the strut until the plane crashed into the water. He was not wearing a life jacket, and it was fortunate he remained conscious, which prevented him from drowning. He managed to drag himself onto the main pontoon, floating nearby. Help reached him 25 minutes later. He was seriously injured; nevertheless, he kept the rescue boat searching the vicinity for Billingsley's body,

No.368-AC-H-13.

ANNAPOLIS, MARYLAND

Naval Engineering Experiment Station,
Aviation Camp.

June 21,1913.

To: Officer in Charge of Aviation, via Head of Naval
        Engineering Experiment Station and Superintendent.

Subject: Report of accident to Navy Hydroaeroplane B-2.

     1.   The Navy Wright hydroaeroplane B-2 with Ensign W.D.
Billingsley as pilot and Lieutenant J.H. Towers as passenger while
returning from a flight to Claiborne,Md., was at about 10 a.m.,
June 20, struck by a violent puff of wind at an altitude of 1600
feet, the machine at this time being about four miles from Kent
Island,Md., and heading for Annapolis with the wind aft.   The
machine then dove suddenly, throwing Ensign Billingsley out of
the machine at an altitude of about 1200 feet.   Lieutenant Towers
held on to the machine, until it struck,and was picked up by the
Navy Aviation Camp launch at about 10:25 a.m., having crawled on
top of the main pontoon, which was floating, and practically un-
injured.   The machine dropped vertically about 900 feet, then
gradually capsized and glided to the water, landing right wing
first.   The wreck at 10:28 a.m. bore SW from Thomas Point and
NW by N from black channel buoy by Aviation launch compass.
Lieutenant Towers was sent to the Naval Hospital at Annapolis and
found to have been injured internally, pronounced serious, but not
necessarily fatal.   Launches were immediately sent out, also the
U.S.S.STRINGHAM, with grapnels to recover the body of Ensign
Billingsley.   The hydroaeroplane was raised aboard the derrick
and brought to the Experiment Station.   The hydroaeroplane is a
total wreck, except the engine, main pontoon and wing tip pontoons.
A board of investigation will meet on Saturday at 10:00 a.m., after
which a full report of the accident will be forwarded.   A verbal
report of the accident was given to the Superintendent immediately
after securing an account of the accident from Lieutenant J.H.
Towers at the Naval Hospital about 12:30 p.m.

                                   V. D. Herbster

                              Acting.

13

but they found nothing. Towers was so badly hurt the doctors would not let him return to duty until October.

After Towers had been rescued, Herbster took command of the camp, got Chevalier and Dortch towed back from a forced landing, and a search started for Billingsley's body. The next day he wrote up the available facts of the crash in the weekly camp report. By Monday he had sent two letters and a wire to Orville Wright. He wanted his opinion on the cause of the crash, and he said of course the Navy would want a new plane. Unlike Towers' report after Ellyson had been injured at North Island, Herbster's correspondence was exclusively concerned with material. There was not a single word of sympathy for the victims. In the weekly report, he merely mentioned Towers, saying he was in the hospital without giving any indication of his condition.

Billingsley was the first Navy man to be killed in an aeroplane accident. His flying career, which had been initiated by an accidental switch of names, lasted a few days over six months, and he had flown only 30 hours and four minutes. His death checked the expansion of naval aviation. For the first time, several senior officers realized that aeroplanes could be dangerous. An alarmed detail officer wiped his slate clear of the orders for flight training. Chambers hesitated; he would have liked to discuss the crisis with Towers, or with Ellyson, but neither of them were available, and he had little faith in Herbster, the most experienced pilot remaining in the aviation camp.

13. A close-up photograph of the B-2 wreckage shows the complete destruction which nearly always results from crashes of such fragile aircraft.

The first reports attributed the accident to a violent gust that had lifted the tail of the plane. The official investigation accepted this explanation and reported that "only ungovernable elements could be held responsible." Herbster was not satisfied. His persistent exchange of data with Wright lasted over a month. Then Orville gave it as his opinion that the trouble had started because the plane was going too fast, with its wings biting the air at too small an angle of attack. Richardson independently had arrived at a similar conclusion.

If "too fast" at fifty-two and one-half miles per hour sounds preposterous in the jet age, it must be remembered that most aeronautical knowledge has been learned since Billingsley died. In a pusher plane the arrangement of weight, drag, and thrus' tended to force the plane into a dive witl power on. This tendency was aggravated by the heavy Curtiss engine and the low pontoon. As long as the pilot flew nosed up five degrees or more, his elevators could hold the machine in level flight even though they had no stabilizer to help them. Billingsley was not flying nose up, but flat and fast. So when a small bump dipped the nose, the big engine took charge and flipped the plane in spite of its little elevators. And even that might not have been fatal if the two men had been strapped to their seats. Then they could have closed the throttle quickly and probably pulled out of the dive.

They were not strapped in because nobody wanted to be lashed to one of the bamboo tails, sitting in front of an engine that would smash him if the plane landed too hard.

When Glenn Curtiss visited Towers in the hospital, this was a topic of discussion. Each of them had escaped injury or death by jumping or being thrown clear, in forced landings, an instant before the engine had crushed their seats. Everyone who had flown very long had had this experience. Both Towers and Curtiss knew that Eugene Ely and others had died of broken necks after being thrown out of crash landings, and they had seen Ellyson badly hurt in a crash at North Island. But these accidents seemed rare exceptions compared to the times a toss-out had saved a man's life.

Ely, Curtiss, and others had tried to compromise by using straps or ropes looped on their seat backs. In rough air, they could wedge a shoulder under these and yet still be free to jump out straight ahead. The straps were only semi-secure. When other men had fallen from planes before Billingsley, it had been assumed that they had fainted and, unconscious, fallen free. But after Towers told his story, Curtiss figured that they might have been thrown like Billingsley. Towers summed it up:

"We need a lashing that will hold a man tight in his seat no matter how the plane turns, and which he can cast off instantly even if he has gloves on stiff fingers."

A few weeks later, Curtiss made a safety belt that met these specifications. He used a link and cam buckle that could be opened by a single swipe of a gloved hand. Soon word was passed from Washington that pilots should always wear belts in flight as soon as they were available. Since that time, Curtiss' original design has changed little. Airliner belts for passengers are dressier, less conspicuous, and less adaptable. World War II fighter pilot shoulder harnesses improved on, but they did not replace, the belt inspired by Billingsley's death, which is still making flight safer for millions.

After the crash, Chambers knew that Towers would not fly again for a long time and that Herbster was unsuited for running the Annapolis camp. Murray, the senior officer flying, had less than ten hours solo but, on the last day of June 1913, Chambers had him ordered from Marblehead to take over at Annapolis.

CHAPTER NINE: POLITICS, NOT PILOTS

During the winter and spring of 1912 and 1913, the name of Bradley A. Fiske became more and more important to naval aviation. He it was who three years before had startled the General Board with his proposal that the Philippines should be defended by naval air stations and torpedo bombing planes. He was then a captain. As an admiral commanding a division of the Atlantic Fleet, he had criticized the Navy Department for its lack of appreciation of "the vast scope of the changes the aeroplane will make in warfare." In the spring of 1912, he had received a patent for a torpedo plane which he claimed to have invented. In January 1913, he became Aide for Operations to Secretary Meyer. For the future of naval aviation, this was a significant event.

In his memoirs, Admiral Fiske recorded his recollection of how, in 1910, as he was passing through the Strait of Magellan, he had watched a giant albatross gliding along in the air beside his ship, and he wrote:

> I realized that the aeroplanes "had come to stay" and that they would get larger and larger, and that then the great speed of which they were capable would make them of tremendous value in war.

Although he and Chambers had known each other since their midshipman days, he did not bother to mention Chambers by name, when he wrote, upon becoming Aide for Operations:

There was a Captain in charge of aviation, but after several conversations with him, I saw that his mind was more occupied with making certain inventions connected with aeroplanes than with the subject of developing an aeronautical service. I finally realized that I should have to get some new blood in.

Chambers' discussions seldom converted an opponent, but, win or lose, they reinforced his confidence that the correctness of his theories would eventually be acknowledged. This often frustrated his pilots. He knew too much of the day-to-day troubles of the fliers to believe that aeroplanes could be effective weapons in his lifetime. And he also knew that many things had to be learned before even a reliable scouting plane could be produced and operated. So he saw the eventual assignment of two scouting planes to each cruiser and battleship as the practicable objective of naval aviation and looked for the hardware to accomplish this.

Fiske was both unconvinced and repelled by Chambers' pessimism.

In March 1913, a new administration came in, and Secretary Meyer, the cold Boston aristocrat, who had never understood the potential of naval aviation, left the Department. He was succeeded by Josephus Daniels of North Carolina. Compared to his predecessor, Mr. Daniels was affable and friendly, polite and serene.

A new naval personnel policy appeared. Captain Templin M. Potts had been taken by Secretary Meyer from command of the USS *Georgia* when Wainwright wanted him to take charge of Naval Intelligence. Later Potts became Aide for Personnel. When his turn for promotion came, an examining

---

1. In March 1913, a new administration took over and Secretary of the Navy Meyer was succeeded by Josephus Daniels (seated). Standing, left to right: Captain A. F. Fechteler, Aide for Inspections; Captain A. G. Winterhalter, Aide for Materiel; Rear Admiral Bradley A. Fiske, Aide for Operations.

1

board had found him qualified for rear admiral, but Daniels disapproved and sent him to sea to command the *Louisiana*. Said the Secretary, an officer should have at least two years' sea duty, in grade, to qualify for promotion.

This new policy threatened not only political pets in sinecures, but able officers who had held key shore billets for long periods because of unique knowledge or ability. Before the end of March, Rear Admiral Philip Andrews turned over the Bureau of Navigation to Rear Admiral Victor Blue, reverted to his permanent rank of commander, and led an exodus to sea.

These events seemed remote to Captain Chambers. He was recognized by civilians as the Navy's aeronautical expert, but nobody in the Navy, not even Lieutenant Ellyson, who was under orders for sea duty, wanted his job. Like Rodgers, Ellyson had married. All around him officers were headed seaward to qualify for promotion under the new regime. Years later, his wife said he had asked for sea duty because "a good aviator must first be a good naval officer," and that promotion had had nothing to do with it. The Bureau of Navigation said the transfer appeared to be one of policy but, as in Rodgers' case, refused to state what the policy was. But Chambers felt as though a favorite son were about to desert him.

On 24 April, Chambers was the principal speaker at a dinner given by the National Aeronautical Society. He was given a gold medal for his own and the Navy's aeronautical achievements and for his personal efforts to get Congress to set up a National

Aeronautical Laboratory. That happy evening was the zenith of Chambers' career. Storm signals were flying, but he ignored them a while longer.

A few days later, Ellyson left Washington and aviation, to become the first lieutenant of the battleship *South Carolina*, and he did not return to the naval air service until 1921.

The tragic death of this first naval aviator seven years after he again joined aviation marked, ironically, a great advance in that service. In 1928, he was the executive officer of the new carrier *Lexington*. On Saturday, 26 February, she lay in Hampton Roads with her planes ashore at the air station. Ellyson obtained permission to fly one of them to Annapolis to visit his daughter, who was ill. Ashore, he telephoned, got a good report on her condition, and waited.

The next evening, on his forty-third birthday, Ellyson was called from a party by a telegram stating that his daughter was worse and was to be operated on the following morning. In company with two pilots, Lieutenant Commander Hugo Schmidt and Lieutenant Rogers Ransehousen, Ellyson called at the air station commander's quarters, and announced that they were flying to An-

2

napolis. There was no question of permission. Ellyson was senior by rank and designation. Commander Read ordered his officer of the day, Lieutenant Clyde Smith, to help get the flight away.

Preparing the Loening amphibian at midnight was a cold, slow job. It had no radio and no lights, but everyone had flown at night that way. Ransehousen, the junior officer but most experienced of the three in this type of aircraft, took off from Willoughby Bay. The plane was never seen again.

Airways communications were then still in the future. Navy plane movement reports, like those of a ship, were passed by the Navy radio net. It was nearly noon before Norfolk learned that Ellyson's plane had not arrived in Annapolis and ordered a search. Three days later, floating wreckage was found near Cape Charles. Over a month later, Ellyson's body washed ashore.

A board of investigation held the cause unknown and the men in the plane responsible. Only Rear Admiral Leigh, Chief of the Bureau of Navigation, disagreed. He blamed Read and Smith for allowing the takeoff. Mr. Warner, the Assistant Secretary of the Navy for Air, pointed out that a station commander had no authority over Fleet plane movements. Some months later, he proposed a General Order permitting flights from naval air stations only in accordance with approved operating schedules or with the station commander's specific authority. After more discussion, Leigh reprimanded Read and Smith. No General Order was issued, but continued discussion eventually led to the establishment of a system of flight re-

leases, and it speeded plane movement reports. Thus his death resulted in the last of Ellyson's many contributions to naval aviation progress. A destroyer and an auxiliary air station at Pensacola have been named in his honor.

In Washington in 1913 the exodus to sea continued. In May, Rear Admiral Cone reverted to the rank of lieutenant commander and left the Bureau of Engineering. Friends kept telling Chambers that he should request sea duty.

The old man could not believe that this new rule really applied to him in his lonely basement office. He had no assistant who could take over. He was sure that no one else knew enough about naval aviation to keep it going. "The authorities," he said, "are blind to all but a few things like sea duty and have neither the time nor the inclination to learn about aviation."

At the end of May, his friends prevailed upon him to write officially to the Secretary. His letter said he understood he was supposed to ask for sea duty. He was "quite willing to go," but he thought the Navy's and the country's interests required that "naval aviation be started right." If necessary, he would take his chance on promotion in order to get aeronautics on the right track.

He felt justly proud of his nearly forty years of service. He had always gone willingly wherever he had been ordered. Asking for duty was something new and strange to him. He sincerely believed that he was the only man adequately informed on naval aviation and that his offer to sacrifice his future for its good would be regarded as a gallant gesture.

Daniels had a talk with Fiske. Then he penciled on the letter, "Don't send him," and sent it to the Chief of the Bureau of Navigation.

The storm broke on 1 July 1913. Without warning the Fiske ambush blasted Chambers with a curt official letter over Daniels' signature:

> The President of the United States having approved the recommendation of the Board of Admirals that you be transferred to the retired list of officers of the Navy, in accordance with the provisions of section 9 of the Navy Personnel Act, approved March 3, 1899, as amended by the Act approved August 22, 1912, you have been, by his direction, transferred to the retired list of the officers of the Navy, from the 30th day of June 1913.

Fiske, who a few months earlier had vigorously protested the Secretary's treatment of Captain Potts, said nothing. Nobody gave Chambers any thanks for doing a job no one else would take. For the time being, Fiske would have to put up with him, and he intended to use him until he found someone more to his liking. The next day Chambers was handed this order:

> Having been placed upon the retired list of officers from June 30, 1913, in accordance with section 9 of the Personnel Act, you will continue your present duties, until further orders, subject to your consent.
>   Josephus Daniels.

He had been scuttled. As he wrote in an agonized letter to Towers, into which he poured all of his suspicions, doubts, and

3. The new Burgess D-1 flying boat arrived in Annapolis in August 1913. (National Archives)

mangled feelings, he had been "dumped into the category of drunks and suspicious characters." He was fully aware that other officers were sometimes "plucked" from active duty into retirement, but he had never expected it to happen to him.

For two days he brooded in his office under the Navy Department stairs. He wondered what had happened. He was aware of no blots on his record. He could think of no personal enemies, but he was sure someone had done him wrong. He did not think of Fiske; their contacts had been too casual.

Newspaper friends had hinted that Towers had had a hand in his destruction, but Chambers wrote that he refused to believe it. He had faith in Towers' loyalty though he wrote they had "differed on matters of policy." Nevertheless, from hints Daniels had previously dropped, he believed that the Secretary was thinking of Towers as his replacement. "Did Daniels or Blue even broach the subject to you of taking my job?" Chambers wrote to hospitalized Towers. He said he wanted to get out as soon as possible. He had a couple of excellent lieutenant commanders in mind for his relief, but if Towers wanted the job he "would not stand in your way." He finished rather stiffly by hoping that "your present illness will not impair your distinguished abilities as a flier."

A few days later, Henry Mustin's request for aviation duty arrived. Chambers still wanted to get out quickly, and he recommended that Mustin relieve him immediately.

3

He can already fly, Chambers said—he had had eight and one-quarter hours total, including one solo hop—so he could take over at once and qualify for his license later.

From Hammondsport, Bellinger sent a letter of sympathy, combined with a request for a crash boat. Civilian air-enthusiasts sent sympathy, and several influential ones offered political assistance. But Chambers was too numb. Plucking was too much like a death for any condolences to make him feel any better.

Nonetheless, and despite his anguished feelings, he had responded affirmatively to the suggestion that he voluntarily continue his duties and, on 11 July, Daniels acknowledged his agreement and promised that "your wishes with regard to time of detachment will be complied with, and it is hoped that an officer can be assigned to duty with you, with a view to becoming your relief." But by this time, Chambers' urge to get out had dulled. He was still more interested in the technical progress of aviation than anything else and he stopped looking for an immediate relief.

Chevalier, who was the Navy's youngest pilot, was doing his best at Annapolis. After Billingsley's body had been recovered, he thought he was carrying out Chambers' wishes when he put the camp back on Towers' routine, which included the weekly cross-country flights. He was instructing Cunningham in the Curtiss, and he tried night flying with Smith. In late July, Smith and Chevy flew in the C-1 to Fortress Mon-

roe for the weekly cross-country flight. Repairs to the plane, and the flight back, took four days. Chambers first heard of this in a letter from Cunningham. He still felt that every hand was against him, and he irritably accused Chevalier of infringing on his authority by making a long flight without his permission.

Then early in August, James McClees Murray arrived to take over the camp. A few days later a sudden squall again flattened the tent hangars and damaged all the planes except the new Burgess D-1 flying boat which was still crated and hence escaped damage. Murray organized the salvage and repair work and then wired the facts to Chambers in Hammondsport. Three days after the storm he followed this up with a progress report, a list of needed repair parts, and the unanimous recommendations of the pilots for a permanent, storm-proof hangar at Annapolis, and the purchase of a Curtiss boat, a Brewster boat, and two military tractor-type planes. The A-2 had been badly damaged. A few days before the storm, Smith had installed a set of experimental controls, which he had devised. These had not been tested and Murray suggested to Chambers that Smith take the machine to Hammondsport to be rebuilt and test his controls there.

For three years Chambers had encouraged his pilots both to experiment and to offer suggestions for improvements. Hence, when he wired Murray to ship the A-2, but keep Smith, and then scolded Murray by mail, the men at Annapolis were startled. Permanent hangars were silly, Chambers wrote. How could they follow the Fleet with them? Pilots must stop infringing on his authority by writing to manufacturers. They should refrain from trying to tell him what kind of planes to buy, from taking off on distant flights, and from making unauthorized changes in the machine. So far as controls were concerned, anyone could build something that pleased only himself. They should stop wasting their time on such things.

The matter of standardized controls in Navy planes had been a problem ever since 1911, when Ellyson and Rodgers had learned to fly with different kinds. By 1913 most of the pilots, while preferring the Curtiss system to the Wrights', wanted something better than either of them. While everyone had ideas, there were few who agreed on what was better. Chambers had proposed a standardized set for both the Army and the Navy but, in the Army, they were leaving the question of controls up to the pilots. As Chambers believed that the pilots could never agree, he thought the Army's solution was silly. He talked of making the decision himself on a "scientific basis" rather than in accordance with pilots' views.

Back in May, while inspecting the D-1, Richardson had proposed, for comparative tests, putting Deperdussin controls in one seat. Chambers did not like these controls because he thought steering with the feet was a "European vogue," which would be awkward for a sailor. A steering wheel, he believed, would be more natural for a Navy man. Warping the wings of a big plane took more force than the other controls, therefore it should be done with the larger leg and foot muscles, as in the Nieuport system.

4. Captain Chambers wanted "a seaworthy plane . . . which will withstand rough water work and has a range of five hundred miles." Smith and Richardson were sent to Hammondsport to help Curtiss develop such an amphibian. The OWL (Over Water and Land) was the result.

Argument waxed warm and the decision was postponed. Then that fall, both the Deperdussin and a modified Nieuport system were tried out in the Burgess planes. When pilots began to favor the former, Chambers remained unconvinced. Lacking any personal experience in the air, it was his notion that they either did not understand his logical reasons or they were just bucking him.

When the Navy pilots asked for tractor planes, Chambers took the position that they were following a fad because they did not understand their future role in the service. He did not need to go up in a fuselage-type machine to know how ridiculous it would be to put an engine in front of a scout and thereby interfere with his vision. Furthermore, the question of tractors or pushers was a policy matter and hence properly within his domain. For what he considered logical reasons, tractors were permanently out.

When Chambers' angry letters arrived, Murray puffed his pipe and felt sorry for the Captain. He realized that all this irritation stemmed largely from personal troubles. He assured the old man that the pilots were only trying to please him and that they had no desire to undermine his authority. At the same time, he kept the Annapolis group working and he got the planes in the air again.

That summer Chambers had troubles coming from all directions. Chief Constructor

4

Watt sent over a memorandum of suggestions on aviation. Chambers objected to all of them. Watt was against dirigibles; Chambers wanted some. The Constructor proposed a hangar ship in lieu of an air station. Chambers said Fleet planes should go on armored cruisers, and all training and experimental work should be done ashore. Watt's Bureau wanted to do aero research at the model basin. Chambers said leave it to the Smithsonian until there is a national laboratory. Watt opposed an Office of Aeronautics in the Department. Chambers insisted that one was required.

Then came an article in a periodical criticizing naval aviation. Two years earlier Chambers might have used such remarks as ammunition in his battle with the conservative admirals. But, after he had been plucked, he took them as personal attacks. Other navies, the article stated, had begun to use aircraft, while the American Navy was still merely experimenting. The Navy Department was "open to severe criticism because of the timid and dawdling policy it has pursued in aviation."

A few days after this, Chambers sent a memorandum to the General Board. It showed that two and a half years after the first naval officer had started to fly, naval aviation consisted of three flying boats and three floatplanes, including the tired B-1. Nobody had asked to be qualified as a Navy Air Pilot under the published rules of the Bureau of Navigation, but Chambers counted everyone who had soloed and reported that fourteen officers had "qualified." He neglected to mention that eight of these—

Ellyson, Rodgers, Dortch, McNair, Cunningham, Billingsley, Richardson, and Mustin— were no longer on flying duty. Almost everyone still assumed that pilots could fly any time they were called upon, just as they might ride a bicycle.

Thus the naval aviation force that made Chambers proud, Wood critical, and Fiske frustrated was actually six pilots and six decrepit aeroplanes. They had no plans for training or for the development of material. There was no organization to put planes in the Fleet or to use them in war. Nonetheless, after three years of trying to organize the naval aviation force without clerical help and in the face of massive opposition, Chambers felt that the mere fact that Navy pilots were flying naval planes was a colossal accomplishment on his part.

Had he not regularly put off purchases in the hope of getting something better, the Navy might have had more planes. This habit was ingrained in him. Admitting the plane shortage to Grover Loening, the Wrights' representative, he said he wanted a shipboard plane—a flying boat that would be a pusher, with an engine between the wings and an outrigger tail like the Curtiss hydroplanes. He specified a hull with a wooden V-bottom, canvas sides and decking, and no wing-tip floats. He was prepared to order ten of these if the Wright Company could deliver in three months so they could make the trip to Guantanamo in January. Then a week later, he asked Loening to build them as amphibians with nonretracting wheels protruding from open wells in the hull bottom. Again, could he get them before the Fleet sailed? But the order was never placed.

In Hammondsport, Chambers commissioned Curtiss to rebuild the A-2 into a prototype of his all-purpose amphibian. He changed the plane's number to E-1 and named it the OWL for Over Water and Land. Smith was transferred to Hammondsport to oversee the project. The Captain was determined that Marines should fly proper pusher amphibians and not the Army's tractor types, which were favored by his two Marine pilots, Cunningham and Smith.

Curtiss was unhappy about the OWL, but he was getting paid to follow Chambers' instructions. He had tried nonretracting wheels on his first Triad, but had never been able to get it off the water. Nonetheless, in order to please Chambers he tried them again on the OWL. However, Smith was unable to get it off the water even with the wheel wells empty and covered. For several days weights were shifted and the surfaces adjusted before it was airborne. Its flying balance was horrible. Bellinger assisted in this pattern of trial and error. On his second trial flight, the plane ran out of gas, the float leaked, and it nearly sank before a boat arrived to pass him a towline.

Then the wheels were installed. They provided a clearance between the keel and the ground of but a scant inch. Nobody could get the plane off the lake. In reporting the week's progress to Chambers, Smith stated that the machine was unsafe to fly as a landplane. Then they took off the wheels, covered the wells, and tried to improve the plane's performance as a hydroplane, but it was too

5. Chambers felt the OWL was the answer to an all-purpose Navy-Marine flying machine, but Curtiss was unhappy because its flying balance was bad and it was heavy and slow. Later, the OWL was assigned to B. L. Smith, and as a result is considered the first Marine Corps aircraft.

heavy and square to do much better. When Smith carried Richardson, his best climb was only a hundred feet per minute, and this was too slow even in 1913.

Sitting in his cubbyhole under the stairs in Washington, Captain Chambers never doubted that his OWL was a big step toward the ultimate all-purpose Navy-Marine flying machine. Like any new mechanism, it had a few bugs to be eliminated. Chambers felt that Smith was just a stubborn Marine who was bucking policies that he could not understand. With chilly politeness, Chambers thanked him for his frank opinions and ordered him to fly the OWL from the field.

Like a good Marine and an excellent pilot, Smith carried out these orders. Since he had never flown a landplane, he spent the first day making short hops and landing straight ahead, as students had done before Curtiss installed dual controls. The flimsy wheel supports began to crumble on the first takeoff. He learned to land on the rear wheels alone because the keel was soon dragging when all three were on the ground. The Curtiss field was small and the OWL had no brakes, so crewmen had to grab his wings to stop him on each landing. The flight ended when they damaged a wing.

The next day's flights threw the wheel supports far out of line, but Smith made one more to oblige a photographer, a favor that

5

no Marine ever refused. Then he took off with Richardson aboard. The heavy machine fell back and dragged its keel four times before he managed to hold it in the air. The wheel supports were beyond use, and he landed in the lake. Then he reported that the landplane tests were complete.

Chambers responded with detailed instructions for modifications. Smith and Curtiss complied. Engine failures slowed their work. During October and November they managed to fly the OWL on only seven days. Then Chambers ordered it rebuilt with more changes, including wheel-retracting screws. Bellinger and Richardson left Hammondsport when the new flying boats were shipped to Annapolis. Smith stayed on alone with Chambers' pet. Ice closed the lake and, in December, Smith shipped the completed but still untested OWL to Philadelphia to embark it for the Fleet's winter maneuvers.

In the preceding August, the General Board, inspired probably by Fiske, had recommended the establishment in the Secretary's office of an Air Department to be headed by a director, who should "proceed with the organization of a naval air service suited to the needs of the Navy in war."

The administration hesitated. Then Roosevelt, "acting," named a board to draw up "a comprehensive plan for the organization of a naval air service." Chambers was the senior member. The junior members—Richardson, Towers, and Cunningham—were the only fliers. The other three had had no previous connection with aviation.

It took Chambers a month with a borrowed stenographer to assemble the data he was to present when he convened the board. In late November, they completed a report which began with eight broad policies and principles and recommended an appropriation of $1,297,700. This sum, the report urged, was to be used for an aeronautical center complete with test facilities, school, and station ship; the purchase of 50 planes and lighter-than-air equipment; an Office of Naval Aeronautics; and a stenographer and typewriter for Chambers.

Pensacola was recommended as the site for the aeronautical center. The old Navy Yard there and a nearby live-oak plantation, where timbers had once been cut for wooden ships, had long been a Navy liability. It had been closed down the year before and, in 1913, unemployed Democratic constituents wanted it reopened. This gave Chambers and Towers their chance to ask for it for naval aviation. The station ship was expected to aid both the school and the experimental work. In addition, the idea was that the school would loan detachments of qualified pilots as needed to other Fleet ships.

The proposed Office of Aeronautics was not the executive agency that had been recommended by the General Board. Rather it was Chambers' old idea of a coordinating, nonflying director, who should preside over an advisory board of assistants and bureau representatives, some of whom "should be qualified pilots whenever practicable."

Chambers was proud of this report. It had been unanimous and it embodied nearly everything he wanted, he wrote the presi-

98 dent of the Aeronautical Society, who was lining up support for Chambers' projected appeal to Congress. Chambers expected that the board's report would enhance his personal prestige, as well as spark a big advance in naval aviation. The most important parts, he wrote, could go into effect with a stroke of a pen, once the funds were assured, and thus aviation would be launched in the right direction.

There was one point that Chambers in his calculations had failed to evaluate. This was the tenacious influence of Admiral Fiske. After the report had been submitted to Secretary Daniels, Chambers and the fliers waited hopefully, but the answers were slow in coming. Towers became impatient. He wanted to know whether he was to take the aviation camp to Guantanamo again or to go to Pensacola. Chambers assured him it would be Pensacola but, as time passed without any orders, they both began to have doubts.

The difficulty lay with Admiral Fiske. He had not liked the report of the Chambers Board because there had been no recommendation that someone be made responsible for creating a large combatant air force. Without his approval, the report was merely stagnating.

Moreover, he wanted to replace Washington Irving Chambers before reorganizing naval aviation. Until he worked on Commander Mark Lambert Bristol, he could find no acceptable officer whom he could interest in taking command of half a dozen decrepit, ineffective aeroplanes. Mark Bristol was an ambitious officer, who was awaiting orders after having been court-martialed for

grounding his ship in a fog off the China coast. He had no aeronautical experience, no desire to fly, and no curiosity about planes, but he was known as a good administrator, and he wanted a job that would enhance his service reputation. Fiske convinced him that common sense and his staff experience fitted him to make any requisite aeronautical decisions. Furthermore, the Admiral pointed out, almost any air service that he might build would be a big improvement on Chambers' picayune assemblage.

In the middle of December, Bristol, who had been promoted to captain, was ordered to report to Fiske for special duty in the division of operations of the Secretary's office. Fiske told him orally to take charge of aviation. He had no title, status, instructions, or clerical help. Nor was there any office space available for him, so Fiske told him to sit down to work on the far side of his own desk. This arrangement made it obvious throughout the department that Bristol was Fiske's man. Thus he was well dug in as Fiske's special assistant before anyone told Chambers that aviation was going to move from the Bureau of Navigation to Fiske's operations division.

A month after Chambers had submitted his report, he reached a new low. His relief had reported. The report had neither been approved, accepted, nor rejected. The day after Christmas he wrote the president of the Aeronautical Society he could get neither action on, nor good publicity from, the report. The administration was scared of a deficit, and he still could not even get a typist.

On 27 December, Fiske released Bureau of Navigation orders for Towers to move to Cuba, whereupon both Bristol and Chambers talked of quitting. Fiske talked Bristol around. Chambers tried again to get action by drafting an order for the Secretary's signature, and Fiske made successful use of this in an attempt to get the Secretary to grant Bristol "enough authority to get a good start in aeronautics."

His success was attested by the succession of events early in 1914. The old battleship *Mississippi*, so outdated that no officer wanted her, was named as the prospective aviation station ship. Mustin, who was considered odd because he wanted to fly, was sent to command her where she lay rusting in the back channel at the Philadelphia Navy Yard, and he sailed her to Annapolis. The part played by determined political interest in Florida was evidenced by a change in the directions to Towers. He was to send the Marine fliers to the Caribbean for maneuvers as "the Marine Section of the Navy Flying School." But the rest of the aviation camp, including Towers himself, was to go to Pensacola. The recommended U. S. Naval Aeronautic Station had come into being, at least on paper.

That same day the Washington papers carried a Navy Department news release, noting that Captain Mark L. Bristol had taken charge of naval aviation, with Chambers remaining as his assistant. When Chambers read this, his injured feelings exploded

in a long letter to Secretary Daniels. He had nearly completed, he said, a plan for air power that was as good as Mahan's for sea power. He did not intend to complete this work merely for Bristol's aggrandizement. He would withdraw his consent to serve on active duty first. In the same letter he forecast dire difficulties for the aviators at Pensacola because the order to move did not provide a station commander. The fliers, he said, should be relieved of administrative duties and protected by a nonflying adviser in the position of commandant.

Though Chambers was still fighting, he knew he was through as the head man of aviation in Washington. If Fiske, or Daniels, had offered to make him commandant at Pensacola, he might have accepted, and he could have served with credit. But he was too proud to beg for the post and it was never offered. On the day after he had protested the news release, he was handed these orders:

1. You are hereby detached from duty in the Bureau of Navigation, Navy Department, Washington, D.C.: will report the same day to the Navy Department for special duty in the Division of Operations.
2. Your assignment to active duty is subject to your consent.
3. The employment on shore duty is required by the public interest.

The next day Bristol went to Annapolis to show the aviators that he was their new boss. He told Mustin and Towers exactly how to set up Pensacola. He wanted the experimental work separated from the school, and a detailed syllabus for training pilots. He either belittled, or perhaps did not know of, the 1913 instructions of the Bureau of Navigation concerning Navy Air Pilot Certificates, and he ordered Towers and Mustin to prepare requirements for such designations. There was a final crack of the whip when he said that Mustin would only remain in charge until a more senior officer could be found to command both the ship and the station.

Fiske now assumed control of naval aviation himself, and his new policy was handed to Chambers in another signed order. Fiske assigned to Bristol the tasks of establishing Pensacola, experimenting with dirigibles, and supervising Richardson's experiments in Washington. Chambers' duties were limited to the development of the OWL boat and liaison with the Smithsonian's Langley laboratory. Now, after three years on his own, he could no longer sign an aviation letter, spend an aviation dollar, or authorize an aviation test without Fiske's personal approval. The old man penciled sarcastic comments on his copy of this order and then complained out loud.

His objections were answered by another memorandum "for the guidance of Captain W. I. Chambers, Captain M. L. Bristol. Subject: Development of Aviation." It began with the statement that Bristol would eventually relieve Chambers. Fiske would set the policy and leave the details to Bristol, who would coordinate the bureaus. Chambers' work was to be limited to "research and investigation," and to liaison with the Smithsonian. Even his pet OWL was taken away from him. He was directed to prepare re-

7. *The battleship* Mississippi, *laid down in 1904 and already outdated, was named station ship for the new air station at Pensacola, 1914.*

ports in the form of "brief compilations of facts, without arguments."

Bristol was still using the other half of Fiske's desk when these memoranda put him firmly in control and isolated Chambers from the Navy's active fliers and flying. Bristol spent two more weeks consolidating his position in Washington. Then he went to Pensacola. He visited the new aeronautical station, not to find out how aeroplanes worked, or to fly in them, for he did not want to become prejudiced about types, confused by facts, or become an aviation enthusiast. He went merely to direct aircraft operations.

In February, Chambers presented a long petition to Congress. It reviewed his service and status and asked that he be restored to the active list as an additional number for special duty with aviation. In two long sets of hearings a host of civilian admirers rallied to his support, but Rear Admiral Victor Blue threw the weight of the Navy Department against him.

In 1915 and 1916, there were long hearings on his appeals and Congress passed general laws permitting the President to reinstate plucked officers and changed the Navy promotion system from seniority and plucking, to selection up.

The Bureau of Navigation sent Chambers' 1915 and 1916 appeals to the White House without comment. President Wilson never re-instated any officer under these laws. In

7

1919, at the age of 63, Chambers went on inactive duty. Too old for restoration to the active list, he asked for promotion on the retired list as a reward for his early aviation work and, as late as 1930 and 1932, Congress considered private bills for this. At that time, Admiral Frank B. Upham, the Chief of the Bureau of Navigation and a former non-flying Pensacola commandant, opposed even honorary promotion without pay. The bills all failed.

Washington Irving Chambers never flew a plane and he never completely grasped the pilot's problems. In trying to help them, he made powerful enemies. Armchair critics with latter-day learning can show the errors of many of his mechanical schemes. Nevertheless, he has properly been called the father of naval aviation. Almost alone in 1910, he envisioned naval aircraft as aids in keeping the sea lanes open and he worked to give America this additional sea power. The original landplane field at the Naval Air Station, Hampton Roads, was named in his honor shortly after he went on inactive duty. Chambers Field is no longer in use.

In the fall of 1913, when Towers again reported for duty after the accident in which Billingsley had lost his life, it appeared that naval aviation had achieved some degree of popularity. There were 34 applications for aviation duty on file, and he was asked to comment on the qualifications of the applicants. On 13 he made no comment because he did not know them well enough. He especially recommended two officers, said two were too heavy, commented on the fact that two others were married, and dismissed 15 with various uncomplimentary comments.

The reaction of the detail officer in the Navy Department was typical. He told Chambers any officer who wanted to should have a chance to fly. He kept Bronson, whom Towers had thought "exceptionally good material," at sea in the *Michigan,* and Dortch, one of the two whom Towers had especially recommended, stayed in a destroyer. He ordered Saufley, who was married, as well as two of the men from the discard list, into flight training.

Second Lieutenant William M. McIlvain was the first new student to report at Greenbury Point after Billingsley's death. He, however, was not from that list. As a student in Washington in 1908, he had been impressed by Orville Wright's flights at Fort Myer. Four years later, McIlvain was serv-

ing on the battleship *North Dakota* when he requested aviation duty; the next morning headlines in the papers told of the Towers-Billingsley crash. He went around to the ship's office to get his request and hold it while he thought things over, but he was too late. The mail had left.

When McIlvain reached Annapolis in October, Sergeant McKeon immediately began to teach the new student about engines, and Chevalier started his air work a few days later.

McIlvain never forgot his solo flight. In December, Towers checked him out and ordered him to "take off. Make three figure eights, then land and taxi in to the beach."

The wind was picking up but everything went well until just as he was about to set the plane down. Then he saw that it was drifting sideways over the water. He gunned the engine, circled, checked everything he could think of, and then carefully tried to land again. Again he found himself in a dizzy skid. So he opened his throttle and pulled up. He was scared and baffled when he climbed away from his third wild skid.

As he stood watching from the beach, Sergeant McKeon suddenly realized that McIlvain did not know which way the wind was blowing. He jumped into a skiff, pulled out into the Severn, and waved the lieutenant into the wind. This time McIlvain landed, and thereupon Towers coldly told him he had flunked. Naval aviation had no room for a man who went flat-hatting when he was ordered to land. But when he found that no one ever told the Marine how to find the wind, Towers thawed out. He pointed out the

---

1. *Naval aviation at last had a home of its own when, in 1914, the old Navy Yard in Pensacola was turned over to the Naval Aeronautic Station. The location was ideal for an aviation training station—it offered a large, sheltered bay and a warm climate. Within a month, the aviators had cleared away the debris, erected tent hangars, and built wooden ramps from each hangar to the water.*

2   3

104 telltale wind streaks on the water, and then sent him up again. This time McIlvain passed.

Three other students reported for training in the fall of 1913—Ensigns Melvin Lewis Stolz, Walter Douglas LaMont, and Richard Caswell Saufley; the latter's orders contradicted the supposed policy of the Department in regard to married aviators.

Soon after Christmas, McIlvain and Smith, the two Marines, loaded the OWL, a Curtiss boat, spares, camp equipment, and 28 men into the transport *Hancock* and sailed for Culebra with the First Marine Advanced Brigade. When Towers was ordered to move the rest of aviation to Pensacola, Saufley, Murray, Chevalier, and Herbster went to Philadelphia to stand watches on Mustin's *Mississippi* when she sailed for Annapolis on 6 January 1914.

The old tub of a battleship was nearly as wide as she was long. Her decks were cluttered, her hatches small, her hoisting gear inadequate. When she anchored in Annapolis Roads, she looked old and stunted beside the big, new collier *Orion,* which was loading planes, camp gear, spares, and Richardson's rebuilt catapult. Four civilians boarded the *Mississippi* before she sailed—Marshal C. Reid; G. S. Curtis, factory manager for Burgess; J. L. Callan, who worked for Glenn Curtiss; and Grover Loening, the Wrights' manager. The Navy Department had invited them to confer with Mustin and the other pilots during the voyage. It was Bristol's hope that the technical details of naval aviation would all be worked out in their five days at sea.

Long before the ship got under way,

2. *Second Lieutenant William M. McIlvain, U. S. Marine Corps, Naval Aviator No. 12.*
3. *Lieutenant Richard C. Saufley, U.S. Navy, reported for training in 1913. He was killed in 1916 when the AH-9 crashed over Santa Rosa Island off Pensacola. After his death, Admiral Benson grounded the old pusher hydros.*
4. *Mustin sent this photograph of Pensacola to the Secretary of the Navy in 1914, to acquaint him with the conditions the aviators encountered when they arrived to set up the new Naval Aeronautic Station. But Mustin was not dismayed—instead, he wrote enthusiastically to Bristol of the aviators' plans.*

Chevalier introduced the guests to the wine mess. Afterwards Loening looked back on this trip as a wonderful junket during which technical matters were never discussed. Nonetheless, the experience did enhance the effectiveness of aviation in the first World War because all these men got to know each other well before they arrived in Pensacola.

Bellinger, Stolz, and LaMont missed the party. They arrived in the *Orion* with most of the men. The next morning the aviators began unloading the collier while Mustin put the battleship alongside the station's only pier. As soon as she was secured, he and Towers scuffed through ankle-deep white sand to survey the U. S. Naval Aeronautic Station.

Most of the first naval air station was covered several feet deep with the debris of hurricanes. The sandy beaches, broken only by the pier and a granite-walled wet-basin, were covered with logs, bridge timbers, sections of broken houses, and shattered boats. Other wreckage surrounded the old oak trees and the brick buildings.

Before Pensacola had been allotted to

aviation, the buildings had been turned over to the Marine Corps for use as an advance base. When the aviators arrived, Marines occupied the only serviceable structures and, while their commanding officer offered Mustin his assistance, he had no intention of moving his men out of the buildings.

On the two landward sides, the nearly square station was enclosed by a 12-foot brick wall. Beyond its main gate, Warrenton, a squatter village on Navy land, nestled against the west wall. At the corner of this station wall, the tracks of an electric interurban train, which ran out from Pensacola, skirted Commodore's Pond. Here hundreds of live-oak knees, relics of the days of wooden ships, were still stored under the black water.

In those days aviation operated largely with "salvaged" material. Thus, instead of being appalled by the torn roofs, broken windows, rusted machinery, and general disorder, Towers saw this desolate station as a source of unguarded riches. He even wondered how he might use the massive oak timbers in the pond.

Before evening his men were at work clearing a section of the south beach for the tent hangars and laying scrap lumber as launching ramps for the seaplanes. They found the balmy weather a pleasant change from Maryland's winter and their work novel enough to be fun. That night Mustin wrote glowingly to Bristol of their plans and progress. He ended:

Again I ask you not to have me superseded in command here. I have had the responsibility of bringing the ship down from Philadelphia, via Annapolis, came into harbor without a pilot and put her alongside the dock without

a tug, so the department might feel that I am competent. Furthermore I feel that I can handle the situation here as you will want it done, and we have started with perfect harmony and enthusiasm in the whole command including those officers who are not directly interested in aeronautics.

The next day Mustin rode the trolley into town. There he discovered that Palafox Street was a dismal ghost of the busy street he had seen on former visits to the port. The railroad had always favored Mobile as a Gulf outlet. The sawmills, which had made Pensacola rich, had cut their last timber before the Navy abandoned the Navy Yard. Then a hurricane had wrecked what was left, and most Pensacola businesses had folded. The old families were penniless and Mustin's acquaintances among them were doubly glad to see him. They hoped that even this slight naval activity might help the city toward better times.

By the beginning of February, Towers had the school in operation. Herbster and Murray were working the Wright machines and getting instruction in the Curtiss from Chevalier and Bellinger, who were also giving dual instruction to the new students. Stolz had been trained with Nieuport controls at the Burgess school before reporting to Annapolis. When Chambers decided against this type, Stolz had to begin all over again in a Curtiss. Then Bristol arrived and boarded the *Mississippi* for a month's temporary duty.

Without relieving Mustin of command or responsibility, he assumed the role of Senior Officer Present. He had accepted the printed requirements for Navy Air Pilot and he

wanted a lot of officers qualified quickly. He demanded that the instructors have the new certificates by the time the next class should arrive, and he heckled Chambers, by mail, until he was assured that the certificates were in the printer's hands.

Flight operations had only routine interruptions until the February day when Murray took off alone in the D-1 for practice. A few minutes later a weather bureau observer atop a Pensacola building saw him start a glide. Flying was still so new that the man waited to watch the machine land off the town's docks. He saw Murray check his speed several times by pulling the nose up and then dropping into a glide again. The inherent instability of the plane made it hard for him to hold a steady speed. At about 200 feet he held the nose up an instant too long. The plane stalled and whipped into the deadly nose dive. Before Murray could regain control, it smacked into the water.

The weatherman grabbed his phone and started rescue operations. Bellinger in the C-1 was the first to reach the wreck. He found his classmate floating face down in his life jacket a few yards away. He held Murray's face out of the water until a boat reached them, but help had come too late. The plane had had no safety belts and a bump on the head had stunned Murray as he was thrown out. He had drowned while unconscious.

Bristol approved the investigation that Mustin convened and wrote to Chambers that he believed it would be practicable to build a plane which "would stand a fall of a couple of hundred feet and keep a pilot from hitting

5. *It was a temptation to unload the hydroaeroplanes and commence flying, but the aviators set up their new air station first. Then Towers, with Chevalier as passenger, made the first flight in a Curtiss flying boat.*
6. *The tents were strictly fair-weather hangars. When a blow came in from the Gulf of Mexico, the planes were quickly moved to old brick structures in a less exposed section of the Navy Yard. A Curtiss flying boat is in the foreground; the other is a Curtiss hydroaeroplane. (Wide World Photo)*

his head." Officers like Bristol, who had never been up in a plane, considered anyone unfit to command a ship, or a Fleet, unless he was a competent seaman. Nevertheless, they never admitted the need for the slightest air experience as a prerequisite for the command and development of an air service. It took 16 years, the efforts of Billy Mitchell, and an act of Congress to change these views.

Mustin disagreed with Bristol from the start. He believed that an air commander should fly in order to understand the problems and guide the development of naval aviation intelligently. Up to that time, he had flown always as a volunteer and had never worried about flight orders or flight pay. But Murray's death made him wonder what would happen to his family if he were killed or seriously hurt in a flying accident. Would it be considered "not in line of duty" or "due to his own misconduct"? When he explained his concern and asked Bristol for flight orders, the Captain put him off. Intelligent administration of the station, he said, was more important than flying.

As Chambers had foreseen, Mustin's status caused the administration of the aeronautic station to be unusually involved. He

6

was legally in command only of the *Mississippi*. Ashore he was a squatter without authority. The Navy's only air station had no commander, no accounting number, no money allotted for any purpose, no lights, power, or even fresh water. The commandant a thousand miles away at Key West was responsible for the old quarters. The Marine brigade controlled the other buildings. A paymaster in Charleston, South Carolina, made out the ship's requisitions and paid her crew. The Bureau of Yards and Docks sent one of their civil engineer officers to watch the aviators camping on their real estate. Under such a complicated arrangement, each small, routine need became a major problem.

Bristol knew all this before he went back to Washington. Orders for Mustin to command the station would have eliminated a lot of red tape, and Mustin repeatedly asked Bristol's help in getting them. If Bristol tried to get such orders, he failed. Then he heckled. His letters to Mustin were full of "I don't understand why you . . ." When Mustin suggested French hydros, Bristol wrote, "If you knew anything about it, you would know the German ones are better." A sudden squall capsized Chevalier and Stolz, wrecking the last of the training hydros. Since the flying boats were considered unfit for primary instruction, Mustin asked for two spare hydros in order to keep training going when some were under repairs. Bristol refused. "Use the [flying] boats for instruction," he said, "when you are short of the others."

Smith and McIlvain arrived from the Caribbean convinced that the Marine Corps

needed its own aviation, trained for troop cooperation. Towers put them to work in the school. Smith was an excellent instructor and his experiences were typical of the times. When he flew with LaMont, a rudder wire snapped. Smith grabbed the controls away from the student and got the plane down to a crash landing. Without belts they were thrown out, but they got off with bruises. The next day, when he was up with Stolz, an air valve broke off their engine. It flew back and splintered the propeller. Fragments nicked the control wires and bamboos, the engine tried to tear loose, but he got the machine onto the water before it fell apart.

A day later, Smith and Stolz had a fire in the air. Again Smith's skill got them safely to the water. Two days later, a carburetor bowl cracked while they were on the water. Gasoline spewed over the hot engine and they had to swim away from another burning plane. This was all routine for a 1914 instructor, but Mustin ordered an investigation, which led to three improvements.

Through it, Mustin heard of the Pyrene fire extinguisher, which was then new on the market. He tested some and was so impressed that he persuaded the Department to put one in every plane. The investigation also led the Bureau of Engineering to require a fuel cock in every plane, with a handle near the pilot's hand. But Bristol bawled Mustin out. "I don't want formal boards," he said, "but I want every accident investigated just the same." This led to the third result, when Mustin and Towers concocted a form that they called a "materiel report." This later grew into the "trouble report" form, which

8

served for many years as a quick means of passing aircraft troubles on to those who could fix them.

Bristol's first contribution to naval aviation advancement and administration was General Order 88. This provided a new system for numbering all kinds of aircraft from kites and balloons to planes, and it renumbered the 14 airplanes the Navy then owned.

By early April, Mustin was completely frustrated by red tape. In order to please Bristol, he had pushed Chevalier and Bellinger into starting tests for Navy Air Pilot tickets, but he never found time any more to fly himself. The bureaus all pestered him. His nerves were edgy and he quibbled with Towers over trifles. His status was so unofficial and complicated that he was always just beating about the bush and never getting necessary things done. He told Bristol, "I'd rather be in Guam." In those days, that remote island was the nearest thing to a concentration camp for unpopular naval officers that Washington could provide.

Then on 10 April, the cruiser *Birmingham,* carrying Rear Admiral William Sims, led a destroyer flotilla into Pensacola. When Sims complimented Mustin on his accomplishments at the air station, he cheered up. Nine days later, the 1914 Mexican affair flared up and put a temporary stop to all operations at the U. S. Naval Aeronautic Station.

Sims was entertaining Mustin at lunch aboard the *Birmingham* when orders from Admiral Bradley Fiske arrived: Take the destroyer flotilla and two planes to Tampico. Mustin rushed ashore and organized the "First Aviation Section." The next morning

7. Lieutenant Commander H. C. Mustin was Commanding Officer of the station ship, the old USS Mississippi. Later, he was designated Naval Aviator No. 11.

8. When the Mexican affair flared up, Admiral Fiske ordered an aviation detachment sent to Veracruz. At the right is the first plane to be hit by hostile gunfire—naval aviation's first combat scars.

9. Commissioned officers of the Aviation Corps of the U.S. Navy, Naval Aeronautic Station, Pensacola, Florida, in the spring of 1914. Left to right: Lieutenant V. D. Herbster, Lieutenant W. M. McIlvain, Lieutenant P. N. L. Bellinger, Lieutenant R. C. Saufley, Lieutenant J. H. Towers, Lieutenant Commander H. C. Mustin, Lieutenant B. L. Smith, Ensign G. deC. Chevalier, and Ensign M. L. Stolz.

Towers, Smith, and Chevalier, with twelve mechanics, a flying boat, and a bamboo-tailed hydroaeroplane, sailed aboard the *Birmingham.* Thus, the *Birmingham,* which had launched Ely's first flight, also became the first ship to carry American planes on an overseas mission that was not a drill.

Before the destroyers were clear of the harbor, Mustin was ordered to take the *Mississippi* to Veracruz. He quickly loaded the five hundred Marines, the two remaining serviceable planes, and parts of others as spare gear, but he had to wait until the next day for food to come from Mobile, because the departing ships had taken all the available provisions in Pensacola. The Navy Department ordered all officers into the ship except Saufley and McIlvain. Herbster was en route to test the first Burgess-Dunne plane, so Mustin took Saufley in Herbster's place as the ship's navigator. Thus, after the *Mississippi* sailed for Veracruz, McIlvain, 11 enlisted men, a broken aeroplane, and a file cabinet were all that remained at the U. S. Naval Aeronautic Station.

9

On 21 April 1914, the Fleet landing force lost 19 men in a poorly conducted seizure of Veracruz against sniper resistance. By the time the *Mississippi* arrived three days later, the occupation had turned into a futile war against a phantom enemy.

Using a boat boom rigged as a crane, Mustin swung Bellinger and Stolz overside in the C-3. They searched the harbor for mines and saw none. They looked over the city for enemy troops, but saw only Americans. After a 50-minute flight, they returned to the ship and logged the first American aerial war mission completed.

The improvised plane hoist and communications with the landing force were both slow and clumsy. Mustin set up an aviation camp on the beach just inside the breakwater and posted a seaman guard to protect the beached planes. Mounted messengers brought requests for scouting flights which Bellinger made, using LaMont, Stolz, or Saufley as his observer. Even with binoculars, they made no startling discoveries. After the first month, this scouting work practically stopped. General Funston had taken command ashore. Mustin complained, "The Army won't ask and the Admiral won't let the pilots volunteer, but he says we must stay until the Army gets some planes here."

As the scouting requests fell off, Bellinger made at least one flight every day just to show the Fleet that it could be done. He was glad to spend the other daylight hours on call at the camp. A slight sea breeze made it the most bearable place in the area. Anchored out in the harbor, the *Mississippi*'s plates soaked up so much sun during the

day that at midnight they were still hot to the touch. Her old ventilating system had never been adequate and, in the stagnant tropical air, her compartments were stifling. Men hung up their perspiration-soaked clothes at night and found them even wetter in the morning. The captain's cabin was as bad as the berth deck. Mustin, never a robust man, sweltered and grew thinner. He tried sleeping on deck, but each night a drenching thunderstorm drove him back to the steaming cabin. By late May he weighed ten pounds less than when he entered the Navy.

His status irked him even more than it had at Pensacola. Officially he was merely the skipper of an antique battleship with a skeleton crew. Nevertheless both Bristol and the fleet admiral expected him to run aviation to suit them, and they seldom wanted the same things.

Bristol wanted some Navy air pilots rated. Who should be assumed to be the "qualified officers" to give the tests? Mustin proposed that the first certificates be issued without test in this sequence: 1. Ellyson, 2. Towers, 3. Herbster, 4. Smith, 5. Chevalier, 6. Bellinger, 7. Mustin. With seven omissions, this was the order in which these officers had soloed. Mustin explained that he had omitted Rodgers because he had qualified only in the Wright controls, "which are now unpopular," and he did not mention the other six who were no longer flying.

But Bristol said, "no." Ellyson and Towers should be designated as the only true pioneers; Bellinger and Mustin as a reward for their operations at Veracruz. Everybody else should go through the prescribed tests.

10

11

Nothing was settled at this time.

At Tampico, Towers, Smith, and Chevalier found their jobs equally uncomfortable and dull. Orders from Washington held planes and pilots idle aboard the *Birmingham*, so Towers asked Bristol to get them sent either to Veracruz, where they could fly, or back to Pensacola, "where so much needs to be done." Bristol answered with the sympathetic hope that they might get some flying. Towers then made a quick trip to the fleet flagship at Veracruz. Two days after he got back to Tampico, the *Birmingham* steamed into Veracruz and landed the First Aviation Section. They were to operate under Mustin at the aviation camp.

That day another student, Clarence King Bronson, reported aboard for aviation duty from the *Michigan*. He was one of several officers whom the fleet commander allowed to report for aviation training at Veracruz. All the others quit or failed physically.

Bronson made rapid progress when Towers started his instruction. At the same time Bellinger tried to instruct Stolz, La-Mont, and Saufley in the flying boat. It was an awkward machine that took a long run to stagger into the air. Landing practice was hazardous inside the harbor on account of the heavy boat traffic, and a long, oily swell made it dangerous outside. Despite these handicaps, Saufley and LaMont were soon flying solo. Watching them from his quarter-deck, Mustin decided that Saufley was going to be very useful for he used his head but, as for LaMont, he looked erratic. His flying was more in the nature of acrobatics than brain work. Stolz alternated be-

10. Clarence K. Bronson began his flight training at Veracruz. Bronson, Naval Aviator No. 15, lost his life in 1916 while on an experimental bomb test flight at Indian Head, Maryland.
11. Richard Harding Davis, war correspondent during the Veracruz skirmish in 1914, on left; P. N. L. Bellinger, right. (Courtesy of Mrs. C. G. Halpine)
12. Curtiss planes on the beach at the first Naval Aeronautic Station, Pensacola, with two flying boats in the foreground.

tween slow progress and slumps. He did not solo until June, but then he did very well.

Soon after the aviation camp had been established, it became a hangout for the war correspondents—Richard Harding Davis, Jack London, and other lesser lights. Most of them had reached Veracruz after the initial excitement. Day after day nothing worth reporting happened. Anything that occurred on a flight, they built into a big news story. One day the mechanics found a bullet hole in the tail of Bellinger's plane. He had absolutely no idea when or where he got it. The correspondents filed long stories of the first American plane in combat.

When absolutely nothing happened that could be exploited, the news men sat in the shade sampling bottles of cerveza and dreaming up fictional releases to keep their employers content. They found handsome, slow-talking Bellinger a convenient hero for their yarns. He was amused. After Towers reached Veracruz, the boys tried to use him, too. But he disliked the fiction. When his mechanics read of Bellinger's combat flight, they found a bullet hole in his plane too. Towers was secretly pleased but he stopped the story. "I was sure the hole was made with a screwdriver, not a bullet," he said.

12

In his hot, stuffy cabin, Mustin brooded over these exaggerated stories about his subordinates. He was the aviator in charge when anybody wanted to complain and every day some senior bawled him out. But, when something good was printed, only Towers and Bellinger were named. Never Mustin.

He began to believe it was a conspiracy. "I am convinced," he wrote to Bristol, "that there is some underground work between someone in this outfit and the Secretary of the Navy." He was sure it was not Smith, who said frankly that he wanted to go ashore and operate as troop support aviation with the Marines. Nor was it Chevalier, who was "a jewel in every way, and I wish we had more of the same mold." But he was uncertain about Towers and Bellinger. "How did the First Section get here when the Admiral wanted it in Tampico?" he asked. "Why are the planes here, when they should be in Pensacola?" He would never have suggested giving Bellinger his license right away, "if I had known he was working himself up with the press." Mustin sent for the pilots, blew his top, and felt better.

When Bristol received Mustin's letter, he understood. He had been the captain of an old ship in the tropics. He remembered the loneliness of the job. He knew how heat and sleeplessness could magnify and multiply problems. He dropped the heckling demands that had previously filled his letters and instead sent encouraging praise to Mustin.

Mustin answered contritely. His suspicion of the pilots had been heat errors. Everything was running smoothly again. Then he vented his frustrations on the planes. "Kill the OWL project," he wrote. "Every flier here knows it is an impossibility until an entirely new system of power, with an enormous saving in weight, is evolved, and that is not likely to occur in this generation." The flying boat hulls soaked up water and the sun ruined wing fabric. They seldom got off the first time they tried and, when they did, they could not climb.

Bristol answered with more praise and sympathy. He was noncommittal about the planes, but he added the news that the *Mississippi* was about to be recalled. On 13 June, she loaded all the planes and sailed away from Veracruz. Naval aviation's first war operation had lasted nearly two months— without firing a shot, injuring anyone, or noticeably affecting the Veracruz incident.

Everyone was glad to leave Veracruz. But the Pensacola station was in worse condition than they had remembered. McIlvain and his few men had kept the seaplane beach and a shop in shape, but no more. The weather was as humid as at Veracruz. The lightest work was exhausting and sleep failed to rest.

In spite of these drawbacks, the pilots were glad to be back. They could fly again without fleet interference. The station might be in sorry shape, but it was naval air's only real estate, the aviators' only haven. The San Carlos bar had cool drinks. Friends gave parties. Officers and men found boarding places ashore that were more comfortable than the hot little ship. They set up the tent hangars, got the planes flying, and visited the ship only on payday.

111

CHAPTER ELEVEN: PENSACOLA'S PIONEERS

The possibility of a flight across the Atlantic was a favorite dream of the early enthusiasts of aeronautics and, early in 1914, it became known that Rodman Wanamaker was planning to finance the construction of a Curtiss flying boat to attempt such a transatlantic flight. Wanamaker had a vision of a great international venture with two pilots, one American and the other English. Even before construction started, the flying boat had come to be known as the *America*. Curtiss had employed B. D. Thomas, who had worked with T. O. M. Sopwith in England, to help him design it, and he applied to the Navy Department, seeking the additional counsel and assistance of his old friend Towers in the planning and development of the plane.

Accordingly, in February, a few days after Murray had been drowned in the D-1 crash, Towers was ordered to proceed from Pensacola to Hammondsport. He stopped in New York, where both Wanamaker and Curtiss urged him to agree to be the American pilot. Towers refused to be rushed into a decision, but he kept an open mind. In Hammondsport, the three of them talked over the design with Thomas, the Sopwith man, who with his helpers had plenty of ideas and was

certain that the flying boat could be designed. Curtiss and Wanamaker were enthusiastic over the possibilities of this first transatlantic airplane.

But Towers, as a prospective pilot, was skeptical. The world distance record for any type of airplane at that time was a little over six hundred miles and the existing Curtiss flying boats seldom made much over two hundred. To build a machine that could fly the 1,288 miles from Newfoundland to the Azores, seemed to Towers to be a leap into the unknown future rather than an orderly step in the evolution of aeronautics. Before he committed himself to fly across any ocean, he wanted something more tangible than the hopes of a designer to demonstrate that the plane could do it.

After the principal characteristics of the plane had been outlined, Towers promised to be on hand in May for its flight tests. Then, before returning to Pensacola, he went to Washington to talk the flight over with Captain Chambers. The Captain agreed with his opinion that the plan was premature, too great a jump in flying-boat development. They both suspected that Curtiss felt the same way, but they knew him well enough to agree that he would keep trying as long as anyone footed the bills. They knew too that he might be lucky. The project might succeed. Then the machine would be a wonderful advance, and of immense value to the Navy.

With that possibility in mind, Chambers promised that the Department would send Towers to Hammondsport for the flight tests. It was also agreed that he would be detailed

113

---

1. *The* America, *a twin-engined, enclosed-cabin flying boat, was designed and built for the purpose of flying the Atlantic to win the* London Daily Mail *prize of $50,000. Rodman Wanamaker, who was financing the construction, envisioned two pilots, one American and the other British, sharing an international venture. Glenn Curtiss (center), builder of the* America, *confers with Lieutenant J. H. Towers (left), the prospective American pilot, and Lieutenant John Porte (right), a former Royal Navy aviator who was the intended British pilot.*

1

2

as one of the transatlantic pilots, if he reported that his flight tests demonstrated the flight to be practicable.

In June, when Towers left the *Mississippi* and returned to Hammondsport after the Mexican interlude, Lieutenant John Porte, a naval aviator, retired from the Royal Navy because of tuberculosis, was there as the prospective British pilot, and the *America* was nearly ready for her first test flight.

The efficient biplane wings were covered with light silk. This fabric was very strong for its weight, but it tended to shrink when it stood in the summer sun. At least once it split from this cause. The plane's rudder and elevator were like those of other Curtiss boats. The ailerons, a new attempt to evade the Wright patents, moved only down and were operated by foot pedals which required a heavy foot for they were big, unbalanced flaps which provided barely enough control in the air. Towers discounted this defect for he saw how they could quickly be connected to work together as soon as the plane was clear of the jurisdiction of United States courts.

The big hull had been framed with oak and ash, planked with thin cedar, and waterproofed by a fabric skin affixed with glue. It carried tanks for three hundred gallons of gasoline, which Curtiss figured would be enough for the 1,288 miles and, for the first time, the pilots were provided with an entirely enclosed cockpit.

Between the wings, two 100-horsepower engines drove pusher propellers. The engines were small for the big plane, but they were the biggest that Curtiss could build at the

2. The America *was christened on 22 June 1914. Towers agreed to flight test the plane in Hammondsport, and during the ensuing summer many changes and improvements were made in anticipation of the transatlantic flight.*
3. *Plans for the flight were canceled by the outbreak of war in Europe, and the plane was sent across the Atlantic by ship. She was the basis for British flying-boat design throughout the war period.*

time. With a light load, the plane flew well on her first flights. But when the fuel tanks were full nothing that the two pilots tried would get it off the water. Before they quit trying, Towers was convinced that the machine was not equal to its projected task. He thought Curtiss knew it, too, but the inventor never admitted it.

The *America,* however, was a big advance over anything previously built. The hull was modified several times, but still it would not get off with its load. Curtiss mounted a third engine—a tractor—on the centerline, high above the hull. While the three engines took off with a full fuel load, they burned it too fast at cruising speed. Then the pilots cut the center engine after takeoff. It windmilled with enough drag so that the other two had to run nearly wide open to hold the plane in the air. At that speed, the fuel consumption made the crossing obviously impossible.

Late in July, it was decided to take out the center engine and rebuild the hull on still different lines. Towers took advantage of this lull for a home leave in Georgia. The proposed flight had been making headlines for months. Each change or delay was news. When Towers went on leave, some reporters started a false report that he had been pulled

3

off the job by the Navy Department because of a question of protocol over who was to be the senior pilot.

The story was entirely erroneous, but Towers never flew the machine again. Before he returned to Hammondsport, World War I had started. Lieutenant Porte left for active duty at the Royal Navy's air stations at Felixstowe, England. Wanamaker canceled his plans and either gave, or sold, the *America* to the Royal Navy. On the basis of Porte's reports, Britain bought more planes of the same design from Curtiss.

The original *America,* modified at Felixstowe to mount higher-powered French engines, went into service as "the Felixstowe boat." She was the direct ancestor of long lines of excellent twin-engine seaplanes on both sides of the Atlantic. After experience with her, the British designed improved versions. In 1917 they were using the F-5, or Felixstowe 5, model. Some were built in American factories and shipped overseas for engine installations. After the United States entered the war, the F-5, modified to take Liberty engines, was built for the U.S. Navy as the F-5-L. For over ten years, this wood, wire, and fabric biplane with 800 semi-reliable horsepower, and over a hundred feet of wingspread, was the darling of the pilots. Later U.S. flying boats have all been indebted to the F-5-L and through her to the original *America.*

Towers was still on leave when the war stopped the *America* tests. He asked for foreign duty. Three weeks later, he was in London as assistant naval attaché for air. This billet held him until late in 1916 and allowed him to see some of the early developments of the Felixstowe flying boat.

Meanwhile, the armoured cruiser *North Carolina* was ordered to replace the *Mississippi.* She was bigger and newer and faster, had a quarter-deck large enough for a catapult, and had more comfortable living spaces. This replacement was not because aviation had come into favor in the Navy, but simply because the old *"Miss"* was being sold to Greece. Mustin was to turn her over at Hampton Roads and return to Pensacola in the cruiser.

Mustin took three planes in the ship and left the others at Pensacola, where Chevalier replaced McIlvain as station keeper. Mustin also left him 31 men and the lone student, Bronson. Since Chevalier, like Towers, was an exceptionally able instructor, Mustin expected Bronson to solo before he got back. The station-keepers' accounts and all the records were kept in the ship because the station still had no separate administration. No inconvenience was anticipated from this arrangement for the ship was expected back in a month. The station had no mess and no quarters for the stay-behinds, but all hands made living arrangements off the station and looked forward to their month of freedom.

The ship's company talked of friends in Newport News and of a rendezvous at the Chamberlain Hotel on Old Point Comfort. Chevalier listened. "Wait till they get out of town," he said to Bronson, "and I'll show you more hot spots in this town than they will find in all of Virginia."

The last newspapers tossed aboard the *Mississippi* before she sailed from Pensacola told of the assassination of an Austrian archduke in a Serbian town. None of the fliers had ever head of him or the town. Anyway, they did not think it important.

At Newport News, on 8 July 1914, Mustin walked across the dock from the *Mississippi* to the *North Carolina* and relieved Commander William A. Moffett, who was destined to become the first chief of the Bureau of Aeronautics. For the next three weeks, there was no time for flying. Everyone was busy moving aeronautical and other gear into the *North Carolina* and turning the *Mississippi* over to the Greeks.

While aviators were moving around Newport News, the European nations swapped notes and ultimatums, using the murdered archduke as an excuse for power politics. Wise men said that if war came, it could only last a few weeks. Modern weapons, they said, made war too horrible for men to stand it longer than that. Furthermore, it would be so expensive that even the richest powers would have to quit inside of a month because they would be bankrupt.

Late in July, Wadleigh Capehart, a classmate of Chevalier's, reported aboard the *North Carolina* from the Burgess factory. When he joined the ship, everyone expected that they would go south in a few days and the new student would take up flight instruction at Pensacola. But this was not to be.

4. Wadleigh Capehart, Naval Aviator No. 19, joined naval aviation in July 1914.

The change-over was completed by the twenty-eighth. The *North Carolina* lay at anchor in Lynnhaven Roads, flew her planes, and prepared to sail for Pensacola. LaMont managed to spin the original Burgess boat into the water and wreck it without killing himself, and this turned out to be his last flight in naval aviation.

On 28 July 1914, Austria declared war on Serbia. The Navy Department held the *North Carolina* at the Virginia Capes to see what was going to happen in Europe. Four days later, when Germany declared war on Russia, the ship was sent to Boston. She unloaded planes and aviation gear, received extra men, and coaled. German troops marched into Belgium and England declared war on Germany. European liners ran for home ports. Thousands of Americans were stranded abroad. "Get them home," demanded their friends and their congressmen. "Send the Navy to protect American interests." In Washington, Fiske told Bristol to confer with the Army and arrange to use both Navy ships and Army transports.

Before daylight on 7 August, Captain Joseph W. Oman took command of the *North Carolina* and declared her in full commission. Mustin, who had commanded her as a reserve ship, became her executive officer. That evening the ship sailed out of Boston under sealed orders. As he watched her go, McIlvain felt out of it again. He had missed the excitement of Veracruz. Now he was

_4_

missing another unusual trip, probably to Europe, while he chaperoned the planes and aviation materials back to Pensacola.

The _North Carolina_ called at Falmouth, England, then sailed to Cherbourg. Mustin, Bellinger, and Smith made a quick trip to Paris, on temporary duty, to find out how aviation was being used in the war. The ship was back in England when Mustin wrote up the report of their trip. This was his last aviation task for several months.

Smith was detached from the ship and sent to Paris as an Assistant Naval Attaché for Air. About the same time, Herbster, who had been on temporary duty in Washington and Marblehead ever since April, was sent to a similar post in Berlin. Without planes, the other aviators were just deck watch officers in the _North Carolina_ when she sailed into the eastern Mediterranean. In October, LaMont was sent home for treatment in the New York Naval Hospital. This first student to solo at Pensacola never returned to flying duty. After he left the _North Carolina,_ the fliers relieved each other on monotonous watches while she steamed back and forth between Alexandria, Beirut, Jaffa, and other eastern Mediterranean ports.

On the evening that the _North Carolina_ sailed from Boston under sealed orders, Chevalier, in Pensacola, was practicing night flying with Chief Electrician Boydler as a passenger. About 2030, as the light was fading into early starlight and they were eight hundred feet above the bay, the engine

sputtered and lost power. Chevalier pushed the plane over into a glide and swivelled to look at the engine behind him. Long, torch-like flames were streaking back through the propeller. He pushed the plane down sharply, then leveled off and felt his way toward the black water. As the plane lost speed, burning gasoline dripped on the lower wing. Flames wrapped around the overhead gasoline tank. Before it exploded, Chevalier and Boydler dove into the warm water and swam for their lives and the beach.

Fortunately no one was hurt in this first serious accident at Chevalier's Pensacola flying club. With the _North Carolina_ away, life had been carefree and gay. The men tried to keep the planes in good shape, to keep their attractive boss from making mistakes, and to play as hard as he did. Parties were frequent. All the ladies between eight and eighty thought Chevalier was wonderful. They made excuses for him when he had too much to drink, which happened now and again. Despite the heat, the carousing, and the absence of supervision, Chevalier flew. He flew early and he flew late. He flew for practice and for fun, to try out new ideas and to teach his pal Bronson.

On or off the station, his personality and his ability as a flier made him the leader, although courtly, good-looking, agreeable, and popular Bronson was his senior. Bronson got used to the heat, drank less than Chevalier, learned quickly, and earned the Aero Club's Seaplane Certificate. Yet forty years later, he was nearly forgotten, but any mention of Chevalier's name in Pensacola would give

118 old ladies stars in their eyes and cause retired mechanics to boast loud and long of their service with him.

When the *North Carolina* steamed east for European ports with their pay accounts, Chevalier's flying club had not been paid in over five weeks. They were all broke, they were thirsty, and their credit was wearing thin. Most of them owed something for their board and lodging. Nobody knew or cared where the ship was going. It was gone. They needed money; it was Chevalier who charmed a local banker into letting all his men sign notes, promising that they would pay the bank when the Navy paid them. Next he negotiated with the supply officer at Charleston, South Carolina, until that worthy began paying for the men's meals in a station mess.

Then Walter Atlee Edwards, who had been at Marblehead with Capehart, arrived for flight training. Chevalier began his instruction soon after he arrived, but Edwards did not learn as rapidly as Bronson.

Lieutenant Kenneth Whiting came aboard and took charge of the station in September. Like Chevalier, who was always known as "Chevy," "Ken" Whiting was another figure of these early days of naval aviation whose name and fame were destined to become legendary. Five years senior to Chevalier, he already had a spectacular and colorful naval career.

At the Academy, he had had a remarkable record as an athlete—quarterback of the first team for four years, a star on the hockey and track teams, a champion boxer and swimmer, president of the Athletic Association, and a wizard with a sailboat. He

never took out much time for studying. Textbooks seemed unimportant. Distinguished by a friendly smile, a modest manner, and innate ability, he had graduated near the bottom of the Class of 1905.

In January 1907, as passed midshipman in the cruiser *West Virginia* on the Asiatic Station, he could not be bothered to study for final examinations. Anything routine bored him. He lived only to enjoy the exciting and the unusual and to achieve the impossible. When his classmates were commissioned ensigns, he never worried about being the bottom man.

In October 1908, after two A-class submarines reached Manila on a collier's deck, Whiting volunteered for submarine duty. He liked the challenge of these erratic, unreliable boats that seldom behaved as they should. If something went wrong on a dive, he fixed it. He was always supremely confident of his ability to handle any emergency he might meet. He argued that if a boat could not be brought up, a man could go out her torpedo tube, swim to the surface, and get help for the others. Everyone said this was impossible. At Newport, some years before, an attempt was made to blow a dog clear of a torpedo tube with an impulse charge, but it was not successful.

In Manila, Ensign Whiting settled the argument. He entered the after end of the torpedo tube in the *Porpoise*, was shut in,

5

made his exit through the forward end, and swam safely to the surface. The whole operation took about 75 seconds.

Back in the States, a year after this submarine escapade, Whiting asked for aviation training, then talked his friend Ellyson into doing the same. Ten days later, Ellyson was pleased, but embarrassed, when the detail officer tapped him instead of Whiting to be the first naval aviator. Whiting was sent to replace Ellyson as the inspector, and prospective commander, of the experimental submarine *Seal,* then building at Newport News.

From San Diego, Ellyson tried to make amends by recommending Whiting as the second man to be trained by Curtiss. Chambers penciled "too slow, and his present duty too important" on the margin of Ellyson's letter and promised to send an ensign who never arrived. Whiting stayed in the *Seal.*

It took him until the spring of 1914 to make the radical boat, re-designated the G-1, perform properly. The craft set several performance records, and proved innovations still used in designing today's submarines. Then a year after Ellyson had left aviation, Ken Whiting was ordered to Dayton.

He was the last naval officer taught to fly in Orville Wright's school. To Ken, flying was just something else he did well easily, like swimming or sailing. Before the end of August, he had won his Aero Club pilot's license and, a few days later, he went to Pensacola, where Chevalier showed him how to fly hydroaeroplanes.

Chevalier was no athlete and he did not have Whiting's service-wide reputation, but

the two men were very alike in important ways. They thought big and they played rough. They saw the future possibilities of naval aviation more clearly than most of their contemporaries, and they worked hard to make those possibilities serve the nation. Concentrating on essentials, they grandly scorned details. Men and machines that could fly were first essentials. Hence at Pensacola they flew to perfect their own skills, to see how better naval planes could be built, and to teach the two students. On the undermanned station they let almost everything else slide.

When flying was over, drinking was pleasanter than worrying about routine problems that could not be solved with the means available. The Pensacola station was a ragtime disorganization where everyone played hard and men did all manner of necessary things without any orders, just because men always want to do right by personalities like Chevalier and Whiting.

In 1917, Chevalier was decorated for his daring flying and successful command of the first naval air station on foreign soil, at Dunkerque, within range of German artillery and bombs. After World War I, he made the first successful torpedo drops from an American plane and flew from the battleship turrets. Then, with Whiting, he worked to develop the arresting gear and landing techniques of the Navy's first carrier, the *Langley,* and he made the first landing on that ship. One Sunday morning in November 1922, Lieutenant Commander Chevalier

6. *Popular Earl W. Spencer, Naval Aviator No. 20.*

120 took off from the Norfolk Air Station to fly to the *Langley* at Yorktown. He circled over a friend's house, crashed, and died. Chevalier Air Field at Pensacola has been named in his honor.

Whiting led the first aviation detachment to Europe and served brilliantly there through the war. After the war, more than any other single officer, he helped plan the U. S. Navy's first carriers, served in, and commanded them. Captain Whiting retired in June 1940, but was kept on active duty. He died in the Bethesda Naval Hospital 24 April 1943. It was later said of him that he was "brilliant, capable, and fearless, but a bottle made him unpredictable." In spite of this, he contributed many sound ideas to the interwar development of naval aviation. A seaplane tender and an auxiliary air station at Pensacola have been named in his honor.

The fall of 1914 brought two more student fliers to Pensacola. Earl Winfield Spencer had been one of Chevalier's most popular classmates. At the Academy, he had been the cheerleader, was active in theatricals, developed a carefree disregard of naval cus-

toms and regulations, and was reputed always to be a good companion. At Pensacola, he wore a close-cropped dark mustache, laughed easily, and liked to be the life of the party. He was comfortable in the irregular operation that was Whiting's Pensacola, but the enlisted men did not trust him. When Chevy started his instruction, the first lesson included the virtue of a few relaxing drinks after a flight. He learned that part quickly. Spencer achieved a footnote of sorts in the annals of time as the man whose wife subsequently became the Duchess of Windsor.

The other new student, Lewis Henry Maxfield, of the Naval Academy Class of 1907, was older than Spencer, more serious about his work, and affable, courteous, and competent. After serving in the Fleet, he had been two years at the Norfolk Receiving Ship when he went to Pensacola. Chevalier found him a very apt pupil at flying. He later pioneered in lighter-than-air and was decorated for heroism in the wartime crash of a French dirigible. He died in 1921 in the crash of the British-built ZR-2 near Hull, England.

CHAPTER TWELVE: THE NAVAL AVIATORS

From the beginning of World War I until
the United States entered it, naval aviation
was in a state of flux. There were several
focal points: the central direction, or in a
sense a lack of it, in Washington; the training of fliers at the nascent air station at
Pensacola; what might be termed armored
cruiser aviation aboard the *North Carolina,*
the *Seattle,* and the *Huntington;* and the
significant improvement of the planes themselves. These facets were developing simultaneously in the years 1915 and 1916.

Ever since 1910, men had been looking
for better naval aircraft. They had never
agreed on what was better or on how to get
it. Early builders and fliers, bogged down by
details, foresaw years of slow evolution before planes could become effective. Captain
Chambers, who had never understood the
weight and horsepower problem, had argued
that a proper use of engineering principles
would expedite their development and quickly
render existing planes obsolete. So he bought
only a few experimental planes and waited
for anticipated improvements.

On the other hand, Admiral Fiske, inventor and strategist, wanted hundreds of
planes that would be able to bomb and torpedo an enemy fleet into oblivion. The problems of builders and pilots he neither under-

stood nor cared about. All such mundane
matters were for underlings.

Like Chambers, Bristol believed in cau-
tious purchasing but he expected that sound
administration would produce an air service
and win for him the recognition that Chambers had missed. By January 1914, design
competitions had produced no acceptable
machines. That spring he disparaged the
recommendations which Mustin had based
on his experience at Pensacola and Veracruz.
Mature officers like Chambers and Bristol
were convinced that young whippersnappers
whose experience had been confined to the
flight of bamboo-tailed kites could not have
learned anything beyond the range of a
captain's knowledge. Like Langley, these
well-intentioned men were sure that their
age, their seniority, and their seagoing backgrounds formed adequate bases for their
aeronautical decisions. Bristol tended to
scorn American builders and ordered only
European-built aircraft.

Late in August of 1914, after he visited
Paris, Mustin wrote:

> They are so far ahead of us that there is no
> chance to catch up. We must avail ourselves
> of the knowledge they already have by buying
> various makes of foreign machines, then select
> and copy. The manufacturers here do not ad-
> vertise in the papers, but by building beauti-
> ful machines and having them flying all of the
> time, the natives think no more of planes than
> they do of a taxi in Philadelphia.

After receiving this corroboration, Bristol,
certain that the war would be short, ordered
three more French planes. Most of the pilots
were away in the *North Carolina.* Hence a
slight delay in plane deliveries seemed to

123

---

*1. Aviation went to war in 1914. Planes quickly
proved their value to the nations in conflict: first as
scouts, then equipped with radio for observation,
with machine-guns, and with bombs. All nations
concentrated upon a tremendous expansion of their
air forces, but U.S. naval aviation lagged behind,
principally because of a shortage of funds. A Curtiss
F-boat at Pensacola, used as a World War I trainer.
Note the simple bombsight on the right side.*

him unimportant. Indeed, what looked like real aeronautical progress to Bristol was the fact that he got a clerk that month.

By late September, Admiral Fiske, who wanted a General Staff, detailed war plans, intensified fleet training, and a fleet of combat planes, had arrived at an impasse with Secretary Daniels. He sent Bristol off with the Secretary to watch Lincoln Beachey, the inventor of the loop, "do twists and turns in the air," and Beachey's stunts helped Bristol to persuade the Secretary. A few days later, Fiske signed a memorandum to the Bureau of Navigation saying that Daniels had approved the relief of the aviation officers in the *North Carolina,* the retention of Towers, Smith, and Herbster as attachés, and the transfer from the *North Carolina* of the records and accounts of the people stranded in Pensacola. Since that station still had no administration, Fiske wanted these records maintained in the *Amphitrite,* the station ship at New Orleans.

With these matters decided, Bristol planned a month's trip to San Diego to observe what the Army was doing in aviation and to keep out of Fiske's way. For some months, Chambers, who had been isolated from naval aviation, had been corresponding about inventions and his appeal to Congress. In October 1914, a memorandum brought him sufficiently up to date so that he could carry on the routine aviation work in Bristol's absence. It said nothing about new planes, equipment, or organization, but it told him where the aviators were. He was to get the new students to the Aeronautic Station with flight orders. The memo read:

2. *Bombing in the U.S. Navy in 1915. Ensign Wadleigh Capehart holds an early Semple bomb device. The tail of the bomb consisted of strips of cloth. The plane was a tailless Burgess-Dunne.*
3. *Before the United States entered World War I, naval aviation numbered just a handful of men. Left to right: H. W. Scofield, W. M. Corry, C. K. Bronson, E. G. Hass, R. R. Paunack, F. T. Evans, E. F. Johnson, A. C. Read, H. C. Mustin, P. N. L. Bellinger, A. A. Cunningham, R. C. Saufley, J. P. Norfleet, W. A. Edwards, H. T. Bartlett, E. W. Spencer, E. O. McDonnell.*

They are to take up flying as soon as they get to Pensacola. When the *North Carolina* gets to Brisindi, Mustin, Bellinger, Saufley, and Capehart will be ordered to Washington. Keep Mustin here for a while. Send the others to Pensacola. Get Capehart flight orders.

When Bristol returned to Washington in November, the students had been ordered to Pensacola, but the *North Carolina* and her aviators were still in the Mediterranean. Secretary Josephus Daniels was busy telling Congress that the Navy was in wonderful shape and equally busy trying to keep Fiske from denying it. The Admiral was working behind the scenes to get called before a congressional committee to tell his side of the preparedness argument.

In less than a week, Bristol charmed the Secretary into signing a "memo to the Department" for the "development of the Aeronautic Service and the establishment of the Aeronautic Station at Pensacola." This put all activities at Pensacola under the command of the senior aviator there; it directed the various bureaus to allot funds for the operation; it recalled the *North Carolina* pilots; it gave Bristol his first office space; and, finally, it promised him the title of Director of Naval Aeronautics. A week later,

orders were issued to both the aviators and to Bristol. Now, as Director of Aeronautics, Bristol was both the coordinator that Chambers had proposed and the executive that Fiske had advocated.

Shortly after Bristol left Fiske's desk for his own office, the Admiral appeared before the House Naval Affairs Committee. He testified that the planes at Veracruz "could just as well have taken bombs and destroyed the city." He did not refer to the existing puny hydros; the kind of planes he had in mind would cost $2,000,000 or more to build. Ships could carry planes, he went on, and, after defeating a defending fleet, use them to destroy coastal cities without landing troops. All this was a part of his argument to replace the Secretary's aides with a Chief of Naval Operations. He intended to make this organization function like the Prussian General Staff. He managed to get all this written into the appropriation bill over Daniels' opposition.

In due course of time the Admiral's ambitious plan to reorganize the Navy command backfired. Instead of Fiske, Daniels chose Captain W. S. Benson as the first Chief of Naval Operations. He ordered Fiske to the Naval War College, where he would have no power. The Admiral described his successor as a handsome, dignified, conscientious gentleman of correct habits, who was an excellent seaman but who had never shown any interest in strategy or the War College. He thought Daniels had picked him because he would be a pliable yes-man.

Captain Benson subscribed to the thesis that the Navy would never need many aero-

planes because they could be used only for scouting or spotting battleship gunfire. Thereupon Bristol, the armchair expert, dropped Fiske's idea of combat planes. Bombing, he told Mustin, had been shown to be most ineffective and useless. The proper objective, he maintained, was a plane that could protect the Fleet by scouting against submarines and torpedo boats.

In January 1915, when Mustin relieved Whiting as officer in charge of the Aeronautic Station at Pensacola, his administrative title was an improvement. Chevalier had taught Bronson to be an expert pilot but everything else had deteriorated. The buildings and grounds were more dilapidated than when the *Mississippi* had first arrived. Government property was being stolen right and left. Station allotments were overexpended. There was liquor in the enlisted barracks. Bartlett and Spencer turned up drunk.

Strict, understanding, and just, Mustin knew and admired the abilities of both Whiting and Chevalier. He too had had to run an unofficial air station with inadequate help and money. He wrote Bristol they were "just swamped and have done wonders under the circumstances" and Bristol for once agreed. Mustin moved everyone into quarters and tried to unravel the mess.

When asking the detail officer to order a batch of candidates to aviation training, Bristol always spoke of "classes" or "the next class." However, until 1917, such candidates never reached Pensacola as classes, but came in as scattered individuals. At the so-

called school, each student started on his flight training as soon after he arrived as the chronic plane shortage would permit.

Weather, accidents, engine failures, and the shortage of parts usually kept some or all of the school's three hydroplanes on the beach. At times the station even ran out of gasoline, but the fliers no longer bought it themselves, as had formerly been the practice at Annapolis. Instruction or practice for everyone came in undesirably scattered flights of short duration. Nonetheless, all these early birds thrilled to the wind whipping their clothes, the whine of the wires, and the detached feeling of being up-in-the-air.

At times, with only one plane in commission and that only part of the time, pilots were using more alcohol than gasoline. Mustin worried about the results of mixing these two combustibles. Early in April, he was forced to suspend Chevalier after a big party at the San Carlos Hotel. It hurt Mustin to punish his favorite, but things were getting out of hand. He consoled himself with the hope that this example would calm down some of his playmates. Chevalier was chagrined. He voluntarily promised to stay on the wagon until Mustin released him.

While Chevalier was by far the most able pilot and instructor on the station, when he took leave to go to his father's funeral, the school was taken over by Saufley, who was meticulous about details and dead serious about his job. Since Chevalier was junior to everyone except Spencer and Bartlett, Mustin used this as an excuse to keep Saufley in charge of the school after Chevy returned.

4. The swept-wing Burgess-Dunne hydroaeroplane, AH-7, in 1916.
5. Another Burgess-Dunne, the AH-10.
6. E. O. McDonnell graduated from the Naval Academy high in the Class of 1912, won the Medal of Honor at Veracruz, then took his Navy flight training at Pensacola in 1915. He was designated Naval Aviator No. 18.

Saufley shunned parties, translated aviation information from foreign papers for recreation, and tried to set up a real school of aeronautics. The students marvelled at his ambition, admired his concentration, but they revolted when he asked Richardson to lecture them on aircraft construction. They only wanted to know enough about inspection and maintenance to save their necks, and Richardson was unable to interest them in structural theory.

Saufley also strove to improve plane performance and reliability. Some of the mechanics thought he was trying to act like an engineer without having a degree, and they preferred to work for Richardson. Nevertheless, by the end of 1915, his persistent efforts had raised the 6-hour seaplane endurance record, set by Towers, to 8 hours and 20 minutes, and he set the American seaplane altitude record at 11,975 feet.

After considerable thought, Mustin tried to segregate alcohol and gasoline by what came to be known as the "Bevo" list. He required each aviator to sign a statement before flying that he had not had an alcoholic drink during the previous 24 hours. Some nonfliers, who were there, have hinted that one or two of the pilots sometimes quibbled about the word "drink" by dipping their

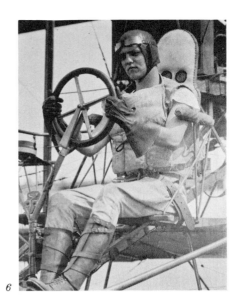

6

bread in whiskey or enjoying a martini served in a consomme cup as the soup course.

The natural result of this Bevo list was a Saturday night routine that made weekend binges compulsory. Since they could no longer enjoy a few drinks after flying during the week, many fliers tried to get enough relaxation on Saturday night to last out the week. The dinner dances at the San Carlos were the occasions for this. Sometimes relaxing got rough. Spencer was one of the first, but far from the last, of the student aviators to put on gymnastic demonstrations in the ballroom. Sundays were devoted to the treatment of hangovers and salvaging ditched cars. The Bevo list and Saturday-nights-at-the-San-Carlos were Pensacola institutions long after Mustin's time.

In addition to the work of instructing these student fliers, the older pilots attempted to get more out of the available planes. Bellinger was the first to fly to Mobile, where the Department sent him to show off a flying boat during Mardi Gras. In the AH-10, a Burgess-Dunne tailless wonder, he was the first American to reach 10,000 feet in a seaplane. For 10 consecutive days, Chevalier tried to keep the same machine in the air for 4 hours. His best was 3 hours and 15 minutes—a little more than half the record that Towers had set 3 years before. Saufley hung extra tanks on another of the type and expected to stay up 10 hours. After an hour, the back of a gasoline tank vibrated loose. This smashed the pusher propeller and flung shrapnel-like pieces through the wings, cutting the spars so nearly through that no one could understand why the wings stayed on long enough to land.

In the middle of July, Bellinger, who was then the Erection and Test superintendent, left that work to his assistant and took the tailless Burgess-Dunne to Hampton Roads. He was to spot the fall of shells from the mortars at Fortress Monroe. The weather was foul. The machine had no radio. It would not carry both an observer and enough fuel for the job. So Bellinger flew solo. He was surprised at how well he could see the splashes from 8,000 feet, but puffs of black smoke fired from a Very's pistol were useless as a quick way to signal corrections. Bellinger had a good time, but his month-long adventure contributed nothing to the business of spotting for naval gunfire.

Student fliers straggled aboard the air station at Pensacola all through 1915 and 1916. Harold Terry (Culis) Bartlett, a tall, dark-haired chap from Connecticut, was one of the country's crack rifle shots. He had entered the Academy with Chevalier, stayed five years, and graduated next to anchor in the Class of 1911. Ordered to flight training in the summer of 1914, he missed the *North Carolina*, was sent to the Burgess school pending her return, and got to Pensacola just in time to do his share of the Christmas drinking in 1914.

Edward Orrick McDonnell, a pride of Baltimore, had a hot temper, strong likes, and even stronger dislikes. At the Academy, he had accumulated some friends, as many

128 enemies, and publicity in the Baltimore papers as an athlete. He graduated high in the Class of 1912, won the Medal of Honor at Veracruz and, late in 1914, became the first man in his class ordered to aviation. He came in from Dayton, where he had been receiving ground instruction.

Even-tempered George Murray spoke softly in a confidential manner with a Boston accent. He loved music, sang well, and enjoyed playing the piano. He never worried about studies at the Academy and had many friends. He served in a battleship, then a destroyer, before starting aviation at the Burgess school at Marblehead in December 1914.

About the time these students checked in, Richardson arrived to qualify as a Navy Air Pilot, try some new floats, help Mustin, and test the catapult that had stood waiting for a year. He had not flown for a long time so he started with several dual flights and then soloed again. He tried out various new ideas, some of which were a bit hair-raising, but at least these theories of his were good enough to keep him from crashing.

Then there was a lull until May, when Cunningham, the first Marine flyer, reported and became a student for the second time. It had taken him nearly two years to convince his wife that he should fly. Then, when he asked for flying duty, Bristol had insisted that he go to Pensacola to "requalify under modern conditions." Three other students reached Pensacola before the Fourth of July.

At the Academy, Albert Cushing Read had been called "Putty" by other midshipmen because his perpetually immobile and colorless face looked as if it had been moulded

7. *Lieutenant Commander Albert C. "Putty" Read found his light weight a decided advantage when he commenced flight training at Pensacola. He became Naval Aviator No. 24, and went on to a distinguished flying career.*

from that lifeless material. Bright, he graduated number four in the Class of 1907. By that time, his associates knew that this poker face masked a pleasant, quiet, unassuming personality. At Pensacola, his light weight was an advantage, but his small stature bothered him. To reach the controls, he perched on the edge of his seat with cushions stacked behind him. Even then, he was seldom able to use the full throw of the controls he clutched. But with patient good humor, he compensated with nerve, confidence, and plain guts. He was hardly big enough to fly, yet he flew anyway—well enough to live to a ripe old age.

Robert Rudolph Paunack, a good-natured, reasonable lad from Wisconsin, also arrived in June. He had organized the Academy's first tennis team, graduated in 1909 along with Billingsley, then served six years in battleships and cruisers of the Atlantic Fleet.

First Lieutenant Francis Thomas (Khaki) Evans, from Ohio, had been a Marine officer since 1909, served in the Fleet and ashore in the States, Panama, Hawaii, and lastly in Guam. Orders to Pensacola rescued him from that isolated outpost.

Three more students reached Pensacola in July. William Merrill Corry, the first arrival, made the most rapid progress of all the summer entrants. Cheerful and popular, Corry's short flying career was spectacular. In 1917, his flying made him a Chevalier of the Legion of Honor. In 1920, he became aviation aide to the commander of the Atlantic Fleet and in October of that year, he flew in a Jenny from a Long Island field, with Lieutenant A. C. Wagner. Near Hartford, Connecticut, their engine quit. In the forced landing, the plane flipped over and burned. Wagner was trapped, and Corry got him out. Both died of burns and Corry was awarded the Medal of Honor:

> For heroic service in attempting to rescue a brother officer from a flame-enveloped airplane. On October 1920, an airplane in which Lieutenant Commander Corry was a passenger crashed and burst into flames. He was thrown 30 feet clear of the plane and, though injured, rushed back to the burning machine and endeavored to release the pilot. In so doing he sustained severe burns from which he died 4 days later.

Three destroyers and two flying fields at Pensacola have been named in his honor.

The junior of the summer arrivals was Harold Wakefield Scofield, a handsome, well-poised man from Michigan. He had been a top wrestler and something of a ladies' man at the Academy. Thereafter he served in a Pacific Fleet cruiser, and in an Atlantic collier, before entering aviation. He was the slowest of the summer candidates to qualify.

Earle Freeman Johnson, the last July arrival, spent two years at Harvard before going to the Naval Academy, where he was a crack tennis player, versatile campus politician, and a socialite.

Three students who eventually qualified reported to the school in September. Grattan Colley Dichman from Georgia—long, lean, and soft-voiced, smiled most of the time, and

had been an intercollegiate fencing champion at the Academy. He served in a battleship, a cruiser, and several Asiatic gunboats and then did two years at the Norfolk Navy Yard.

George Samuel Gillespie, born in Missouri, spent his boyhood in Michigan, then worked hard for a passing mark at the Naval Academy, where he finished close to the bottom of his class. He was a medium-sized, nice-looking lad, who always spit out his words in irregular bursts like the starting explosion of a cold gasoline engine. He spent most of the time between the Academy and flight school in the battleship *Arkansas*.

Robert Todd Young, the third student, a big man from Michigan, was destined for a short aviation career. Outspoken and unceremonious, he had served in the Pacific, Asiatic, and Atlantic Fleets in the five years after his graduation. He never liked flying after he started but qualified in June 1916, went to the Curtiss plant for duty that September, and quit flying by Christmas.

There were two more students who entered Saufley's school. Tall, lank Glenn Beauregard Strickland of Georgia seldom smiled, and he always spoke and moved slowly. After two years at Georgia Tech, he went to the Naval Academy and finished near the bottom of his class. Thereafter he served in a half dozen ships. On the Asiatic Station in 1913, he asked for flight training. At that time, neither Towers nor Chambers knew him well enough to comment on his qualifications. His progress proved to be slow.

The other October arrival was a slightly built, blue-eyed, dour little fellow named Marc Andrew Mitscher. Academy classmates

8. *Naval Aviator No. 23, Lieutenant W. M. Corry, died in 1920 while attempting to rescue a companion from a burning plane in which they had crashed. He was posthumously awarded the Congressional Medal of Honor. Corry Field, an auxiliary air station at Pensacola, was named in his memory.*

130 remembered him as the world's most stubbornly determined and persistent man. Always on the moody side, he tended toward grouchiness. He was wont to speak softly and briefly. He never abandoned a friend nor forgave a slight. His career in naval aviation reached a spectacular climax in World War II, when Vice Admiral Marc A. Mitscher commanded the powerful carrier task force which helped defeat Japan.

The troublesome question of rank in the air was inextricably entangled with the training of student aviators. When the Navy Air Pilot certificates were first proposed in 1912, Ellyson and the others assumed that they would be like commissions. In a ship, the line officer with the lowest numbered, or oldest, commission was always in command. Fliers expected that in the air, the aviator with the lowest numbered certificate would be in command irrespective of his relative naval rank. Consequently everyone wanted the lowest possible number of his designation. Under the 1913 rules issued by the Bureau of Navigation, there was a necessary assumption that some officers were qualified, and they would examine the others. These, then, would always be the seniors. But argument over the issue of the original certificates held up all certificates.

The matter became urgent in January 1915 when pilots and students assembled again at Pensacola. Director Bristol got Fiske to sign a memorandum to the Bureau of Navigation, which pointed out that, since there were no Navy Air Pilots, it was impossible to appoint

the "qualified aviators" required by that Bureau's instructions to conduct candidate's tests. In order to get some legal examiners at Pensacola and to give status to the foreign air attachés, it was proposed that certificates be issued to the seven officers Mustin had named in June 1914 but with their precedence shuffled in order to promote Bellinger and Mustin for the Veracruz operation. This was done and, on 21 January 1915, the first designations, or Navy Air Pilot certificates, were mailed to the following officers:

1	1/1/14	Ellyson
2	1/1/14	Towers
3	6/1/14	Mustin
4	6/1/14	Bellinger
5	7/1/14	Herbster
6	7/1/14	B. L. Smith
7	7/1/14	Chevalier

Then in March, Congress passed its Naval Appropriation Bill. It contained something for everybody. It prescribed Fiske's organization for a Chief of Naval Operations. It established the National Advisory Committee for Aeronautics—NACA—which was destined soon to develop into the national laboratory Chambers wanted. It made $1,000,-000 available for aviation. The Bureau of Construction and Repair got money for a wind tunnel. The Bureau of Yards and Docks got funds to fix up Pensacola. The bill raised flight pay "for qualified Naval Aviators" to 50 per cent of base pay, gave "student Naval

Aviators" 35 per cent extra, doubled pensions and death gratuities for men killed or disabled in aviation, and appropriated a fund to pay a death benefit to Billingsley's mother.

Bristol on the whole was happy about the bill until somebody asked, "What is a 'qualified Naval Aviator'?" The phrase had never before been used as a specific term or as a title. But now this new law, without defining it, made it the key to flight pay.

Then in order to sort out the confusion about the certificates, Secretary Daniels signed a circular letter directing the change of "Navy Air Pilot" to "Naval Aviator" wherever it appeared in the 1913 pamphlet of the Bureau of Navigation. But nothing was said about the certificates that had already been issued. Early in April, when Bronson, Whiting, and Richardson passed their Navy Air Pilot tests, the air board at Pensacola recommended them for Naval Aviator certificates. No such certificates had yet been printed. So the Bureau used what they had and issued the following Navy Air Pilot certificates:

8	3/6/15	Saufley
9	3/10/15	McIlvain
10	4/6/15	Bronson
11	4/10/15	Whiting
12	4/12/15	Richardson

Six more such certificates were issued in the same way by the end of September 1915.

But as early as the preceding May, paymasters had been arguing about who was legally entitled to flight pay under the 1915 law. In order to protect them and to get the pilots paid, Secretary Daniels signed a letter to each flier:

You are hereby designated as a Naval Aviator for duty involving flying in aircraft, including balloons, dirigibles, and airplanes, in accordance with the Act of Congress approved March 3, 1915.

For the future, a circular letter authorized commanding officers to issue similar orders to officers required to operate aircraft.

These letters, which designated the recipient a "Naval Aviator," were dated long after the first Navy Air Pilot certificates and they ran in a different sequence. Then the pilots began to wonder. Did the letters change their seniority in the air? Mustin put it up to the Bureau of Navigation by asking them to change his Navy Air Pilot certificate to read "Naval Aviator." Thereupon Navy Department bureaucrats wrote notes to each other for three weeks before they concocted this official reply:

... it is not believed by the Bureau that the Department's circular of May 21, 1915, authorizes the antedating of orders designating officers and men of the Navy and Marine Corps as student Naval Aviators or Naval Aviators.

Towers watched all this maneuvering from London. Ten months later, the Bureau of Navigation asked him some questions about his flying. Is it any wonder that in his reply from London, he wrote, "I do not know upon what date the Department considered I became a qualified aviator."

The next stage of the confused pattern came in January 1916, when the Bureau of Navigation replaced the 1913 instructions with a pamphlet called "Courses of Instruction and Required Qualifications of Personnel for the Air Service of the Navy." This contained several splendid innovations, most of

10

9

which could never be carried out. It provided for revisions every six months by a board of aviators to be appointed by the Commandant of Pensacola. Arrangements for the ordering up of quarterly classes of eight officers and 16 enlisted men were described in great detail. No such class ever arrived at the air station. Candidates continued to start their training individually.

Flight physical examinations were required before students were ordered to the school, weekly during the first month, monthly thereafter, and before soloing.

Besides flying, the students were required to attend lectures and to learn-by-doing—administration, records, shop work, and plane maintenance. Each student was to be assigned a plane, which he was to inspect, maintain, and fly himself. During the first half of 1916, the school averaged five planes in commission for 41 students. Thereafter the average grew less. Nobody at Pensacola ever attempted to carry out this training routine. They never had the planes.

There were to be written examinations monthly and "after passing the final written and practical examinations and having at least 50 hours flying, students, upon recommendation of the officer in charge of the flying school and approval of the Commandant, will take the flying tests prescribed for qualification as Naval Aviators." These were to be observed by a board of "at least two Naval Aviators." One of the tougher flying requirements added at this time was "ability to fly in very bad weather." This, on the open end of a pusher without any instruments of any kind, no pilot would attempt

9. *Marc A. Mitscher's career in naval aviation began in October 1915, and reached a spectacular climax in World War II, when as a vice admiral he commanded the carrier task force which helped defeat Japan.*
10. *Lieutenant J. V. Rockwell was Pensacola's public works officer and had volunteered for flying lessons. He lost his life when one of the old hydroaeroplane pushers went into a nose dive. These planes were declared obsolete shortly after Rockwell's death.*
11. *"Wings for the Fleet"—an accomplished fact after January 1918, when a list of 282 names was prepared in the Office of Aviation, listing the early designations according to the date of qualification.*

today. "Landing in a seaway where the wave height is at least three feet, without damage to any part of the aeroplane" was another of the requirements. The landing could be made with luck, but the machines would never take off in such a sea. A third difficult requirement stipulated, "start a flight from the catapult after personally making all adjustments." This had been Mustin's idea, but in his day the station never had a catapult that could be used that way.

After passing the flight test, a student was to be designated a Naval Aviator and "become eligible for further training in aeronautics to qualify as a Navy Air Pilot. . . ." This further training was to include aerial navigation, for which there were no instruments; open sea scouting flights, most unhealthy without navigating facilities; and spotting gunfire, for which there was neither equipment nor procedure. But the book said, "Only those line officers who have qualified as Navy Air Pilots (aeroplane) are eligible to command Navy aeroplanes."

Nobody ever qualified as a Navy Air Pilot under these rules. The precedence set by the Navy Air Pilot certificate, however, was still

accepted as determining seniority in the air. It was to be determined by a complicated weighing of training grades and dates.

In 1917, when Captain Noble E. Irwin became Director of Aviation, with Towers as his assistant, a revision of these training instructions was published. The provision restricting command of Navy planes to Navy Air Pilots was dropped.

Late in the summer of 1917, the Commandant at Pensacola asked for instructors and equipment to qualify Navy Air Pilots. Since he suspected that they did not exist, he suggested an alternate self-training course. The Chief of Naval Operations told him there were not enough Naval Aviators to spare any for advanced training. All facilities were needed to make more Naval Aviators. They would have to pick up extra skills on the job. Self-instruction was not practicable and hence the Navy Air Pilot rating would not be granted until an advanced school could be maintained for all Naval Aviators.

Before that could happen, the title of Navy Air Pilot was removed from the manuals and it was never reinstated. It should not be confused with the entirely different NAP, or Naval Aviation Pilot, which was later given to enlisted men who qualified as pilots.

In the meantime, the Bureau of Navigation decided to issue gold wings, with the aviator's name and designation number engraved on the back, just as in the case of medals. When the first wings were issued the early designations were numbered as they appeared on a list of 282 names prepared in

Captain Irwin's Office of Aviation. This list, dated 18 January 1918, assigned numbers

> . . . according to the date of qualification as Naval Aviator in all cases where such date is shown by the records; but due to the fact that those officers of the regular service who were first to enter aviation were not required to take a naval aviator's test but were merely designated "Naval Aviator" or "Navy Air Pilot" because of their recognized qualification as such, the numbers assigned in such cases were determined by the date upon which they were ordered to aviation duty, and the length of such duty, full consideration being given to each and every individual case so effected.

This list omitted McNair, Dortch, Stolz, Rockwell, and LaMont, who had soloed in the bamboo tails. For the first time it designated Rodgers, J. M. Murray, and Billingsley. Bristol's brevet promotions were eliminated. The sequence was the start of the official list of Naval Aviators.

Engraved gold wings were given to each new Naval Aviator until April 1924, when the Secretary of the Navy ordered their issue stopped. At that time, slightly over three thousand had been issued.

Until 1917 the Navy had no flying uniform. Without official sanction, the early pilots wore Marine officer's breeches, with leather puttees to protect their shins in case of a crash, and they topped this off with a Marine blouse decked with Navy insignia. After the United States entered the first World War, the Bureau of Navigation prescribed a similar uniform for the Naval Reserve Flying Corps. It included the first Navy gold wings as the insignia of a qualified Naval Aviator.

CHAPTER THIRTEEN: THE CATAPULT CRUISERS

In Washington, soon after Bristol had become director, Fiske had cautioned him against building up a top-heavy organization. However, a director needs workers to direct and, when Bristol found that the only thing that everyone knew about aircraft engines was that they were undependable, he asked the Engineer in Chief to make someone an expert. In April 1915, Lieutenant Warren Gerald Child was detailed and moved into Bristol's office.

A thin chap from Utah, with a habitually worried look on his narrow, serious face, Child graduated from the Naval Academy in 1907, served four years in the battleship *Georgia,* and then was ordered to submarines. His aviation experience had been limited to a few observation flights with Towers in 1912, when he was skipper of the submarine C-5 at Annapolis.

His first step in his new job was to start an engine test facility in the Washington Navy Yard. His second step was to achieve designation as a student naval aviator. Unlike Bristol, he decided that, if he was to know how engines behaved in the air and how to improve them, he should learn to fly. So he wedged instruction and practice in between his engine research and departmental work. He never reached Pensacola but, a year after entering Bristol's office, he passed the Naval Aviator's test.

Child was typical of the early fliers who never really learned how to fly, but flew any-

way. His early training was too scattered and too unorganized. Later in the 1920's, he always flew in a crash helmet, seldom soloed, but religiously handled the controls for at least four hours a month in order to keep his hand in. Usually he flew with a younger pilot and would scare the poor devil by floundering around the sky on the verge of a stall without ever being aware of it.

About the time Child joined him, Bristol organized lighter-than-air craft as another part of his sprouting empire. While dirigibles looked slow and rather cumbersome for naval use, most pilots thought that they should be investigated. But they looked like flying battleships to Bristol, and he liked them.

In 1915, Fiske, Bristol, and Benson all tried to expand naval aviation and to make it useful. As a result the Navy received six bamboo-tailed pushers from Curtiss and an experimental type from the Gallaudet Company that cost more and did less. Nineteen officers had qualification certificates. But the Navy still lacked a way to use an aeroplane in war.

Bristol's annual report, submitted on the first of January 1916, outlined the vicissitudes of naval aviation since he had taken charge two years before. Thereby he explained why progress had been so slow. He did not discuss plane types, and his recommendations were limited to administrative matters. This logical explanation might have served him as a good alibi had it not been for the fact that congressional committees kept asking Daniels and Benson embarrassing questions about naval aviation. They, in turn, began looking around for a goat and

135

1. Lieutenant Commander H. C. Mustin, flying the AB-2, makes the first catapult launch from the deck of the armored cruiser USS North Carolina, *5 November 1915. (National Archives)*

1

2

3

136 Bristol felt them growing increasingly cool and polite.

The disgruntled Chambers, still trying for reinstatement, exemplified what could happen to a troublesome captain who stayed in Washington too long. Every time they met, Bristol was reminded that he, too, had had no sea service as a captain. He began to think that the official Washington climate was unhealthy. He might have left aviation to the aviators and asked for a sea command but for two things. The job was unfinished and he was no quitter. In addition, he liked the prestige of being the Navy's air expert, a member of the National Advisory Committee for Aeronautics, and head of a naval service, even if it was only a puny thing. So, by the end of February 1916, he arranged to have his cake and eat it too, with orders in which he was detached from duty as Director of Naval Aeronautics and ordered to

> . . . proceed to Pensacola, Fla., and assume duty in command of the Air Service, and in command of the *North Carolina* in connection therewith. You will also assume supervision over all aircraft and aircraft stations, and the further development of aeronautics in the Navy.

Bristol pulled Lieutenant Bronson out of Pensacola for temporary duty in Washington as his messenger boy. Bronson occupied an aviation desk but not an office in the Chief of Naval Operations division of the Department. Child took his aircraft engine work back to the Bureau of Engineering and once again Richardson worked only for the Bureau of Construction and Repair. The Office of Naval Aeronautics was closed and

2. *Some unusual and interesting designs in experimental aeroplanes made their appearance during this period of naval aviation. The Gallaudet was a biplane with exaggerated sweep-back, and its engine was mounted in the fuselage aft of the cockpit. The four-bladed propeller revolved in a section of the fuselage midway between the wings and tail surfaces. The plane was not popular with the pilots.*
3. *Pioneer naval air photographer Walter L. Richardson, armed with his 5 x 7 Speed Graphic, shown with Pilot E. F. Johnson, Naval Aviator No. 25. Richardson is often referred to as the "father of naval photography," and it is said he took the first aerial photograph at Pensacola in 1914. At one time a ship's cook, he was largely responsible for establishing the Navy School of Photography, Pensacola, Florida.*
4. *Curtiss hydroaeroplane, the AH-18, at Naval Aeronautic Station, Pensacola.*

no new director was appointed. At the War College in Newport, Admiral Fiske grumbled about this destruction of the aviation organization he claimed to have built single-handedly.

Before he left Washington, Bristol sent orders to Pensacola to ready the *North Carolina* for a Caribbean cruise with a complement of planes and pilots. If he could not get anyone else to do it, he was determined to put aviation in the Fleet himself. So, on 10 March 1916, Captain Bristol arrived in Pensacola and assumed command of the Air Service and of the *North Carolina*.

Other officers side-by-side at Pensacola might have cooperated to break some of the bottlenecks in the development of naval aviation, but not Bristol and Mustin. Those two rugged personalities had opposite approaches to all problems; for over two years they had disagreed on everything. Mustin had backed a suggestion of Whiting's that the big sea-

4

going train ferry of the Florida East Coast Railway be acquired and converted into an experimental aeroplane carrier. Bristol, who held to the theory of catapults only, had stopped it. Mustin wanted to develop several types of combat planes. Bristol, following Benson's lead, demanded that naval aviation use only an all-purpose, non-combat, scout. Mustin thought the head man should fly in order to understand his job. Bristol said no.

When Bristol took command of the *North Carolina*, Commander John Hyland became the executive officer and navigator. Bristol was pleased because Hyland and the engineer had the ship rigged for coaling and otherwise ready for sea. He had harsh words for Mustin because the other attached officers never went near the ship. As student aviators, they worked entirely on the station. Furthermore, the station had put no planes aboard, had not proved the ship's torpedoes, had done nothing about installing the new catapult, had not worked out a plan for operating planes from the ship, and had not even heard of the radios Bristol had sent from Washington long before for immediate testing in planes.

Trying to work Bristol and Mustin together at this small station was like welding in a powder magazine. Something was bound to blow up.

The new commander of the air service wasted no time. The day after he took over, he had all of the attached students check in aboard ship. At the same time, he had station officers—Chevalier, Scofield, Corry, Read, Bartlett, and Bellinger—report aboard

for temporary duty. That morning, they all began standing deck watches aboard the moored ship. During the following week, they all coaled ship.

Bristol fumed when he found his radios in a storehouse, where they had been sitting untested since January. He had to give up on the catapult. Too many parts were still being made in the Washington Navy Yard. After coaling was finished, 24 men were transferred from the station to the ship. They brought aboard the three newest Curtiss pusher hydros, AH-16, 17, 18 and the Navy's first tractor hydro, the Martin AH-19. The Captain temporarily released six of the least experienced students for flight training on the station while the ship was away. Then, early on the morning of 20 March 1916, the *North Carolina* sailed for Guantanamo.

The ship had no way to fly off planes. No one had had any experience in landing or in picking up a plane at sea. Everyone aboard knew they were unprepared to be a Fleet aviation ship. Bristol also knew that his time was running out. Either his air service had to do something to show it could help the Fleet win battles or he would be discredited. At the outset, he planned to send the hydroplanes from Guantanamo Bay to observe the target practices the ships were firing just outside. With radios working in the planes, they might develop a spotting procedure. The cruise would also explore ways to work planes from a ship.

The day after the *North Carolina* anchored in Guantanamo, the planes were

6

138 hoisted out at daylight. Two fliers went in each of the Curtiss planes and Bellinger took the Martin alone. Everyone managed a short flight before they secured the planes on Hicacal Beach, an isolated and unused strip of white coral sand near the southwest corner of the bay.

During target practice the next week, Bristol sent pilots to Hicacal and then took the *North Carolina* outside to guard their flights while they observed the firing of the *Delaware*. The pilot of one plane got out there to see a few rounds. Mere chance alone put them on station at the right time; they could not stay long and had no way to receive a message from the firing ship.

During the next three weeks, the usual engine failures plagued the fliers. Any flight beyond gliding distance of the harbor entrance was a matter of pure luck. But despite the difficulties, several so-called spotting flights were logged. Of course, no actual spotting could be done for the reason that, while the pilot could see the splashes if he happened to be on station, he had no way to signal his corrections. After a few days, Bellinger installed a transmitter in one of the Curtiss planes. Like Maddox's 1912 model, it could only send out dots and dashes blind and there was no provision for reception. No spotting procedure to use it was even proposed.

One day Read and Chevalier made a few dummy attacks on a small ship. Her skipper asked for antiaircraft guns because he believed they reached a drop point without coming within range where his guns could

5. *The experimental catapult developed at Pensacola was mounted on a coal barge. This was H. C. Richardson's pet project, and by April 1915 it was ready for the first live launch.*
6. *P. N. L. Bellinger, in the Curtiss AB-2 flying boat, made the first catapult takeoff, 16 April 1915, with Richardson firing the machine. Then Ken Whiting tried it, too. These were tests of the catapult before it was placed on the* North Carolina.
7. *An AB-3 flying boat on the* North Carolina, *about mid-1916, after a permanent catapult had been installed.*

bear. He, at least, apparently did not believe that other navies would restrict their naval planes merely to scouting.

Bristol's air circus closed in the middle of April. On the fifteenth, the *North Carolina* coaled ship, hoisted the planes aboard, and sailed for Pensacola. On the trip, Bellinger drew up a report of the operation. He put the best possible face on everything that had been done, but there was nothing to refute the opinion of those conservative senior line officers who believed aircraft were useless at sea. He had to conclude that none of the Navy planes were fit for proper naval aviation tasks. He did not blame the plane builders. The Navy should find out what it needed and specify it. He suggested that prototypes be built and tested at Pensacola. Then these problems would be solved by trial and error.

Bristol disapproved this suggestion but forwarded the report. His theory was simple. Pensacola should only train pilots. The *North Carolina* should develop tactics. Planes should be designed by engineers and built by the bureaus—"like other ships."

After this cruise, the conclusion of the General Board was that planes were "far

7

from becoming a compelling force against an enemy." Bombers had never been able to hit anything but big-area land targets. The Board thought the machines too small, short-legged, and unreliable to have much potential even as scouts. Until the fliers had something better to fly than the bamboo tails, these judgments could not be disproved. Thus there was a stalemate, but no one concerned stopped trying or arguing.

There was one achievement, however, that came to final fruition after the *North Carolina* returned to Pensacola in the spring of 1916. This was the successful development of a catapult. In addition to Richardson's work on pontoons, this had been his pet project. All through February and March of 1915, he had worked on a catapult that had been partially assembled on a barge since the previous spring. It was a semi-portable compressed air engine bolted to a long track, which was supported on short legs. In late February, he fired a dead load at 30 miles per hour. While the test was successful, it took six days to get ready for another shot. This time the end speed was increased to 50 miles per hour, but more parts broke. Then he had to appeal to the Bureau of Construction and Repair for money and parts.

In April, Bellinger helped Richardson reassemble, adjust, and fire some more dead loads. They had it ready for its first live launching when they quit one afternoon in the middle of the month. That night every-

one went to a fancy dress ball at the San Carlos. Whiting and Richardson called for a bit extra, celebrating their qualifications. The others all pitched in and helped them.

The next morning, when Bellinger climbed onto the barge and checked the AB-2 on the catapult car, his head seemed too big for his helmet. He revved up the engine and Richardson fired the machine. The car flew off the end of the track, and Bellinger was airborne. Mustin had been at the San Carlos the night before, too. He was relieved when he wired Bristol, "Very satisfactory run from catapult this morning. Bellinger in AB-2." The Bevo list was invented soon after.

The catapult worked but it always needed fixing between shots. If there was nothing else wrong, the car had to be retrieved and refitted to the track. Richardson was full of ideas for improvement when he left for Washington a few days later.

On the first of September, the *North Carolina* came into Pensacola where, as the station ship, she lay idle beside the pier for two months. Her return renewed the aviators' interest in the catapult, still on the barge. Could they install it on the ship? On 27 September in the same AB-2 Bellinger had used, Saufley made the second live shot from the barge. In the next two weeks, they made two more shots, once with Bronson, once with Whiting. The catapult was disassembled late in October and taken aboard the *North Carolina*. Mechanics bolted it to the quarter-deck with its engine near the after turret. The track, on legs just high enough to clear hatch, coamings and skylights, ran straight

aft to the stern. "The "cat" was ready on the fourth of November. Chief of Naval Operations Benson watched a dead-load test of it. He still believed that scouting planes were all the Navy should have, but he was facing increasing criticism in Washington because even these were not in service with the Fleet. Bristol's promises no longer satisfied him. He had come down to see progress for himself.

On Friday morning, 5 November, the ship moved out from the dock and anchored off the station. There the AB-2 was hoisted into the catapult car. Mustin climbed into the plane, warmed it up and, just before noon, with Admiral Benson watching, he became the first person to be catapulted from a ship in an aeroplane. Fifteen minutes later, Benson went ashore in a boat. He was not converted, but he hoped he had an answer for some of his critics.

The next morning Richardson himself took a plane off the catapult, and he was followed by Bellinger. This was the first time the catapult had held up for two shots on the same day. Two within 35 minutes of each other was phenomenal. The pilots all knocked off and celebrated with the usual Saturday night routine at the San Carlos.

On Monday, the *North Carolina* prepared to move back to the station dock, but waited, at short stay, for one more catapult launching, with Cunningham in the AB-2. The plane left the catapult, smacked into the water, and rolled up into a tangle of wreckage. A boat fished Cunningham out, unhurt, and towed the plane back to the ship. The ship moved back to the station pier, and lay

8. AB-3 leaving the catapult of the North Carolina, *12 July 1916. The permanent catapult installation on the ship was higher than the first experimental catapult, and extended over the after turret, on a level with a Y track around the mainmast on which additional aircraft could be carried.*
9. By 1916 the Seattle *was carrying N-9 seaplanes with as much pride as the modern carrier does its jets. This ship was the third in the U.S. Navy equipped to operate aircraft.*

there until spring. The catapult was taken down. Richardson went to work on a better one, and four months were to elapse before a plane went aboard a ship again.

A week after the *North Carolina* reached Pensacola in April 1916, parts for her new catapult began to come aboard. Designed as a permanent addition to the vessel, the track, which was raised on stanchions, was the longest yet. At boat-deck level, it ran aft from the base of the mainmast along the center line over the after turret to the stern. Most cruiser captains disliked so restricting the fire of half of their heavy guns. However, Bristol was as anxious as Richardson to prove the catapult in service. For nearly two months, from 25 to 30 yard workmen labored on it every day. Bristol called impatiently for overtime and kept them at it on Sundays and half the night on other days.

In the middle of June, they fired the first low-pressure test shot of the new catapult. One of the buffer springs snapped and let the car go off the end of the track. For the next two weeks each test broke something that had to be repaired before the machine could be used again. At last they were able to fire three full-load shots without trouble. Then the next morning, a hurricane struck Pensacola.

9

Bristol backed the *North Carolina* away from the dock, dropped an anchor in the bay and steamed to it. Before the boats could be hauled in, a motor launch swamped at the boom and had to be cut away. A bit later, the main top with all the wireless antennae crashed. Twice the wind veered, took the ship broadside, and started her anchor. Bristol was lucky; both times he got the ship under way and shifted her to a more sheltered anchorage. Two days after the storm had passed, they were cleaned up enough to get back to the catapult job. On 11 July another dead load went off without damage. The next afternoon, the ship got under way. In the Gulf of Mexico 20 minutes later, Chevalier strapped himself into the AB-3, the catapult slammed the plane along the track, and he was flying out over the ship's wake. Other claims notwithstanding, this appears to have been the first time that an aeroplane was launched from an American vessel while she was under way.

The priority of catapult work had been only one of the many sources of friction between Bristol, as Commander of the Air Service, and Mustin, as Commandant of the Aeronautic Station. Bristol had wanted to replace Mustin with a good administrator, and he did not care whether the new man could fly or not.

Admiral Benson tried diplomatically to separate these two antagonists. He arranged for the *North Carolina* to operate with the Fleet as the nucleus of a division of aviation cruisers. As a part of this plan, he asked Daniels to relieve Bristol "of the responsibility of the 'supervision over all aircraft and aircraft stations and the further development of aeronautics in the Navy.'" He recommended instead giving Bristol command of the *North Carolina* and aircraft serving in the Fleet.

The very next day after Chevalier's successful catapult flight, the *North Carolina* took aboard two flying boats and a hydro-aeroplane and got under way. Aboard her were five qualified aviators—Bellinger, Bartlett, Johnson, Chevalier, and Read—for permanent ship duty. All students had been transferred back to the station. Bristol never again visited Pensacola while he was connected with aviation.

When she sailed from Pensacola in July 1916, the *North Carolina* joined the Fleet on the Southern Drill Grounds. In summer weather, the ship anchored there and rolled gently to the long, flat swells. The pilots assembled the flying boats on deck. On two exceptionally calm days, they hoisted a plane overside and took off from the water. Maxfield joined the ship at the end of July. During August and September, they cruised with the Fleet in New England waters, visiting various summer-colony ports. In port, pilots hoisted out planes and flew for practice, but the unreliable engines bothered them and kept them out of the only fleet exercise that had been planned to give them a minor role.

Soon after the Fleet returned to the Southern Drill Grounds in October, the *North Carolina* was detached for overhaul at the Portsmouth Navy Yard. Since leaving Pensacola, no one had been hurt and no machines had been lost. The catapult had not been

10

used. Aviators had done nothing to show that planes could be useful at sea and nothing to disprove the derogatory opinion of the General Board in June. But the social climate in Boston, Bar Harbor, Rockport, and Newport had been very pleasant for Bristol and his fliers.

That fall, with less than half a year to go before the nation became involved in a world war, naval aviation reached a new low. At Portsmouth, the pilots on the *North Carolina* flew their one tractor hydro occasionally. Bristol was away most of the time on temporary duty—visiting aircraft factories, attending NACA meetings, or mending his fences in Washington. Read, Chevalier, and Bartlett moved over into the *Washington*, the *North Carolina*'s sister ship, to become the nucleus of her new air detachment.

In November 1916, President Wilson was re-elected. The Naval Affairs Committee called Fiske in from Newport, heard him say again that the Navy was not ready for war and propose again masses of attack planes, which he thought would be quicker to build than an equally effective Fleet. Towers told the General Board and the committeemen of his observations in Britain. A German Zeppelin did the work of a cruiser squadron. To chase them off, the British launched landplane fighters from battleship turrets. The plane was expendable but destroyers usually recovered the pilot.

Daniels and Benson told Congress that the Navy was ready for anything. It would use planes "only for legitimate naval uses"— scouting and spotting. The catapult was

10. *Lieutenant Lawrence B. Sperry joined the* Seattle *with Whiting, Corry, and Murray. He was known as "Gyro" Sperry, because as early as 1912 he worked for months, with the help of Richardson and Bellinger, trying to perfect a gyroscopic stabilizer for planes. Young Sperry lost his life on a flight in 1923; his father, Elmer Sperry, went on to make many improvements in his son's invention and the gyro pilot is now to be found on all major aircraft designed for long flights. (Sperry-Gyroscope Company)*
11. *The cruiser* Huntington *left Mare Island Navy Yard in May 1917 equipped with a catapult of the* North Carolina *type. She arrived in Pensacola on 28 May and began her air operations. Above, Curtiss R-6's on the* Huntington.

working on the *North Carolina*, and that of the *Washington* would soon be ready. The one on the *Huntington* was coming along.

In mid-December, Bristol resigned from the NACA, was detached from the *North Carolina*, and went to take the senior course at the War College. Read Admiral Albert Gleaves inherited fleet aviation. Bristol told him he had come to believe in planes for naval use, but that the facts concerning them were befogged by romance, exaggerated news reports, sales talk of the plane builders, pilots' one-sided reports, and propaganda for military reasons.

Whiting, Corry, Murray, and Lieutenant Lawrence Sperry, USNRF, joined the *Washington*, renamed the *Seattle*, and wished that she were a carrier. They tested the new catapult with a dead load before the *Seattle* sailed for the Caribbean early in 1917. The cruiser's five planes were all different and none of them had a reliable engine. During her short cruise most flights had trouble getting off, averaged twelve minutes in length, and ended with forced landings or crashes. Nevertheless, the *Seattle* pilots,

11

under Whiting's leadership, pioneered useful shipboard aviation.

Whiting made the trip rugged and active. He believed in doing things to learn how, he had unlimited confidence in his pilots, and he persuaded a conservative admiral and captain to let him try a variety of experiments. They started flying while the Fleet operated off Culebra Island. Chevalier and Bartlett expended one plane when they hit the forestay of the gunboat *Dubuque* and crashed alongside. An hour after the gunboat's crew had fished them unhurt from the wreck, Admiral Gleaves boarded the *Dubuque,* looked over the salvaged scrap, and ordered it sent back to the *Seattle.* He did nothing about the crash, but a few days later, while Chevalier was officer of the deck, he suspended him from duty for letting the cruiser get slightly out of cruising position.

The pilots flew at Port au Prince and from Hicacal Beach at Guantanamo. Lieutenant (junior grade) R. A. Lavender, the staff radio officer, flew with them repeatedly in the course of improving their temperamental wireless sets. And then, for the first time, an American ship, while she was firing, received radio spots from a plane.

Lavender's aerial work came to an end in Hungry Gulf on 11 February. The AH-47 was heavy and Chevalier had trouble in getting it off the water with Lavender, who weighed two hundred pounds, aboard. In the air, it climbed slowly, fluttering on the verge of a stall. When the radio officer signaled that he had no voltage from the generator,

Chevalier turned sharply in order to land near the ship. The plane stalled and whipped down into a spin. Chevalier stopped the spin, but he was too low to pull out of the dive. The machine hit the water nose down like a "bamboo tail," but, with the engine out in front of them, the two men lived. Chevalier was a mess of cuts and bruises; Lavender broke both his legs.

An admiral ordered an investigation because he had prohibited turns below four hundred feet. When witnesses agreed that Chevalier had been at least that high, neither the board nor the admiral had any further interest. Chevy was held to be "at fault but not culpable." Friends wondered if his flying was suffering because the ships no longer had wine messes.

Later, when Bartlett crashed, Whiting commandeered the Admiral's barge, which was the only boat at hand, to go to the rescue. The pilot, wet but unhurt, was atop the wreck, and they returned to find Admiral Gleaves in a rage because his barge had been taken. He promptly put Bartlett under arrest for destroying government property.

On the second of March, near Culebra, the *Seattle* fired two planes from the catapult into the following trade wind. The sea was too rough for safe landings so the pilots flew into the Fleet anchorage and waited for the ship to return. A few days later, the Fleet steamed north. When war with Germany began, the *Seattle* was anchored in the York River. All of her aviators were detached before she went to sea again.

Meanwhile, out on the West Coast, the Mare Island Navy Yard was building a

144 catapult of the *North Carolina* type on the quarter-deck of the cruiser *Huntington.* Captain J. K. Robison took command of that ship early in April. Later that month, Lieutenant (junior grade) Marc Mitscher arrived to be her senior aviator. He had no plane, but he saw the catapult tested with a dead load just before the ship sailed for the East Coast.

Moody young Mitscher kept to himself during the voyage. He failed to find cracks about "damaviators" funny. After the ship reached Pensacola, he was joined by Lieutenants Stone and Donahue, newly qualified Coast Guard aviators, and a detail of aviation enlisted men. The first plane went aboard the *Huntington* in June, but the ship never accepted aviation as belonging to her. For two months at Pensacola, aircraft were merely a show for the cruiser people. They saw a balloon break loose on the beach. Seaplanes crashed nearby. The ship's officers observed, but they offered no help. A boat brought out a captive balloon and passed its mooring line aboard. Captain Robison tried to tow it from the maintop, but without success.

Nobody asked Mitscher's advice on aviation problems. He volunteered nothing and, with his mouth welded into a thin, straight line, just carried out the orders he received. One day the station commandant went along when the ship stood out of the harbor towing a balloon. Reasoning like Professor Langley, the two captains decided that a seaplane could be dropped into the sea with the ship moving, just like a whaleboat on a sea painter. Then it should take off from the

12. Lieutenant Marc Mitscher was the Huntington's *senior aviator in 1917.*

water. The catapult would then be unnecessary clutter on the quarter-deck.

The *Huntington* was making over 12 knots when Captain Robison ordered plane No. 26 dropped overside. When the pontoon touched, the machine did a flip, dove under water, and was wrecked. The two captains were surprised. Mitscher, glumly silent, went below for a cup of coffee. Robison stopped his ship, backed down on the plane, and spent over an hour fishing the remains out of the water.

After the two captains had lunch, the log records: "At 1429 shot Navy seaplane from the catapult without pilot or passenger. Plane and car dove into the sea 50 yards astern." It took two hours to pick up that wreck. At 1745, they anchored again off the station pier. Unsmiling, Mitscher watched the commandant go ashore.

A few days later, with the commandant again aboard, airplane No. 20 blew up and caught fire. The crew put the fire out without any damage to the ship. Captain Robison got rid of this damaged plane by shooting it off the catapult and letting it drift out with an ebb tide. Three hours later, the officer of the deck indifferently watched the *Mary Ann,* the station salvage lighter, pass by with the remains, which she had recovered near the harbor entrance.

In spite of such dismal events, Mitscher got both planes and stores aboard. In late July, he and Donohue both catapulted, tested radios, and flew into the harbor. The ship's company learned something about aviation, but they still thought planes were nuisances and considered pilots as aliens. On 1 August, the *Huntington* sailed for New York and a month later, with her planes dismantled and stowed below, she led a convoy into the Atlantic.

With her return to port, all cruiser aviation was dropped for the next six years.

At midnight on 13 October 1917, Mitscher's men began tearing down the catapult tracks and emptying the storerooms. By morning they had finished loading the *Huntington*'s aviation gear onto a lighter. Most of them rode the tug that took it to the Brooklyn Navy Yard. That afternoon, Mitscher was the last aviator to leave the cruiser. He went off to command a new naval air station at Montauk Point.

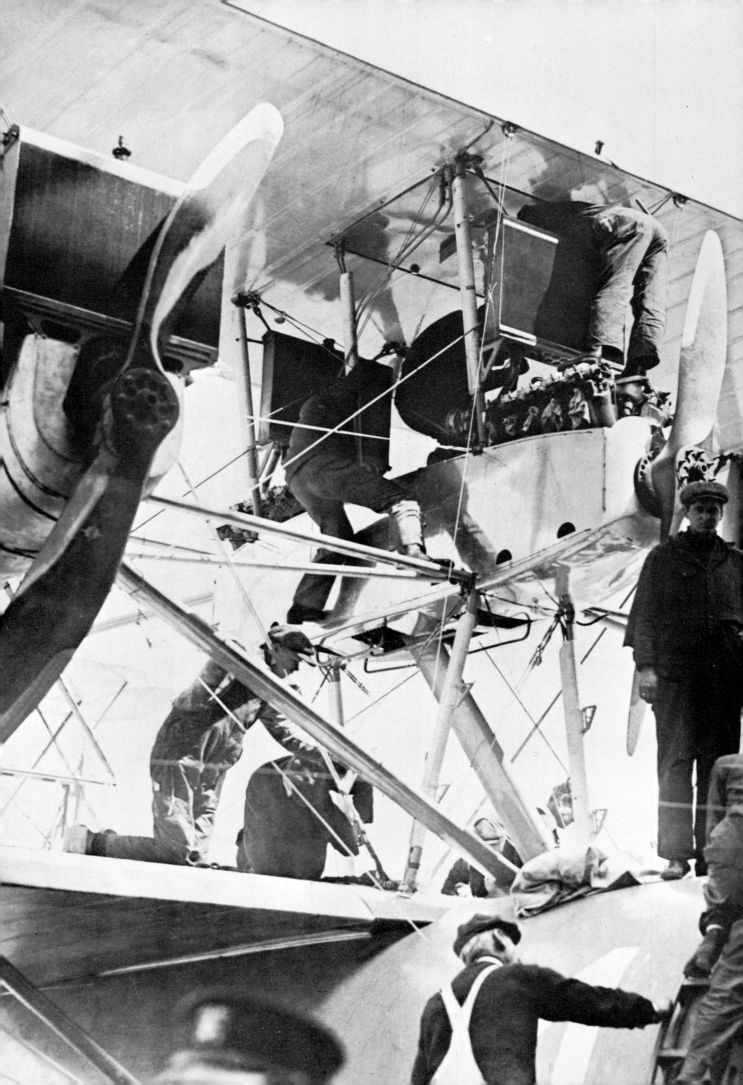

CHAPTER FOURTEEN: NAVAL AVIATION

Flying in the early days of aviation was a hazardous game. Nonetheless, the United States Navy had been fortunate with but two fatalities until the year 1915: Billingsley, who had fallen out of a plane over Chesapeake Bay; and Murray, who drowned following a crash. But in 1915 there came a series of accidents and fatalities, the consequences of which, in the development of naval aviation, were far-reaching.

Late in February 1915, Capehart narrowly escaped Billingsley's fate. He was flying solo in the Curtiss hydroplane that had no safety belt but only a strap across the top of the shoulder yoke. He was so short that this shoulder strap was closer to the top of his head than to his shoulder and it was completely ineffective. Suddenly a bump dropped his machine. Losing his hold on the wheel, he flew out of the seat. He grabbed something—he never was able to remember just what—and the machine nosed up toward a stall as he struggled to pull himself back into his seat. When he got to the wheel again and slammed it forward, just in time, the plane was on the verge of a spin or the deadly nose dive. Thereafter, Mustin ordered him to use a "waist strap," or Curtiss belt, and hoped there would soon be enough of them for all the planes.

---

1. *The decade following World War I was a period of controversy, experimentation, and great achievement in naval aviation. The Atlantic Ocean crossing was first attempted in May 1919 by three NC (Navy-Curtiss) flying boats. At left, the high-compression Liberty motors of the NC-4, the plane which successfully completed the trip from Newfoundland to England by way of the Azores and Portugal. (Wide World Photo)*

About a month later, Saufley and McDonnell stalled a hydro while flying at about 60 feet. The machine whipped down in a diving turn and crashed. In those early days, spins were a complete mystery. In the split seconds between the stall and the crash, the fliers thought an aileron wire must have parted because their controls would not pick up the low wing. The plane was demolished, but the men were lucky. They had only bruises when they were fished from the bay. The stolid Saufley was back in the air next day, but the high-strung McDonnell had a bad case of shock. For two weeks, he was no good at all and Mustin feared that his flying career was finished. But the doctor said, "Give him ten days' leave." There is no record of the therapy he found on that leave, but he came back in shape to fly again.

By the spring of 1915, Mustin, Whiting, and other fliers had come to realize that seagoing aviation needed different planes as well as better engines. They were certain that safer and more useful planes could be built. But Bristol belittled their suggestions, and he refused either to let Richardson design or Pensacola build any experimental machines. He had spent a month at North Island after the Army had scrapped the pushers there as unstable man-killers. He knew that the Army fatality rate had dropped after they shifted to Glenn Martin's tractors and he had received reports from Towers and other air attachés in Europe that tractor planes were proving themselves in war.

In spite of this evidence, Bristol clung to Chambers' old opinion that, in order to see, a scout had to sit out in front of everything.

"Tractor planes are probably through for military use," he wrote in April 1915. Not long after writing that letter, he and Richardson became the Navy members when the National Advisory Committee on Aeronautics was organized. That membership and his office title set him up in business as an air expert. Although he had scarcely been off the ground, he was soon lecturing on aviation in East Coast cities. Then, three days before Benson took office in May, tragedy struck at Pensacola, and interrupted Bristol's lectures, again focusing attention on plane types.

Mel Stolz had stood deck watches on the *North Carolina* until late in January before he was able to wangle orders back to aviation. In mid-March, when he reached Pensacola, he had not flown in nine months. For a month and a half, he worked hard to catch up. Then he asked for a board to test him for naval aviator. On 8 May, Saufley started him out in the AH-9, a two-year-old Curtiss hydroaeroplane.

Stolz took off straight out from the beach, turned left, climbed slowly to a hundred feet, flew a mile, and turned in over the bay. Suddenly, observers saw his machine nose over and crash into the water.

In those days, few people understood the "deadly nose dive," as the newspapermen called it. Men only saw planes dive suddenly into the ground. Their pilots were then too dead to relate what had happened. Later, men learned that a stalled pusher seldom spun. It usually pushed its nose nearly straight down. The pilot suddenly saw the landscape coming straight at his face. If

2. *One of the last of the Curtiss pusher hydros. This was the type in which M. L. Stolz, J. V. Rockwell, and R. C. Saufley lost their lives. As a result, these planes were declared obsolete, and grounded.*

instinctively he pulled the controls to level off, he was finished, for then the hard-up flippers kept the stalled machine from gaining the necessary speed to start flying again.

From another hydro, Bronson saw Stolz dive in. He landed alongside, dove under the wreck, but could not free Stolz from his seat. Bartlett, Maxfield, and Machinist's Mate Rhodes manned the crash boat. The time they lost with a balky engine was unimportant. When Rhodes and Maxfield went overboard and helped Bronson bring up Stolz, they found his head had been crushed by the engine.

Whiting presided at the subsequent investigation. The finding was that the crash had been due to a stall in a turn. Nobody was sure whether or not the engine had quit, but the OX engine was so unreliable that the board added, "probably following an engine failure."

In the board's opinion, instruments such as an airspeed or an incidence meter might warn a pilot before a stall. The Navy had none. A crash helmet and a seat in a padded nacelle might also improve the chances of survival. They concluded that "the pusher-type planes, with the pilot in front of all the weights, should be abandoned in favor of a tractor-type with the personnel in a fuselage aft of the concentrated masses."

Mustin heartily concurred in these opinions, but the expert Bristol was unimpressed. Planes should be designed to fly, not to crash, he said. The evidence merely showed that Stolz was inexperienced. Bristol went on with his lecture dates and, before the end of May, he ordered three more pusher hydros from Burgess.

The argument about the plane types continued and, in the end, Bristol decided to try something different. In July, the Navy ordered two tractor hydros from Thomas, the designer of the seaplane *America,* who had left Curtiss and started an aircraft company of his own. He promised September delivery.

The day that contract was signed, Bristol left Washington for Pensacola. He said he wanted to see what the Air Service needed and to start writing the year-end report he was planning to submit on aeronautics. As soon as Bristol reached the air station, Mustin tried to interest him in newer and safer planes. He backed his own opinions with specific recommendations drawn up independently by his pilots. They all wanted a slow tractor training plane with the crew in a fuselage aft of the tanks, radiator, and engine. Whiting, who had the best grasp of the problem, listed many details to make the machine tough, stable, and safe. Maxfield and Bronson contributed other good ideas and Saufley, thinking like the school man that he was, wanted interphones and other instructor aids.

Unfortunately, Bristol and Mustin had developed such different viewpoints that every conversation drove them farther apart. Bristol felt that he had conceded enough when he had ordered the Thomas planes. He wanted to see how they performed before ordering anything else. For three weeks,

while he checked on buildings, clerks, the labor board, and the supply department, he ducked any discussion of planes. Then he went back to Washington. Two days later, Mustin sent in his recommendations officially. The letter amounted to a petition for tractor trainers.

Pensacola remained short of planes while Bristol waited for the delivery of the two Thomas tractors. Instead of meeting the promised date, Thomas wrecked both planes and had to begin rebuilding them. In October, Bristol ordered six more Curtiss pushers as stopgaps and, two weeks later, gave Curtiss and Glenn Martin each an order for two experimental tractors. Then he left for an extended tour of the aircraft factories. Curtiss delivered three of the pushers in November. They were basically the same machine he had been selling for four years. In January 1916, the delivery of the four tractors was overdue when Bristol ordered another dozen pushers.

That spring tragedy again struck at Pensacola. Lieutenant James Vincent Rockwell had entered the Navy Civil Engineer Corps in 1903. He became Pensacola's public works officer in July 1915. Chambers' old order, to give flying lessons to any volunteer officer, had never been countermanded and, pursuant to it, Rockwell began flight instruction in January 1916 as one of McDonnell's students. By late May, he had accumulated 35 hours of solo time. On 24 May, he took one of the Curtiss pushers for an altitude hop. Nearly an hour later, the station lookout saw him

150 spiraling down almost over the spot where Stolz had died the year before. As he watched, the machine dove into the water.

The rescue facilities had been improved since Stolz's accident. A boat officer got the crash boat away in a hurry. A few minutes later, Read, Capehart, and Schrieber followed in a motor dory. None of them could find the pilot. Whiting, who arrived in a third boat, dove under the wrecked plane and found Rockwell strapped in his seat. He freed him and brought him up. Just as in the case of Stolz, his head had been crushed by the engine.

As the Senior Officer Present, Bristol appointed a board of investigation composed of Whiting, Bellinger, and Saufley. They reported that the crash had been due to a sideslip and nose dive, following the loss of control. They ascribed the loss of control either to a stall or to the broken tail bamboo found in the wreckage. The opinions of the board sharply criticized the entire aviation setup.

Since January the chronic shortage of planes had made each man's instruction and practice too scattered to be either safe or effective. The fatality would not have occurred had the station been using the kind of planes that Mustin had recommended the previous August. Instead, only pushers were available. These had been repeatedly condemned for instability, because of the weights that were massed up behind the pilot and for the reason that the propellers often cut the bamboos or control wires. In the board's considered judgment, only urgent necessity for training additional pilots could justify the continued use of such ma-

3. Officers attached to the Navy's Flight School, Pensacola, in 1914-15. Standing, left to right: Paunack, Spencer, Bartlett, Edwards, Bronson, Corry, Norfleet, McDonnell, Scofield. Seated, left to right: Saufley, Bellinger, Whiting, Mustin, Read, Johnson, Cunningham, Evans, Hass.

chines, which, the board said, were sure to kill more fliers.

When Whiting's report of the Rockwell crash, with Mustin's concurrence, reached Bristol, he read it bitterly. The aviators were all unjust. Pushers were obviously the ideal planes for their work. However, he had tried to humor them by ordering three kinds of tractors for test. Was it his fault that neither Thomas nor Curtiss had delivered? Or that nobody liked the Martin craft? Bristol put a long endorsement on the Rockwell report, disagreeing with all of its opinions. It was not shortages of planes but his regular duties that had kept Rockwell from flying more frequently. True, the station had had three deaths due to stalls, but the proper correction was not more stable planes. The present type merely needed proper instruments and men trained to fly by them instead of by instinct and the seat of their pants.

After he put that opinion in the mail, Bristol took a train to Washington for the regular meeting of the NACA. Possibly he discussed the Rockwell investigation while he was there. In due time, Secretary Daniels backed him handsomely. In disapproving the findings and opinions of the board of investigation, he called them irresponsible, extrajudicial, not based on the evidence, and lacking in pertinency. As to the ratio of students to planes, the commandant should

3

have said something about that long before the accident. The plane type was irrelevant. The only question was the individual plane. Was it safe at the time? If not, who was to blame? He directed the Chief of Naval Operations to find some means "to fix responsibility" for future plane safety. He said nothing about improving planes.

Before Bristol returned from Washington, Pensacola's air board waived enough impractical requirements to qualify Dichman, Young, Gillespie, Mitscher, and Strickland as Naval Aviators. They were the last students to qualify in the bamboo tails.

In March of that year, Saufley had swapped jobs with Bellinger. In the Erection and Test Division, he endeavored to improve the performance of the old machines and kept working for flight records. There was no separate inspection organization. As superintendent, Saufley both directed and approved the shop work.

A year after Stolz had been killed in the AH-9, Saufley's shops finished rebuilding it. It had extra tanks for an endurance flight. Saufley hoped for a record before the float got waterlogged, or the wing fabric became slack. He balanced it during approximately eight hours of short flights. Then, very early in the morning of 9 June, he took off with full tanks. Some eight hours later, at 1240, he was flying east about three hundred feet above Santa Rosa Island. Mitscher, watching from the ground, saw the machine nose over, drop, level off, and suddenly plunge down out of sight behind a clump of scrub trees.

McDonnell and Spencer were in a restaurant near the hangars when they heard

the alarm. They took off in a hydro beached nearby, sighted the wreckage on the island, and landed in the bay near it. They found Saufley's body strapped in the seat. His head, chest, and legs had been crushed by the engine and the radiator.

On the board of investigation, Whiting, Spencer, and Bellinger all felt like saying "I told you so," except that this never helps when a friend has been killed. It merely increases one's feelings of frustration. They decided that the plane stalled when one of its two elevators had pulled loose because an inexperienced shop mechanic had failed to properly fasten three of its four flimsy hinges. The board was also of the opinion that in a pusher, death was certain in this sort of crash. And they pointed out that, in other places, pilots flying in tractors had survived similar crashes. They declared pushers obsolete and dangerous, as had been reported after the deaths of Stolz and Rockwell, and that they would kill others if they were continued in service.

Again Mustin concurred. Again Bristol took issue with the opinions. The board had not been thorough. Their opinions of the pushers were unsupported by any evidence. Rockwell and Stolz had died because of inexperience, Saufley because of poor workmanship. Secretary Daniels approved the proceedings, disapproved the opinions, and sent the papers on to Benson.

While these papers were circulating in the Navy Department, Bristol's status changed in accordance with previously issued orders. The orders removed him from the chain of command of shore-based aviation, while leav-

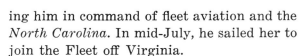

ing him in command of fleet aviation and the *North Carolina*. In mid-July, he sailed her to join the Fleet off Virginia.

About that time, Benson sent the records of the Rockwell and Saufley investigations directly to Mustin and asked him how to fix responsibility for future plane safety. Which was it? To make flying safe, or merely to fix responsibility: that is, to offer up someone to blame for the unnecessary slaughter of his shipmates? Mustin burned. Was the Navy Department going to let more pilots die before they tried to ascertain the real cause?

Mustin analyzed the problem and presented his answer in three parts: faulty workmanship; poor plane design; and a stubborn refusal to look at the problem from a pilot's point of view. He covered the first by a letter in which he explained that, after Saufley's accident, he had formed a separate inspection department, responsible directly to the commandant, to check all work as it progressed through the shops. This later became standard air station procedure for the entire Navy.

Three days later, he proposed a board of inspection for aircraft consisting of three pilots and representatives from the Bureaus of Engineering and Construction and Repair. If practicable, these latter should also be pilots. The board would approve each proposed design, check its mock-up, recommend changes as needed, and then, after a contractor's demonstration, each pilot on the board would fly the machine. Final acceptance or rejection of the design would, after these flights, be up to the board alone, and

4. *The first of the N-9 seaplanes which replaced the old bamboo tails, on the beach at Pensacola, November 1916.*
5. *Naval Aviator No. 26, Francis T. Evans, U.S. Marine Corps, discovered the spin recovery technique in 1917, while flying alone in an N-9. From that day, spin recovery has been taught every new flight student. Evans was awarded the Distinguished Flying Cross sixteen years later for his discovery. (U.S. Marine Corps)*

the members of the board would be held personally responsible for the results.

Mustin wrapped up the rest of the question with a lengthy endorsement on the Rockwell report. He began with a list of 21 references, which comprised the letters, recommendations, and reports with which the station had endeavored to improve the plane situation. Then he listed the instances when Bristol had delayed corrective action or had filed the complaints without any action. He maintained that a commander of the Air Service, who was not a trained pilot, could not understand aviation problems and that Bristol had had only two very short flights as a passenger since he had undertaken the job. On the next two pages of the endorsement, Mustin endeavored to prove that Bristol had no real understanding of either aerodynamics or of flight instruction.

Mustin stoutly objected to the classification of his recommendations as irresponsible opinions by a nonflier. His record as a pilot and his service in aviation entitled his statements to the status of expert testimony whether each of them was documented or not. He concluded by asking for an investigation of his competence if the Department should be unwilling to accept his views on that basis.

5

This fighting endorsement marked Lieutenant Commander Mustin forever as the pilot's champion. It undoubtedly saved many lives.

While Secretary Daniels still refused to approve the opinions of Mustin and Whiting's board, he told the Chief of Naval Operations to handle the materiel problem and to file the report. Benson was out of sympathy with Bristol. He reflected on the three deaths. He called in Bronson from the aviation desk and listened while the latter lauded Mustin and Whiting. Before July was out, Admiral Benson grounded the old pusher hydros and ordered them used only for testing pontoons. Then he told Daniels that he had ordered Chief Constructor D. W. Taylor to furnish Pensacola with tractor types.

This action by Admiral Benson cut naval aviation to four planes, none of which was suitable for training. Pensacola's students, idled for months, did some serious drinking and lost most of the little piloting skill they had acquired, but they all stayed alive. Scofield, Gillespie, and Capehart left the station for inspection jobs. Whiting left for sea duty in the *Seattle*. Before training in the new planes commenced, Spencer married Wallis Warfield of Baltimore, and succeeded to the Chief Instructor's billet.

In order to replace the bamboo tails quickly, the Bureau of Construction and Repair turned to the JN—the landplane trainer that Curtiss was then building for the Allies— known to all aviators as the Jenny. Richardson designed an amazingly tough and efficient

pontoon to hang under it, and Curtiss fitted extra center wing panels and bigger tail surfaces to handle this added weight. The first of these N-9's, as the modification was called, was ordered in October of 1916.

These were the first machines built for the Navy with controls connected as they are in modern planes, and they were the first to be delivered with safety belts installed. The fuselage was a rectangular box truss of four ash longerons, which were spread by wooden struts, cross braced with fine steel wires, and sheathed with doped cotton fabric. The engine, the gas tank, and the radiator were all in the nose. Behind them came the instructor's cockpit, which boasted a tachometer, an airspeed meter, and an inclinometer. The rear cockpit, for a student, had no instruments. The plane needed a long run to get off the water with the original 100-horsepower Curtiss engine; the performance improved somewhat when 130-150 horsepower Hispano-Suiza engines were installed.

One of the first of these N-9's was tested at Washington early in November. The Bureau of Ordnance wanted to use the new plane to test an antisubmarine bomb, but no pilot was available. Bronson volunteered. Bronson, who was still on the Chief of Naval Operations' aviation desk, had been ordered to nonflying duty because he had a wife and an infant son. When he flew the plane to the proving ground at Indian Head, Maryland, Lieutenant T. S. Wilkinson and Luther Welsh met him with four bombs. One was far too heavy for the OX engine, but Bronson agreed to carry the smaller ones, one at a time. The plane had no bomb racks. Wilkin-

153

6

son, a very heavy man, climbed into the rear seat with a bomb in his lap. A thousand feet up over the bay, he removed the safety cap and pulled the safety pin, which set the fuse to explode either on contact with a solid object or after traveling a set distance through the water. Then he simply threw the bomb out and away from the plane.

The first two flights went as planned, but the wind died before they were ready for the third. Without wind to assist the takeoff, Bronson declared, Wilkinson was too heavy. He got out and thus lived to become an amphibious admiral. Luther Welsh, some 50 pounds lighter, took his place in the plane.

Bronson climbed to the drop position. Through glasses, ground observers watched Welsh drop the bomb over the side. Then they saw an explosion just under the machine. The last bomb had exploded when it hit the pontoon. Bronson, the first pilot to be killed in an N-9, was buried in Arlington. Since then bomb fuses have required air travel after release to arm them.

Jack Towers, who had recently returned from London to get enough sea duty to avoid Chambers' fate, was still in Washington. Benson assigned him temporarily to Bronson's desk, and he stayed there until after World War I.

When an N-9 stalled, instead of going into the deadly nose dive like the old pushers, they went into a spin. At first the result was the same. They spun in, and for some time nobody in the Navy ever recovered from such a spin.

6. At the beginning of World War I, Pensacola was the only Naval Air Station; by the time of the Armistice, the U.S. Navy had 39 air stations. This is the way the main thoroughfare through the Pensacola Naval Air Station looked in 1917.
7. By 1917, the old tent hangars at Pensacola had been replaced. The planes in the foreground are Sturtevants.

In England there was talk of a rather dumb student pilot who had accidentally discovered the recovery technique in 1915, but in 1917 spins were still a mystery to American fliers; they caused many crashes before they were understood.

Instructors argued about the new N-9's. Evans and McDonnell held that, because they had stabilizers and a fuselage, one could do things in them that would have been impossible in the old pushers. Probably they could loop just like a landplane. Others insisted that, if anyone dived a seaplane to such speed and then pulled up, the wings would come off.

Early in February 1917, Evans was flying alone for an altitude hop. After half an hour he just reached 3,500 feet and he was bored. At the far end of the bay, he decided to try a loop. He nosed over, gained a little speed, then pulled back. The nose went up, stalled, and snapped down in a spin. He recognized the stall. He did not realize that he was spinning. He thought he was just turning fast. Pushing the wheel forward to get speed, he recovered from the stall and then just naturally stopped the turn with his rudder. Again he tried it a little faster and got a little higher before he spun. After several tries, each one a little faster, he got the plane on its back by easing back gently on his pull

7

up, and at the top he snapped the wheel to his chest and went around in the loop.

On the way back to the station, he suddenly realized that not only had he looped, but he had also recovered from spins. The arguments on the beach had been so heated that he feared no one would believe him when he went back and told what he had done. He was unaware that the crew of a captive balloon had nearly fallen out of the basket, watching.

Evans flew along the bay in front of the seaplane beach. At 2,000 feet he pulled the plane into a smooth loop, then stalled into a spin. He let it go around about three times before he recovered. Then he landed and came roaring into the beach with the plane on the step. From that day, spin recovery became a part of every student's first instruction. Evans was sent around to all the new aviation training stations to demonstrate his discovery. Sixteen years later, the authorities finally awarded Evans the Distinguished Flying Cross for discovering the spin recovery technique.

As summer drew to a close in 1916, the imminence of war made an expansion of naval aviation inevitable. The problem was to obtain and train more naval aviators. Admiral Victor Blue, Chief of the Bureau of Navigation, favored establishing a reserve flying corps as the only practicable way in the time available. Mustin was of the view that all aviation should be a separate corps with a flying commandant controlling materiel and personnel, and charged with the responsibility of developing combatant naval air

power. Towers wanted all pilots to be regular line officers. Benson was opposed to commissioning civilians after only six months' training. He envisioned enlisted pilots acting as chauffeurs for officers on combat missions. Bristol objected to this because he thought command of an aircraft called for the same responsibilities as command of a surface ship. He wanted regular officers to be pilots and argued that they could be obtained by using civilians in their places for submarine and coast defense work.

The upshot was, Congress authorized the Naval Reserve Flying Corps with an initial strength of 150 officers and 350 enlisted men. Towers, who had just taken Bronson's place in the office of the Chief of Naval Operations, was given additional duty in the Bureau of Navigation to supervise this corps.

By December 1916, the Navy had 19 planes and 70 more on order. None of them could make an open sea landing even in good weather. The Department asked for 86 more, 30 of which were to be for the Fleet. Many thought this an excessive request since no American had as yet scouted, spotted, or in any other manner made a plane serve any naval purpose at sea. After Congress voted the planes, the Department refused to order 75 of them "until the type the General Board had particularly recommended has been developed."

By this time Pensacola was training both new and old students in 25 new N-9's, the type used there until 1928. Mustin, who had been largely responsible for this improvement, was ordered to nonflying duty as the executive officer of the battleship *North*

8

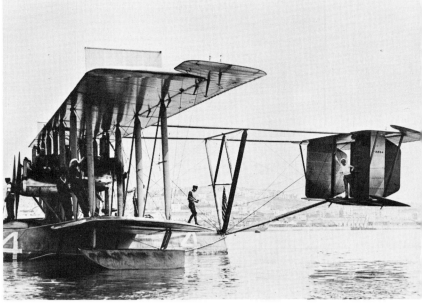

9

156 *Dakota.* Benson had selected a nonflying administrator, an "officer of high rank from the War College," to relieve Mustin. There was no doubt about the high rank; the new officer was Captain Joseph L. Jayne. He had graduated from the Naval Academy in 1882, and he quickly saw that the reason planes crashed in spins and stalls was because they flew around the corners too fast. So he ordered pilots to *slow down on all turns,* and charged those who crashed with the destruction of government property. The survivors were punished with sentry duty, carrying a rifle and knapsack full of sand.

8. The NC-4, under the command of Lieutenant Commander A. C. Read, successfully crossed the Atlantic in 1919. Lieutenant R. E. Byrd developed a drift indicator which proved invaluable in the crossing.

9. The NC flying boats were designed to carry tremendous bomb loads and fly long distances, but the wartime need for these planes ended with the Armistice; by then ten had been completed. The NC-4 had four Liberty motors and a wingspan of 126 feet. She is shown here refueling at Lisbon, Portugal, 28 May 1919.

10. Instrument panel of the NC-4. (Wide World Photo)

11. Secretary of the Navy Josephus Daniels officially welcomes back the crew of the NC-4 after the first transatlantic flight. Sitting next to Mr. Daniels is Franklin D. Roosevelt, Assistant Secretary of the Navy in 1919.

The spur of war gave impetus to the industrial system of the nation and provided full scope for the American genius for swift organization. The bare statistics in themselves tell a startling tale. On 6 April 1917, the day the United States entered the war, naval aviation consisted of 43 qualified Naval Aviators, five of whom were Marines; 239 enlisted men; and 54 planes. Nineteen months later, on 11 November 1918, naval aviation had grown to 6,716 officers and 30,693 men in Navy units; 282 officers, 2,180 men in Marine Corps units; and 2,107 planes.

The expansion of the service was equally impressive. At the outset, Pensacola was the only U. S. naval air station in existence, but by the time of the Armistice, there were 39. Of these, 12 were in the United States, 27 were in France, the British Isles, Italy, and the Azores. In addition, six bases in France and one in England supported the operations

of the Northern Bombing Group.

In the field of procurement the outstanding achievement was the creation and production of the Liberty motor, the first one being completed five weeks after the plans for it came off the drafting board. The mass production of this motor laid the basis for the successful series of American flying boats—the HS-2-L, the H-16, and the F-5-L.

Significantly for the future, five of the French stations and one in Ireland were equipped for lighter-than-air operations, and from these bases both blimps and kite balloons performed services in antisubmarine warfare and in patrolling and observation for the protection of convoys. The decade after the war saw a large expansion of this service until the destruction of the *Shenandoah,* the *Akron,* and the *Macon* brought to an end the construction of rigid airships. After that the blimp—the nonrigid dirigible —evolved to a high degree of efficiency.

10

11

The decade of the twenties was the great formative period in the development of naval aviation. It was a period of controversy, of experiment, and of great achievement. The Atlantic crossing was first attempted in the spring of 1919 by three NC (Navy-Curtiss) flying boats, with the NC-4 commanded by Lieutenant Commander Albert C. Read actually completing the trip from Newfoundland to England by way of the Azores and Lisbon, Portugal.

Then came a confused period of agitation for and controversy with Brigadier General William Mitchell over a separate air force, in the course of which, between the years 1921 and 1924, various obsolete naval vessels were bombed from the air off the Virginia Capes by both Army and Navy aircraft. The culmination of the controversy came in 1925 following the loss of the rigid airship *Shenandoah,* when Mitchell's serious charges led to his court-martial and President Coolidge appointed a board dominated by civilians under the chairmanship of Dwight W. Morrow to study the problem of "aircraft in national defense." This action greatly strengthened naval aviation, and, most important, for the first time a law required commanders of aircraft operating units and aviation ships to be qualified airmen.

Meanwhile, a start had been made in the development of a new type of naval craft that was destined within a generation literally to revolutionize the Navy and naval warfare. On 20 March 1922, Commander Ken Whiting commissioned the USS *Langley,* the Navy's first aircraft carrier. The ship

had been converted from the former *Jupiter,* a collier. By the end of the decade two more carriers, the *Lexington* and the *Saratoga,* were commissioned. Converted from unfinished battle cruisers, these 35-knot ships of 33,000 tons each had flight decks measuring 800 by 100 feet. Their performance in the war games of 1929 was an augury of the future.

The opposed fleets were charged with the attack and defense of the Panama Canal. By a clever ruse the *Saratoga,* of the attacking force, under cover of darkness and bad weather, was able to launch a force of 69 planes, which arrived on target without interference. The canal was theoretically destroyed, and the place of the fast carrier with the Fleet was indicated 12 years before the Japanese attack on Pearl Harbor.

Many persons, both in and out of the Navy, deserve credit for these radical ships, which most naval architects said would not prove practical, with big hangars opening in their centers. Conservative sea officers believed they would be both useless and a handicap to the Fleet in battle. A small group of persistent men, led by Whiting, deserves most of the credit for solving the problems involved and overcoming opposition to the carriers.

Whiting agitated for carriers from the spring of 1916 until 1919, when the *Langley* conversion was authorized. Then he worked on her plans, organized her, and directed the pilots who used her as a laboratory to study the efficient operation of planes at sea. Later, in Washington, he applied the accumulated

157

12

13

158 knowledge to the plans for the *Saratoga* and the *Lexington;* then he served as the *Saratoga's* first executive officer, and later commanded her. Gene Ely may have been the first pilot to point the way to the use of carriers, but Whiting deserves credit as their parent and guardian.

Between 1929 and Pearl Harbor a few hundred carrier pilots developed carrier aircraft tactics that proved remarkably successful in war. Ship tactics were still being debated, however, when Pearl Harbor was attacked. Until then, even many enthusiastic naval aviators could not forget the traditional line-of-battle formations for naval fighting. The winning tactics of the carrier forces were forged by the hard lessons of the early months of World War II, when naval battles were first decided between ships which never saw each other.

In December 1941, the Navy had eight aircraft carriers. Luckily, none of the five Pacific Fleet carriers were in Pearl Harbor at the time of the Japanese attack. When the United States entered World War II, naval aviation strength consisted of 6,750 pilots, 1,874 ground officers, 21,678 enlisted men, and 5,260 aircraft. The growth experienced during World War I was repeated on a far greater scale; by V-J Day, naval air counted 60,747 pilots, 32,827 ground officers, 344,424 enlisted men, and 42,272 aircraft. A total of 99 aircraft carriers, of which eleven were lost in combat operations, had served with the Fleet in World War II.

Among the flag rank officers who helped the Navy achieve victory over the Japanese, there were five admirals who had qualified

12, 13, 14. A revolutionary new type of naval craft joined the U.S. fleet in 1922 when Commander Ken Whiting commissioned the USS Langley, *the Navy's first aircraft carrier. The* Langley *was followed shortly by the* Saratoga *and the* Lexington. *They were to point the way to the future, when naval aviation came of age in the great air battles of World War II.*

as naval aviators in the old bamboo-tailed pusher crates prior to World War I: John H. Towers, Patrick N. L. Bellinger, Marc A. Mitscher, George D. Murray, and Albert C. Read.

In the naval war with Japan, air superiority was a determining factor. In the first all-air battle in history, the Battle of the Coral Sea, U. S. forces halted Japanese expansion across the sea lanes to Australia. At Midway, the turning point of the war in the Pacific, U. S. carrier-based planes destroyed four Japanese aircraft carriers; the remainder of Japanese naval aviation was nearly wiped out in the famous "Marianas turkey shoot." As the war neared its end, fast U. S. carrier task forces lashed the Japanese homeland with a rain of fire. The dreams and determination of the daring young men who flew frail crates at Annapolis and Pensacola years earlier had paid off. The gold wings and medals they may have won could only acknowledge, but never repay, the debt owed them by the nation.

Supersonic Navy jet fighters armed with nuclear weapons now streak across the continent in a couple of hours; the Navy's huge aircraft carriers can launch air strikes from any ocean in the world, against any target on

14

earth. In the dark void above the earth, naval astronauts have piloted space vehicles around the globe at speeds of five miles per second. Even as these pages in the history of naval aviation are written, a U. S. space vehicle is hurtling across millions of miles of deep space on its voyage to Mars. Men will follow it; all human achievement is bound in a belief that what can be done must be done.

The bamboo tails have long been museum relics. But there is every prospect that in the life span of men who won their gold wings flying those strange craft at Annapolis and Pensacola, other men will land even stranger craft on the surface of the moon. These adventurers into space may·well be wearing the same gold wings as the bamboo-tail pioneers.

APPENDIX A: EARLY NAVAL AVIATORS

Naval Aviators Who Trained in the Bamboo Tails (Pusher-type Aircraft)

Naval Aviator No.	Name	Service	Reported to Aviation	Soloed	Aero Club Test Date	Seaplane Certificate No.	Aviator License No.	Navy Air Pilot No.	Date
1.	Theodore G. Ellyson	USN	1/ 2/11	2/—/11	7/ 2/11		28	1	1/ 1/14
2.	John Rodgers	USN	3/17/11	4/—/11	8/ 3/11		48		
3.	John H. Towers	USN	6/27/11	6/28/11	9/14/11		62	2	1/ 1/14
4.	Victor D. Herbster	USN	11/ 8/11	2/19/12	2/28/12		103	5	7/ 1/14
5.	Alfred A. Cunningham	USMC	5/22/12	8/ 1/12	5/26/13	2		14	9/17/15
	*Laurance N. McNair	USN		9/21/12					
	*Isaac F. Dortch	USN		10/28/12					
6.	Bernard L. Smith	USMC	9/18/12	12/ 2/12	5/ 3/13	3		6	7/ 1/14
					10/ 6/13		285		
7.	Godfrey deC. Chevalier	USN	10/25/12	1/18/13	5/ 3/13	5		7	7/ 1/14
8.	Patrick N. L. Bellinger	USN	11/26/12	2/ 1/13	5/ 3/13	4		4	6/ 1/14
9.	William D. Billingsley	USN	12/ 2/12	3/ 8/13	5/13/13				
10.	James M. Murray	USN	1/20/13	—/—/13	10/17/13	13			
11.	Henry C. Mustin	USN	12/31/13	3/13/13	11/26/13	14		3	6/ 1/14
12.	William M. McIlvain	USMC	11/ 1/13	12/16/13	12/22/13	15		9	3/10/15
13.	Holden C. Richardson	USN	10/10/11	4/22/12	10/—/12		174	12	4/12/15
	*Walter D. LaMont	USN	11/ 8/13		4/17/14	17			
	*Melvin L. Stolz	USN	10/24/13	6/ 4/14	6/22/14	19			
14.	Richard C. Saufley	USN	11/10/13	4/11/14	6/20/14	18		8	3/ 6/15
15.	Clarence K. Bronson	USN	5/24/14		10/22/14	23		10	4/ 6/15
16.	Kenneth Whiting	USN	6/29/14		8/26/14	24	304	11	4/10/15
					11/30/14				
17.	Louis H. Maxfield	USN	11/—/14		3/27/15	25		13	7/13/15
18.	Edward O. McDonnell	USN	12/—/14			33		15	9/19/15
19.	Wadleigh Capehart	USN	6/—/14	1/—/15				16	9/19/15
20.	Earl W. Spencer	USN	10/—/14		4/ 6/15	27		18	9/27/15
21.	Harold T. Bartlett	USN	9/—/14		10/16/15	39			
22.	George D. Murray	USN	12/—/14					17	9/20/15
	*James V. Rockwell	USN		1/—/16					
23.	William M. Corry	USN	7/—/15						
24.	Albert C. Read	USN	6/—/15						
25.	Earle F. Johnson	USN	7/—/15						
26.	Francis T. Evans	USMC	6/—/15						
27.	Robert R. Paunack	USN	6/—/15						
28.	Harold W. Scofield	USN	7/—/15						
29.	Warren G. Child	USN	4/—/15						
30.	Grattan C. Dichman	USN	9/—/15						
31.	Robert T. Young	USN	9/—/15						
32.	George S. Gillespie	USN	9/—/15						
33.	Marc A. Mitscher	USN	10/—/15						
34.	Glenn B. Strickland	USN	10/—/15						

Note: Where blanks appear, data is not available. Other student naval aviators reported to Pensacola before Admiral Benson grounded the pusher hydros in the summer of 1916. Some of these started their training in the bamboo tails, but qualified in the replacement machines.

* Started training in bamboo tails, but did not qualify as Naval Aviators.

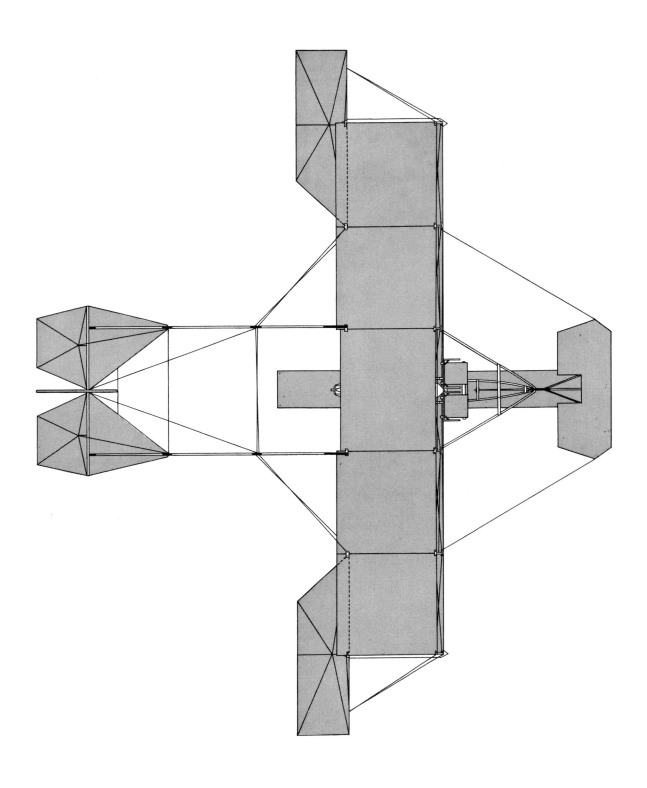

Curtiss Hydroaeroplane, Navy No. A-1.
Rendering based on drawings of the A-1 as produced
by the Curtiss Aeroplane Company, Hammondsport, New York, 1911.

APPENDIX B: EARLY AIRCRAFT OF THE U. S. NAVY

	A-1	A-2[3]
Manufacturer	*Curtiss*	*Curtiss*
Type	*Pusher, Biplane Triad*[1]	*Pusher, Biplane Landplane*[4]
Year Delivered	*July 1911*	*July 1911*
Year Expended	*Oct. 1912*	*July 1913*[5]
Overall —Length	*28'7⅛"*	*27'2"*
Span	*37'*	*37'1"*
Height	*8'10"*	*8'5"*
Weight —Empty	*925*	*967*
Gross	*1575*	*547*
Wing —Type	*Voisin*	*Curtiss*
Span	*28'8"*	*28'8"*
Chord	*5'*	*5'*
Gap	*5'*	*5'*
Area	*286 sq. ft.*	*286 sq. ft.*
Hull or Pontoon—Type	*Curtiss, Single Pontoon*	*Curtiss, Single Pontoon*
Length	*16'*	*16'*
Beam	*1'11⅝"*	*1'11⅝"*
Draft	*11½"*	*1'1"*
Engine —Type	*Curtiss V-8, W.C.*	*Curtiss V-8, W.C.*[6]
B.H.P.	*75*[2]	*80*
RPM	*1050-1250*	*1050-1250*
Screw —Type	*1 Curtiss, 2-Blade*	*1 Curtiss, 2-Blade*
Diam.	*7'6"*	*7'6"*
Pitch	*5'4"*	*5'4"*
Speed	*60 mph.*	*60 mph.*
Number of Flights	*285*	*575*[7]

General.—All data, except for N-9, taken from aircraft Log Books. The extent to which these early aircraft were modified and used for testing various kinds of equipment makes it practically impossible to determine whether these data represent the original or some later configuration. When known, the variations are indicated.

[1]Triad rig was removed 12 July 1911 and plane operated as a landplane. Changed to a hydro rig 21 July 1911 and apparently operated as such from then on.

[2]Installed 7 July 1911 but was originally fitted with a 50 h.p. Curtiss.

[3]Redesignated E-1 on 22 September 1913 and AX-1 on 27 March 1914.

[4]Purchased as a landplane and originally operated as such. Was rebuilt as a hydro 20 Mar.–26 June 1912. Was converted to an amphibian in summer 1913 and upon completion was redesignated E-1, 22 Sept. 1913. By general change in designation system 27 Mar. 1914 became AX-1. As an amphibian was also called OWL.

[5]Month in which conversion to amphibian began, not the end of service. E-1(AX-1) was wrecked at Pensacola 27 Nov. 1915.

[6]Originally equipped with a Curtiss 4 cylinder; on 15 Oct. 1911 shifted to a 60 h.p. 8 cylinder, and in June 1912 to a 75 h.p. Accuracy of 80 h.p. figure is not known.

[7]As the A-2. Record for E-1 (AX-1) is incomplete but 91 flights are recorded.

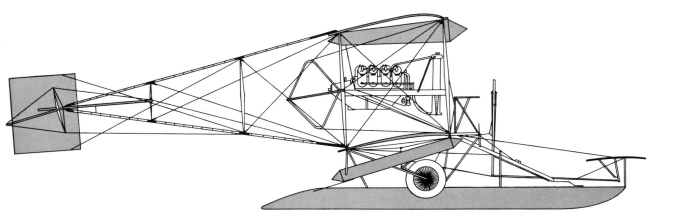

Curtiss Hydroaeroplane, Navy No. A-1.

	B-1	B-2
Manufacturer	*Wright Bros.*	*U.S. Navy*[10]
Type	*Pusher, Biplane* *Landplane*[8]	*Pusher, Biplane* *Hydro*
Year Delivered	*Sept. 1911*	*Oct. 1912*
Year Expended	*June 1913*[9]	*June 1913*[11]
Overall —Length Span Height	*28'9"* *38'10"* *9'3"*	[12]
Weight —Empty Gross	*960* *1274*	*1040* *1522*
Wing —Type Span Chord Gap Area	*Wright* *38'10"* *6'3"* *5'4"* *485 sq. ft.*	*Wright* *39'* *6'2"* *5'4"* *480 sq. ft.*
Hull or Pontoon—Type Length Beam Draft	*Burgess-* *Curtiss Pontoon* *17'* *2'6"* *12"*	*Curtiss Pontoon* *15'6"* *2'6"*
Engine —Type B.H.P. RPM	*Sturtevant 4 cyl.* *40-46* *1350-1450*	*Wright 6 cyl. W.C.*[13] *50-52* *1350-1450*
Screw —Type Diam. Pitch	*2 Wright, 2-Blade* *8'6"* *10'*	*2 Wright, 2-Blade* *8' 6"* *10'*
Speed	*45 mph.*	*50*
Number of Flights	*393*	*298*

[8]Purchased as a landplane but converted to hydro 8-9 Dec. 1911.
[9]Date of last Log entry is 5 June 1913.
[10]A Wright aeroplane constructed from spare parts by Navy at Annapolis.
[11]Plane in which Billingsley crashed to his death at Annapolis, 20 June 1913.
[12]Dimensions not reported in Log but assumed to be same as B-1.
[13]Replaced by Curtiss 6 cyl. W.C. in April 1913.

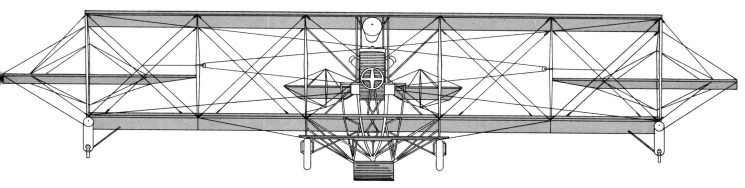

Curtiss Hydroaeroplane, Navy No. A-1.

C-1	D-1	N-9
Curtiss	*Burgess Co. & Curtiss*	*Curtiss A&M Co.*[17]
Pusher, Biplane	*Pusher, Biplane*	*Tractor Biplane*
Flying Boat	*Flying Boat*	*Seaplane*
Dec. 1912	*May 1913*	
Apr. 1914[14]	[15]	
27'4"	*30.8*[16]	*32'7¼"*
37'1"	*43.3*	*53'3¾"*
8'6"	*9.0*	*10'8½"*
1286	*1450*	*1860*
	2091	*2390*
		RAF-6
37'1" upper; 28'8" lower	*40.3 upper; 33 lower*	*53'3¾" upper; 43'3⅜" lower*
5'	*5.5*	*5'*
5'	*5.5*	*5'*
308 sq. ft.	*397 sq. ft.*	*488 sq. ft.*
Curtiss Boat	*Boat*	*Single Pontoon*
23'3"	*28'4"*	
2'6"	*2'5"*	
12"	*12"*	
Curtiss V-8, W.C.	*Renault A.C.*	*Curtiss OXX*
80	*78*	*100*
1150–1275	*1800*	*1400*
1 Curtiss, 2-Blade	*Chauviene*	
8'2"	*9.5*	
5'4"		
59–65	*60*	*65 mph.*
262	*130*	

[14]Date of last Log entry is 1 April 1914.

[15]Plane in which J. M. Murray crashed to his death at Pensacola, 16 Feb. 1914.

[16]Dimensions as given in Log without indication as to whether these are in fact tenths of feet.

[17]Also built by Burgess; some with Hispano engines. A total of 460 N-9's were procured in the years 1917 and 1918. Used as a trainer during WWI and in postwar years as late as 1927.

BIBLIOGRAPHY

Unpublished Material

Much of the material for this work was found in unpublished manuscripts in the National Archives, in the Library of Congress, in various Departments of the Navy, and other miscellaneous sources.

1. National Archives, Navy Section, Washington, D.C.

Investigations:

Death of Lieutenant C. K. Bronson at Indian Head, Maryland, 11/8/16.
Death of Lieutenant (jg) J. M. Murray at Pensacola, Florida, 2/16/14.
Death of Civil Engineer J. V. Rockwell at Pensacola, Florida, 5/26/16, with endorsements.
Death of Lieutenant R. C. Saufley at Pensacola, Florida, 6/9/16.
Fire, plane A–3, at Pensacola, Florida, 3/20/14 (B. L. Smith and M. L. Stolz).
Death of Lieutenant M. L. Stolz at Pensacola, Florida, 5/8/15.
Crash of G. deC. Chevalier and R. A. Lavender at Guacanayabo Bay, Cuba, 2/11/17.
Death of Lieutenant Commander G. deC. Chevalier at Norfolk, 11/12/22.
Death of Commander John Rodgers at Philadelphia, 8/27/26.

Reports:

Captain W. I Chambers' Aeronautical Inventions (N.A. No. 736–65235).
G. deC. Chevalier's fire in the air, 8/7/14 (N.A. No. 736–135276).
Memo to Secretary of the Navy Metcalf, 12/2/08. (Signed by Rear Admiral Cowles, prepared by George Sweet), file 187781, GCS-H.
J. H. Towers' report on the Flying Boat *America*, 7/28/14 (N.A. No. 736–132192).

Ships' Logs:

USS *Bailey*, 1911.
USS *Birmingham*, 1910 and 1914.
USS *Dubuque*, 1917.
USS *Huntington*, 1917.
USS *Iris*, 1912.
USS *Jason*, 1915.
USS *Langley*.
USS *Mississippi*, 1913, 1914.
USS *North Carolina*, 1914, 1915, 1916, 1917.
USS *Pennsylvania*, 1911.
USS *Washington*, 1916.
USS *Seattle*, 1916, 1917.
USS *Yankton*, 1912.

Miscellaneous:

Daniels, Josephus. "Memo for All Bureaus." 11/16/14 (N.A. No. 736–139986).
———. "General Order Number 88." 3/27/14

2. Navy Department, Washington, D.C.

Aviation Logs:

Aviation History Unit, Office of Chief of Naval Operations, Navy Department, Washington, D.C., holds files of old aviation records, including:
Aviation Log, Curtiss Hydroaeroplane, Navy No. A–1.
Aviation Log, Curtiss Hydroaeroplane, Navy No. AX–1 (Converted from A–2).
Aviation Log, Wright Hydroaeroplane, Navy No. B–1 (15 July 1911 to 5 June 1913).
Aviation Log, Wright Hydroaeroplane, Navy No. B–2, photo reproduction 1961, including pertinent letters from the files.

Miscellaneous:

Bellinger, P. M. L., filmed interview, held at Navy Photo Center, Anacostia, D.C.
———. Memoirs. Unpublished manuscript, Technical Historian's Office, Bureau of Naval Weapons, Washington, D.C.
Chambers, W. I., "Findings of the Board appointed to investigate the circumstances attending the death of Ensign William D. Billingsley, USN," contained in 1961 photo reproduction of the B-2 log book.
Ely, Mabel (Mrs. Eugene), scrapbooks of news clippings on early aviation, 1910–1911. Navy Historical Foundation, Washington, D.C.
McIlvain, William M., filmed interview, held at Navy Photo Center, Anacostia, D.C.
Welborn, Mary Catherine, "History of the Technical Development of Naval Aircraft." An unpublished manuscript with source notes. Aviation History Unit, Office of the Chief of Naval Operations, Navy Department, Washington, D.C.
Zogbaum, Rufus F., filmed interview, held at the Navy Photo Center, Anacostia, D.C.

Biography of each early aviator. Biographies Branch (OI-450) Office of Information, Navy Department, Washington, D.C.

Weekly Reports from the Aviation Camp, November–December 1911; May 1912 to January 1914. In Technical Historian's Office, Bureau of Naval Weapons, Navy Department, Washington, D.C.

168   3. Library of Congress, Washington, D.C.

Bristol, Mark L. "Annual report on Aeronautics, 1/19/16," copy with collection of his papers.

———. Personal papers.

Chambers, W. I. Personal papers.

Ellyson, T. G. Letters to Chambers, among Chambers papers in Library of Congress collection.

———. Letters to his wife, Helen.

Loening, Grover. Personal papers.

Wright Brothers. Personal papers.

4. Miscellaneous

Aero Club of America, original card file of Aviator's licenses and Seaplane Certificates, in custody of National Aeronautical Association, Washington, D.C.

Towers, John H. Talk before the Institute of Aeronautical Sciences, New York, 1/26/54, as recorded. (Held by Mrs. J. H. Towers.)

Newspapers and Periodicals

Anonymous

News items, *Aero* magazine, 1911.

News items, *Aero and Hydro* magazine, 1913 and 1914.

"Accidents to the LeBaudy and Langley Flying Machines," *Scientific American*, Vol. 89, No. 25 (19 December 1903), 462.

News items, *Aeronautics*, Vols. 7, 8, and 9.

News items, *Aircraft*, 1911 and 1912.

"Airplanes in Naval War," *The Naval and Military Record*, quoted in *U.S. Naval Institute Proceedings*, Vol. 37 (1910), 1088.

"The Airplane in War," *The Engineering Magazine*, quoted in *U.S. Naval Institute Proceedings*, Vol. 35 (1909), 321.

"Airships and Warships," *Independent*, Vol. 69 (21 July 1910), 150–151.

"Fact and Fancy in Aeronautics," *Scientific American*, quoted in *U.S. Naval Institute Proceedings*, Vol. 35 (1909), 1010.

"The Failure of Langley's Aerodrome," *Scientific American*, Vol. 89, No. 16 (17 October 1903), 272.

"Flying Men of America," *Current Literature*, Vol. 49 (December 1910), 615–620.

"Hydroplanes for the Navy," *New York Sun*, quoted in *U.S. Naval Institute Proceedings*, Vol. 37 (1911), 1480.

News items (Ely), *Portland Oregonian*, January–May 1910.

News items (Langley), *San Francisco Call*, October–December 1903.

News item (Wright), *San Francisco Examiner*, 13 December 1903.

Bartlett, Harold T. "Mission of Aircraft with the Fleet," *U.S. Naval Institute Proceedings*, Vol. 44 (1917), 729 ff.

Bell, Alexander Graham. Photographs of Langley's aerodrome in flight, *Scientific American Supplement*, Vol. 54, No. 1405 (6 December 1902), cover and p. 22510.

Bellinger, P. N. L. "Sailors in the Sky," *National Geographic*, Vol. 120, No. 2 (August 1961), 277 ff.

Chambers, Washington Irving. "Aviation and Aeroplanes," *U.S. Naval Institute Proceedings*, Vol. 37 (1911), 162 ff.

———. "Aviation Today," *U.S. Naval Institute Proceedings*, Vol. 38 (1912), 1491.

———. "Naval Aviation," *Scientific American*, Vol. 105 (8 July 1911), 26–27.

Davis, Bob. "A Startling Operation of the Law of Coincidence," *New York Sun*, 5 April 1928.

Duval, Ruby R. ". . . figures cut in mid-air," *Shipmate*, Vol. 22, No. 5 (May 1959), 6 ff.

Eisenberg, Howard. "The Record-Making Ride of the Vin Fizz Whiz," *Cavalier*, Vol. 8, No. 72 (June 1959), 28 ff.

Foulois, Benjamin D. "Why Write a Book?" *The Air Power Historian*, April 1955.

Fretheim, Fred K. "The Nose Spin Problem," *U.S. Naval Institute Proceedings*, Vol. 44 (1917), quoted from the *Scientific American*, 27 July 1917.

Langley, Samuel P. "The Flying Machine," *McClure's*, Vol. 9, No. 2 (June 1897), 647 ff.

———. "The Greatest Flying Creature," *Scientific American Supplement*, Vol. 55 (31 January 1903), 22644 ff.

———. "The Langley Aerodrome." *Smithsonian Institution 1900 Annual Report*, quoted in *Scientific American Supplement*, Vol. 54, No. 1405 (6 December 1902), 22509 ff.

———. "Mechanical Flight," *Cosmopolitan*, May 1892, 55 ff.

———. "The Possibility of Mechanical Flight," *Century*, Vol. XLII, No. 5, 783 ff.

———. "A Successful Trial of the Aerodrome," *Science*, Vol. 3, No. 73 (22 May 1896), 753–54.

Mason, Charles P. "The Bald Eagles," *Shipmate*, Vol. 22, No. 5 (May 1959), 12 ff.

Perry, Pat. "Flier's Widow Reminisces," *Virginia Pilot* 1961.

Reynolds, Bruce. "Pioneer Mechanic," *Flying*, Vol. 62, No. 4 (April 1958), 40 ff.

Wright, Wilbur. "The Wright Experiments in Flying," *Independent,* quoted in *Scientific American Supplement,* Vol. 57, No. 1471 (12 March 1904), 23571.

Books

Arnold, Hap. *Global Mission.* New York: Harper and Bros., 1949.

Chandler, Charles D., and Frank P. Lahm. *How Our Army Grew Wings.* New York: Ronald Press Company, 1943.

Curtiss, Glenn H. and Augustus Post. *The Curtiss Aviation Book.* New York: Frederick A. Stokes Company, 1912.

Dixon, Charles. *The Conquest of the Atlantic by Air.* Philadelphia: Lippincott, 1931.

Fiske, Bradley A. *From Midshipman to Rear Admiral.* New York: Century Company, 1919.

Furlong, William Rea (ed.). *The First Twenty-five Years* (Class of 1905). Annapolis: U.S. Naval Academy, 1930.

Gann, Ernest K. *Fate is the Hunter.* New York: York: Simon and Schuster, 1961.

Halsey, William F., and J. Bryan, III. *Admiral Halsey's Story.* New York and London: McGraw-Hill Book Company, 1947.

Hartney, Harold. *Up and At 'Em.* New York: Stackpole Sons, 1940.

Howe, M. A. DeWolf. *George Von Lengerke Meyer.* New York: Dodd, Mead and Company, 1920.

Jane, Fred T. (ed.). *Fighting Ships.* London: Sampson Low, Marston and Co., Ltd., 1910 and 1912 editions.

Kelly, Fred C. *The Wright Brothers.* New York: Harcourt Brace and Company, 1943.

Langley, S. P., and Charles M. Manley. *The Langley Memoir on Mechanical Flight.* Washington, D.C.: Smithsonian Institution (publication No. 1948), 1911.

Loening, Grover. *Our Wings Grow Faster.* New York: Doubleday Doran and Company, 1935.

Magoun, F. A., and E. Hodgin. *History of Aircraft.* New York and London: McGraw Hill, 1931.

Miller, Harold Blaine. *Navy Wings.* New York: Dodd, Mead and Company, 1942.

Paine, R. D. *The First Yale Unit, A Story of Naval Aviation, 1916–1919.* 2 vols. Locust Valley, Long Island, New York: Privately printed, 1925.

Sherrod, Robert. *History of Marine Corps Aviation in World War II.* Washington, D.C.: Combat Forces Press, 1952.

Sims, William Snowden. *Victory at Sea.* New York: Doubleday Page and Company, 1921.

Studer, Clara. *Sky Storming Yankee, The Life of Glenn Curtiss.* New York: Stackpole Sons, 1937.

Sullivan, Mark. *Our Times, The United States, 1900–1925.* (*America Finding Herself,* Vol. II). New York and London: Charles Scribner and Sons, 1927.

Taylor, Theodore. *The Magnificent Mitscher.* New York: W. W. Norton and Company, 1954.

Turnbull, A. D., and C. L. Lord. *History of United States Naval Aviation.* New Haven: Yale University Press, 1949.

Windsor, Wallis, Duchess of. *The Heart Has Its Reasons.* New York: D. McKay Company, 1956.

Zogbaum, Rufus Fairchild. *From Sail to Saratoga.* Rome: Tipografia Italo-Oriental S. Nilo, 1961.

Government and Other Publications

U.S. House of Representatives. Committee on Naval Affairs. *Additional Facts Bearing on the Petition of Captain W. I. Chambers, USN, dated 15 December 1915.* Hearing Pamphlet No. 499. 71 Cong., 2 Sess., 1915.

U.S. House of Representatives, Committee on Naval Affairs. *Report of a Board on Naval Aeronautics convened by Navy Department Order No. 2309-89, 9 October 1913.* 14 February 1914.

Congressional Record, 58th Congress, January 1904.

Dictionary of American Fighting Ships, Vol. 1. Washington, D.C.: Government Printing Office, 1959.

First Annual Report of the National Advisory Committee for Aeronautics. Washington, D.C.: Government Printing Office, 1916.

Lucky Bag, U.S. Naval Academy Annual. Various publishers.

Navy Department, Bureau of Navigation, *Courses of Instruction and Required Qualifications of Personnel for the Air Service of the Navy.* 26 January 1916.

Navy Directory, various dates.

Navy Register, published annually.

New International Year Book. New York: Dodd, Mead and Company, 1910 to 1914.

Register of Alumni 1845–1961. Annapolis, Maryland: The U.S.N.A. Alumni Association, Inc.

Secretary of the Navy's Annual Report. 1911 and 1913 issues.

U.S. Naval Aviation 1898–1956. Washington, D.C.: Bureau of Aeronautics, Navy Department, 1957.

United States Naval Aviation, 1910–1960. Washington, D.C.: Government Printing Office, 1961.

INDEX

THE AUTHOR

Graduated from the U. S. Naval Academy in 1920, Rear Admiral George van Deurs (Retired) had a long, distinguished career in naval aviation. As Naval Aviator No. 3109, he first flew in the old N-9's, later, in cruiser and battleship catapult seaplanes, and finally, in the Navy's first jet fighters. He was a ship's officer in the *Saratoga,* and commanded Patrol Squadron 23 at Pearl Harbor.

During World War II he served as Superintendent of Aviation Training, Naval Air Training Center, Corpus Christi; Plans Officer and then Chief of Staff for ComAirSoPac during the Solomons campaign; Commanding Officer of the escort carrier *Chenango* (CVE 28) at Morotai, Leyte Gulf, and Okinawa; and Chief of Staff to Commander Battleship Squadron One during the Okinawa campaign. At the close of World War II, he commanded the naval occupation forces in western Japan.

After leaving Japan in the spring of 1946, he subsequently commanded Fleet Air Wing 14, the carrier *Philippine Sea,* and served on the Naval Staff in London.

Since his retirement in 1951, Admiral van Deurs has obtained his Master's degree, and has kept busy with writing, photography, and travel. His writings include some thirty articles on the Navy, aviation, and travel. *Wings for the Fleet* is his first book.

The text of this book is set in ten-point Century Expanded, with three points of leading. The chapter titles are set in fourteen-point Century Expanded.

The book is printed offset on sixty-pound Warren's Patina text paper.

The cover is Lindenmeyr Schlosser Elephant Hide paper, Gray 15, and Holliston coated fabric, white.

Editorial production by Louise Gerretson.

Design by Gerard Valerio.

The book was composed and printed by the John D. Lucas Company, Baltimore, Maryland, and bound by Moore & Company, Baltimore, Maryland.